Counting Bodies

D1672682

COUNTING BODIES
Population in Colonial American Writing

MOLLY FARRELL

Oxford University Press is a department of the University of Oxford. It furthers
the University's objective of excellence in research, scholarship, and education
by publishing worldwide. Oxford is a registered trade mark of Oxford University
Press in the UK and certain other countries.

Published in the United States of America by Oxford University Press
198 Madison Avenue, New York, NY 10016, United States of America.

© Oxford University Press 2016

First issued as an Oxford University Press paperback, 2019

Library of Congress Cataloging-in-Publication Data
Names: Farrell, Molly.
Title: Counting bodies : population in colonial American writing / Molly Farrell.
Description: New York : Oxford University Press, 2016. | Includes bibliographical
references and index.
Identifiers: LCCN 2015040571 | ISBN 9780190277314 (cloth) | ISBN 9780190934026
(paper) | ISBN 9780190277321 (updf) | ISBN 9780190607654 (epub)
Subjects: LCSH: American literature—Colonial period, ca. 1600–1775—History
and criticism. | American literature—Revolutionary period, 1775–1783—History and
criticism. | Population in literature. | Minorities in literature. | Literature and society—
United States—History.
Classification: LCC PS195.P66 F38 2016 | DDC 810.9/355—dc23 LC record available
at https://lccn.loc.gov/2015040571

For Jesse and Hattie

And again the anger of the LORD was kindled against Israel,
and he moved David against them to say,
Go, number Israel and Judah.
—2 Samuel 24:1

It is a negative concept this multitude: it is that which
did not make itself fit to become people.
—Paolo Virno, *A Grammar of the Multitude*

Contents

Acknowledgments

This book would not have been possible, materially or intellectually, without the work of feminist, anti-racist, and other anti-oppression movements. I thank all those who have dedicated themselves to these ongoing struggles.

At a crucial time, a fellowship from the American Society for Eighteenth Century Studies at the American Antiquarian Society supported my work on this project. More personally, it appears thanks to the generosity of friends and colleagues, many of whom I am lucky to consider as both. My early Americanist colleagues have been tremendous sources of wisdom and assistance, and I am particularly grateful to Elizabeth Maddock Dillon, Donald Pease, Cristobal Silva, Kathleen Donegan, Jason Shaffer, Jeffrey Glover, Dennis Moore, Timothy Sweet, Duncan Faherty, Paul Erickson, Meredith Neumann, Susan Scott Parrish, Kristina Garvin, Anna Brickhouse, Russ Castronovo, Monique Allewaert, Jonathan Senchyne, Brigitte Fielder, and Justine Murison. Beginning when I was at Yale and continuing well beyond, I have benefitted from the invaluable insights and support of Wai Chee Dimock, Caleb Smith, Elliott Visconsi, Linda Peterson, Katie Trumpener, Sam See, Sarah Novacich, Julia Fawcett, Laura Saetveit Miles, Liz Appel, Caroline Murphree, Hilary Menges, Andrew Heisel, David Currell, and Daniel Gustafson. Since coming to Ohio State I have been immensely grateful to be surrounded by colleagues and friends in Columbus whose comments and encouragement have touched nearly every aspect of this work, especially Elizabeth Hewitt, Jared Gardner, Lisa Voigt, Elizabeth Renker, Byron Hamann, Roxann Wheeler, David Brewer, Chadwick Allen, Jill Galvan, Sean O'Sullivan, Leslie Lockett, Lynn M. Itagaki, Thomas S. Davis, Ruth Friedman, Christa Teston, Sarah Neville, Lauren Squires, Richard Dutton, Debra Moddelmog, Karl Whittington, Adam Fazio, Namiko Kunimoto, Max Woodworth, George Rush, and Khara Nemitz. Since my days at Kenyon, Pamela Scully, Sergei Lobanov-Rostovsky, and Clifton Crais have nurtured my growth as a scholar. The work of the staff and my fellow volunteers at the Sexual Assault Response Network of Central Ohio and at the abortion fund Women Have Options has inspired me, as has the extraordinary kindness and fortification of Kelly Morrissey, Patrick Morrissey, Nikki Rae Strong, Lucinda Currell, Kate Kennedy, Roni Schotter, Richard Schotter, and Barnacle.

Most of all I thank Jesse and Hattie Schotter. Words cannot express my gratitude for the countless hours of labor Jesse has devoted to the task of bringing this manuscript to print, or for the innumerable moments he has spent lovingly restoring my spirit. He is the best partner I could imagine: "If ever two were one, then surely we." This manuscript was completed before the birth of Hattie, and I'm so grateful for all the joy and love she's already brought into my life.

Counting Bodies

Introduction

Stories of Cataclysm and Population

In 1616, Powhatan, the most powerful ruler in what is today Virginia, ordered an emissary named Uttamatomakkin to accompany Pocahontas on her visit to England and to "number the people" there.[1] According to the English captain and explorer John Smith, Uttamatomakkin could not complete his mission because his method of counting proved inadequate. "Arriving at Plimoth," Smith writes, "according to his directions, he got a long stick, whereon by notches hee did think to have kept the number of all the men hee could see, but he was quickly weary of that task."[2]

In this anecdote, Smith implies that the indigenous people of the Americas in particular have to face the frustration of a gap between their desire to count people and their ability to do so. He ignores the fact that Uttamatomakkin's journey took him through a densely populated region, and assumes that English counting methods would have protected him from growing similarly "weary of that task."[3] At the same time, he shows that efforts to count population in order to gain power within colonial interactions are undertaken by both English and indigenous people. Colonialism itself draws attention to counts of people as representative tools, which help make sense of threateningly unfamiliar relationships. Powhatan and Uttamatomakkin already know how to conduct reconnaissance, but the trip to England stretches, tests, and renders urgent their methods of doing so. This colonial encounter serves as a catalyst to "number the people," and to compare numerically the strengths and vulnerabilities of the two groups in question. For Smith, the failure of Uttamatomakkin's survey is an opportunity to depict a powerful adversary as overwhelmed by the task at hand.

During the time period when Uttamatomakkin went to England to carve his notches, Europeans were beginning to consider the counting of populations in fundamentally new and different ways. Whereas today birth certificates, census forms, immigration quotas, and other tools of quantifiable citizenship are so ubiquitous that they appear ahistorical, English readers and writers in 1616 were neither familiar with the word "population" in the sense of numbers of people, nor universally accepting of the idea that states should even count their subjects in peacetime at all. Much of the work of naturalizing the view that people can be represented as populations took place far outside government institutions and philosophical treatises. It occurred instead in writings like that of Smith—an anecdote that turns to an act of counting to disarm a colonial threat. This book explores the imaginative, personal, and narrative writings that performed the cultural work of normalizing the enumeration of colonial bodies. By repositioning and unearthing a literary prehistory of population science, *Counting Bodies: Population in Colonial American Writing* shows that representing individuals as numbers was a central element of colonial projects.

Early colonial writings that describe routine interactions (such as Uttamatomakkin's abandonment of his stick) offer a window into the way that the quantifiable forms of subjectivity made a-vailable by population counts crept into everyday life. Whether trying to make sense of frontier warfare, plantation slavery, rapid migration, or global commerce, writers framed questions about human relationships across different cultures and generations in terms of population. These writers include witnesses to the earliest colonial encounters, from Smith to the indigenous writer Felipe Guaman Poma de Ayala; New England Puritans from Anne Bradstreet to Mary Rowlandson; and natural philosophers from Richard Ligon to Benjamin Franklin. Taken together, their considerations of population do not so much mount a critique of biopolitics, as they present us with a forgotten history of how beginning to conceive of people as populations spurred numerical representations of communities. *Counting Bodies* maps the development of a countable colonial subjectivity by exploring in depth key representative case studies from the seventeenth- and early-eighteenth-century British colonial Atlantic, including New England, Barbados, and North American port cities. In this Introduction, I draw connections between the European roots of population discourse and the work of a contemporaneous indigenous writer in Peru in order to show how the proliferation of investigations into counting people did not arise solely from a particular strain of state activity. My methodology resists traditional political histories of state intervention, in favor of a narrative about how women, indigenous people, and slaves performed essential roles in the cultural work of solidifying statistics as an unquestioned and ingrained means of understanding society. The variety of texts I consider show how the experience of colonialism itself drove the turn toward representing human relationships through numbers, emphasizing that this phenomenon did not simply arise from one coterie of closely interrelated thinkers.

New numerical ways of thinking about societies helped structure the migratory and cross-racial social relationships produced by colonialism. *Counting Bodies* returns to moments, like Uttamatomakkin's journey to England, when population counts retained a sense of strangeness, or even an aura of creative playfulness. By focusing on writings from a time when population science was neither a "science" nor concerned with what its practitioners would name "population," I can explore how numerical representations of communities profoundly shaped approaches to problems of reproduction and family life that were nowhere more urgent than in colonial spheres. Because of this focus on a broad epistemological shift, rather than solely on state demographic projects, I trace the development of early applications of population thinking across genres of colonial writing. Poetry, captivity narratives, travel histories, newspaper mortality bills, and chronicles of conquest, when interrogated side by side, show how the tendency to speak about groups of people as quantities or calculations circulated around the colonial Atlantic and gathered momentum. Working together, these various forms of writing wove numerical representations of human groups into a means of understanding subjectivity and community quantitatively that is now so ingrained that it seems natural.

Yet the proposition that states should count population on a regular basis was once controversial. Advocates of state censuses repeatedly had to argue against the idea that the Bible explicitly forbade any count of people that was not specifically ordained by God. The story that kept reappearing as fodder for criticizing state attempts to obtain an accurate count was known as the "sin of David," and it arises from a moment in the book of Samuel in which God sent a pestilence as punishment for David's desire to "number Israel and Judah" out of triumphant pride (2 Samuel 24:1). Although an adviser hesitates, David tells him to make the count anyway, giving only a tautological reason: "Go . . . number ye the people," David commands, "that I may know the number of the people" (2 Samuel 24: 2). As a result of David's sin, hunger and epidemics ravage the land, killing tens of thousands of people. This biblical episode firmly links the desire, apparent in Smith's story of Powhatan, to "number the people" with the threat of cataclysmic depopulating events.

Understanding the role of the "sin of David" within early population discourse helps explain why fears of cataclysm continue to motivate twenty-first-century cultural texts about population, whether they are concerned with climate change or the eclipse of white racial majorities.[4] Writings from the early years of state interest in population show how, as in the biblical story, expressing the desire to "know" numerically the extent of human multitudes carries with it the risk of confronting the fragility of the life pulsing within them. Texts that applied counting to the task of understanding colonial upheaval play an essential part in the story of how census-taking like David's became widely accepted as a modern state activity, rather than rejected as an offense against God.

Complicating matters further is the fact that anyone discussing population in the early modern period had to contend not only with the devastating threats arising from invocations of the "sin of David," but also with the utter lack of words with which to talk about numbers of living people. The link, broadcast in the story of David's census, between keeping an account of human numbers and decimating those numbers is deeply embedded in the origins of the word "population" itself. Seventeenth-century writers fashioned the word "population" from the Latin abstract noun *populatio*, denoting "multitude," "colonization," "settlement," or "populousness." Both words share a root with *populus*, which derives in part from the word *populāri*, meaning "to ravage, plunder." This "ravaging" comes from a root, *poplo-,* meaning "army." Because of these martial connotations, variations of the Latin term can refer to an army and what the army does to a place when passing through it. Indeed, by adding the suffix "-ion" that signifies past actions, "population" points directly to the (presumably devastating) aftereffects of that army—or even, since this is one sense of *populatio*, the aftereffects of colonization. Therefore, the etymology of "population" includes the meanings both of a gathering of people and a wasting of people; of a deliberate collection of bodies and the havoc those bodies have wrought.[5]

As a result of the association between an army's capacity for destruction and an army's collection of men embedded in *populāri*, speaking of population brought *de*population to mind long before

Thomas Malthus schematized the link between population growth and famine in his 1798 *Essay on the Principle of Population*. In fact, the English word "population" first denoted the negative sense of the Latin root, meaning destruction or "wasting," and only referred to positive numbers of people much later on. Etymologically then, the concept of population loss preceded that of living numbers of humans. According to the *Oxford English Dictionary*, the word "population" first appeared in English in the mid-sixteenth century in two senses. One referred to centers of habitation, like towns: for example, the 1605 English translation of the French poet Guillaume Du Bartas's biblical epic includes the line, "[s]ing the Worlds so divers populations; / And of least Cities showe the first Foundations."[6] The other definition of population circulating in the 1600s meant "the act of laying waste," or a devastation. This negative connotation of "population" persisted for over a century: as late as 1692, dictionaries listed the only definition of "population" to be "a wasting or unpeopling."[7] During the same period in which English rulers made political arithmetic an imperial policy and commentators first began analyzing public health statistics, the majority of English readers and writers would have thought of the word "population" in terms of its negative sense of loss and destruction.

Just four years before Powhatan gave his order, Francis Bacon used the word "population" to refer to numbers of people in the first recorded instance.[8] In a 1612 essay, Bacon turns the Latin *populatio* into "population" in the context of a warning against class imbalance, leaving it unclear whether he means the positive or negative sense of the neologism: "Let states that aim at greatness take heed how their nobility and gentlemen do multiply too fast. . . . [I]n countries, if the gentlemen be too many, the commons will be base; and you will bring it to that, that not the hundred poll will be fit for an helmet; especially as to the infantry, which is the nerve of an army; and so there will be great population and little strength."[9] Because of the complexity of the Latin roots, Bacon might mean destruction when he writes of "great population," even though the *OED* assumes that this last clause contrasts large numbers of people with "little strength." Perhaps Bacon means that the gentlemen will be numerous when he uses the words "great population," but he also might be warning that unruly commoners will form weak armies that will be capable only of leaving disorder—"great population"—in their wake. The shifting etymology of "population" means that readers cannot now know for sure.

This uncertainty exemplifies how, especially during the seventeenth century, concepts of measuring destruction and growth, cataclysm and regeneration, and depopulation and population attended one another so closely that readers and writers had difficulty teasing them apart. Even with the increasing institutionalization of population discourse as a science and the imbuing of numbers with what Mary Poovey calls "the aura of fact," ways of speaking about population repeatedly circled back to the conundrum of how to distinguish population from depopulation, of peopling from wasting, and of growth from decline.[10]

Just as the words "population" and "depopulation" tangle semantically in the seventeenth century, writing about this early period of population science involves terminological difficulty. "Science" did not yet exist as the discipline we understand it to be today; instead, writers might refer to "natural philosophy" or "natural history" instead as the closest relatives of modern science. And of course, many thinkers and philosophers who would become influential for later writers about population like Malthus did not even use the word "population." Early statisticians, who collected and analyzed data about burials and causes of death, did not use the word "statistics" to describe what they were interested in; that term, meaning "facts about the state," appeared only in the late eighteenth century. And it would still be another century before "demography" as a word denoted the branch of studying groups of people using statistics. "Political arithmetic" was a seventeenth-century term for thinking about state accounting of populations, though it relates specifically to imperial strategy: William Petty, a royal adviser, wrote a pamphlet entitled *Political Arithmetick* outlining a plan for unifying the British Empire through accounting methods in 1690. To make sense of the semantic morass characterizing a period crucial to the later development of population science, yet during which neither "population" nor "science" circulated as terms with much stability, I use the phrase "human accounting" to denote the various emerging attempts to quantify social life. "Human accounting" describes the experimental conceptual field out of which colonial writers drew creative ways of understanding human relationships through numbers. Population science codified a particular expert-driven form of systematically counting human bodies, but this book investigates moments around the colonial Atlantic world when writers explored the implications of enumerating people before censuses and birth registries shaped everyday life. In the two centuries before Malthus's *Essay*, human accounting as a way of representing community was experimental, speculative, and available to many different kinds of writers. Though the prehistory of population science has previously been told as the purview of philosophers, political officials, and bookkeepers, I show here how the representative potential of ordering colonial movements and environments through numbers drew a far wider array of people into the task of human accounting.[11]

The inaugural century of confusion about the word "population" is also the first century of Atlantic colonialism, a historical phenomenon marked by the encountering, migrating, and enslaving of previously separate populations. Itself a cataclysmic event for those subject to it—and itself an endeavor the Latin word *populatio* names—colonization gave rise to plagues and wars, and the sea journey across the Atlantic recalled Noah's journey in Genesis through the great Flood to a new post-diluvian world on Ararat. People across the Atlantic world drew upon emerging quantitative discourses in order to make sense of these colonial encounters, while simultaneously confronting the dissonances and resonances that resulted from quantifying social life.

   Early population theorists like Jean Bodin, Giovanni Botero, and Petty advocated monitoring masses of people by representing them with a numerical system that effaces difference in the service of uniform control. This human accounting was a representative tactic that served the political and economic strategy of imperialism. There were several ways in which British colonial interest in the Americas, especially, fueled the development of human accounting. For policymakers and theorists, colonies presented an opportunity for transferring undesirable people out of the metropole.[12] Moreover, colonial territorial conflicts with indigenous groups led to pervasive interest in the numbers and growth rates of native populations—data that was very difficult for colonizers to obtain. The slave trade, especially, instituted a system that normalized the counting of human bodies. When Europeans forced Africans to labor on enormously profitable Caribbean plantations—plantations that constituted the economic engine for Atlantic colonialism—colonial economics morphed seamlessly into social engineering. Long before Britain passed the census bill in 1800, or the newly created United States instituted its first census in 1790, merchants on slave ships tracked and enumerated people kidnapped and deported across the Atlantic in the service of someone else's wealth. Through this economy, slaves, indentured servants, indigenous people, sailors, traders, bookkeepers, insurers, and plantation owners all became accustomed to viewing human bodies as numbers in a ledger.[13]

   A sense of oneself as a single number within an enumerable whole took hold so thoroughly as part of modern citizenship because it proved so useful, especially in colonial environments. When stable geographic borders no longer separated social groups from one another, counting served as a serviceable representative tool to denote the sameness or difference of individual bodies. Distinguishing communities by attempting to count them was a way for colonial subjects and imperial policymakers to impose an imaginative order over the conflicted, constantly changing sphere of colonial encounters. Early colonial writing about population produced and consumed by those working outside metropolitan centers of power dramatizes the tension between the way censuses work to consolidate social landscapes and the way colonial spaces call borders into question. By applying new ideas about bodies as countable to respond in real time to their local environments, these idiosyncratic texts also show how authoritative forms of counting themselves craft stories about people, places, and power. The ad hoc application of population thinking in colonial writing shows how, as Geoffrey C. Bowker puts it, "'raw data' is . . . an oxymoron"[14]; or in other words, how every act of enumerating people—not just those by, say, a poet or a precocious newspaper printer—reflects a particular subjectivity. Contemporary demographers are beginning to recognize that even when scrupulous attention is paid to data collection methods, "there is very little evidence of any thought given, for example, to what an individual or a person may be, [or] to the notion of time."[15] Early colonial writers, by contrast, surrounded as they were by foreign cultures, ecologies, and social organizations, considered these questions at length and drew upon new population theories to attempt to answer them. In the ferment of writing about their experience in the colonies, writers like Smith formed new ideas about subjectivity—about "what an individual or a person may be"—when they experimented with methods of counting themselves and others around them as numbered populations.

I am primarily interested in how what we might think of as "official" imperial strategies of tracking population, in the form of political philosophy and the writings of policymakers who applied those philosophies, became "normative frameworks" that were "*manipulated by users*," to borrow phrasing from Michel de Certeau.[16] The texts that make up these "normative frameworks" tell fascinating stories about colonialism and the encroachment of state power into family life in themselves, and early colonial writers who encountered them embraced the creative opportunities they provided. In particular, they tested the applicability of quantification to the tasks of representing women, children, and sexual desire. Colonialism reshaped sexuality as much as it did territory, and population science in particular turned reproductive practices into political problems. Reproduction is the process of slowly creating two people out of one through pregnancy, birth, and weaning, thereby calling individuality into question. The act of counting insists on drawing clear boundaries between individuals, even when those boundaries are necessarily blurred or dissolved, such as those between a parent and a dependent child, a subject and an object of desire, or a woman and her fetus. A rigidly numerical view of human bodies instigates ongoing political problems around the same fraught boundaries it insists on creating. I show that when writers from the seventeenth to the early eighteenth century engaged with the growing tendency to enumerate themselves and others, they consistently produced figures of bodies that seem to exist between quantification and innumerability.

Human accounting colonized minds as well as bodies, changing the way people around the Atlantic viewed themselves and their communities. Bookkeeping methods applied to humans in groups affected early modern assumptions about what kind of matter bodies are and how those bodies exist in historical time. The variety of these assumptions as illuminated within early colonial writing contributes to a genealogy of contemporary forms of subjectivity and political recognition. When the US census apportions congressional representation based on population once every decade, it gives a certain form of numerical representation of bodies the force of law. One implication of this representation is that an individual body has a clear boundary separating it from its environment; without these distinctions between what is inside and outside of bodies, counting would be impossible. Also, because today's census counts all residents equally, whether young or old, male or female, citizen or non-citizen, it ignores (for the purposes of reapportionment) relationships of interdependence. A small child, a disabled person, or a nursing mother might be inextricably linked with another person in a way that simple quantification is not able to express.[17] Taking into account relationships of fundamental interdependence, certain pairs of bodies might be described numerically as neither one nor two, but rather something in between. Moreover, because bodies are counted using the same numbers that can be applied to crops or commodities, the representation implies that humans share an ontological status with other kinds of animate or inanimate objects. Numerical representations of population, such as the contemporary US census, are historical phenomena, and the assumptions about human bodies in community that enable them to function culturally have seventeenth-century foundations.

Cataclysm and Early Population Thought

The intertwining of censuses and death pervades both the political and discursive histories of population thought—as though enumerating a multitude was an archetypal narrative in which cataclysm has to make an appearance to satisfy generic conventions. Among English speakers, this intertwining hearkens back not only to the etymology of "population," but also to the apocalyptic Anglo-Saxon name for William the Conqueror's eleventh-century *Great Inquisition* or *Survey of the Lands of England*, the Domesday Book. The Middle English word "Domesday" and the more common contemporary word "doomsday" come from the Old English *domes dæg*, referring to the biblical Day of Judgment at the end of the world. William the Conqueror ordered the survey in order to make a written record of the value and titles of all land holdings and obligations in his new realm in 1086. Although the ruler presented the extraordinary effort as the most authoritative accounting in England, the Domesday Book appeared at a time of transition in the function of written records. As M. T. Clanchy has shown, even after the Domesday Book, oral testimony and mnemonics held as much if not more legal and political authority than written titles.[18] Still, the name "Domesday" gave the unprecedented survey a world-ending resonance. The name comes not from the conquering Normans, but from the language of the newly subjugated Anglo-Saxons: in the words of a twelfth-century historian, the Anglo-Saxons viewed the new ruler's extensive numerical accounting as akin to "The Book of Judgment [*Domesday*] ... because its decisions, like those of the Last Judgment, are unalterable."[19] Even though the historian likely overstates the actual finality of the 1086 census, the Anglo-Saxon name of *domes dæg* does show that either the rulers wanted the census to evoke cataclysmic finality, or the conquered people being counted interpreted the survey as akin to such an apocalyptic judgment.

Perpetuating this connection between disaster and sovereign accounting, historians and theorists of state interest in population generally agree that the earliest European censuses took place primarily as a response to labor shortages in the wake of the devastating plagues that swept Europe in the Middle Ages.[20] Counting people served as a practical reactive strategy as well as a way to recast catastrophic events like war, pandemic, fire, or flood into a communal narrative that restored social order.

In 1576, the French legal philosopher Jean Bodin advocated the taking of regular state censuses in his influential *Six Books of the Commonwealth*. Considered to be the foundation of what is now population science, this book's rationale for keeping count of a king's subjects directly refers to colonialism. For Bodin, colonial spaces simultaneously reveal Europe's inadequate fertility and create an opportunity for absorbing imperial migrants. Bodin mentions the West Indies several times to excuse slavery as an institution endemic across the globe, as well as to insist that Europe lags behind in population: "[T]he people of the West Indies, which are three times greater than all Europe, who never heard speech of the lawes of God or man, have alwaies bene full of slaves."[21] Colonial spaces become crucial to Bodin's philosophy, however, when the treatise discusses how to maintain social harmony within the national home. As the commonwealth moves toward greater stability and a larger share of happiness for its people, colonies operate as a site for depositing excess elements: Bodin describes a process of peaceful and slow social change, one that is "least subject unto tumults and sturres," and argues that these tumults can be avoided "by keeping of strangers from entering into the citie: or by sending of them out into colonies" (*SB*, 428). Bodin, recalling ancient Rome's legacy in France, praises Rome as an example of how this policy could work through colonial conquest: "[T]he Romans ... [sent] Colonies from their citie to inhabit the conquered countryes, distributing to every one a certayne quantitie: and by this meanes they freed their Citie from beggers, mutinies, and idle persons" (*SB*, 655–656). For Bodin, Rome showed how colonies are necessary for "freeing" metropolitan spaces of their unwanted elements.

Bodin advocates using the power of reproduction, not simply conquest, to turn a foreign place into an imperial territory. These colonies must not be military outposts: rather, they should be settlements amenable to "marriages" that can "[fill] the world" (*SB*, 656). Another essential element for Bodin's commonwealth is the careful selection of a "certayne quantitie" which is sent away from the city. The amount of people to be removed must be deliberately chosen; the number must not simply be determined by natural forces or by the independent will of the people. Hovering above all of this work of colonizing through reproduction and protecting peace at home by shipping human "waste" abroad is the state census, the necessary step in arranging this social redistribution, and Bodin argues for its institution in earnest.

In addition to the prospect of colonialism, the memory of population cataclysm also lingered in Bodin's advocacy of state monitoring of numbers of people. The bubonic plague had catastrophically devastated France's population two centuries earlier; it still had not recovered by the late 1500s (Bodin himself died of plague in 1596).[22] Historians of political economy have argued that the book for which Bodin was best known in his lifetime, *On the Demon-mania of Witches* (1580) was a pronatalist plan for increasing the birth rate by eradicating wise women who stewarded knowledge of birth control methods.[23] Framing the growth of state and intellectual interest in reproduction and population growth as a response to the devastating plagues, Sylvia Federici links "the intensification of the persecution of 'witches'" around Europe in general to the resulting population crisis.[24] Viewed this way, Bodin's work on witches complements his advocacy of the census and seeks to make up for the devastating loss of population after the late medieval plagues by removing obstacles to increased human reproduction.

The Italian Machiavellian philosopher Giovanni Botero expanded and solidified the tie between colonialism and population thought a little over a decade after Bodin's *Six Books* appeared. Published in 1588, Botero's *The Greatness of Cities* became available to English readers simultaneously with Bodin's *Six Books of the Commonwealth* when they were both published in English translation in 1606.[25] Botero goes further than Bodin in arguing that colonialism contributes to the health of the state at home. Whereas Bodin described the social harmony made possible by removing undesirable elements, Botero proposes that increased metropolitan population is the greater good that will be brought about when people migrate to colonies. For Botero, propagation is the goal, and colonialism provides the means:

> For if any man think by taking the people out and sending them to colonies elsewhere that the city thereby comes rather to diminish than increase, haply for all that the contrary may happen. For as plants cannot prosper so well nor multiply so fast in a nursery where they are set and planted near together as where they are transplanted into an open ground, even so men make no such fruitful propagation of children where they are enclosed and shut up within the walls of the city they are bred and born in as they do abroad in the divers other parts where they are sent unto. [26]

Botero yokes conquest of "open ground" to the "increase" of population, imbuing colonialism with a direct focus on the "fruitful propagation of children." Bodin and Botero's books calling for states to keep count of their people were published in London just six years before Sir Francis Bacon included the complex neologism "population" in his essay, "On the True Greatness of Kingdoms and Estates"—a title that recalls Botero's work.

By the eighteenth century, population concerns were everywhere in European political discourse. Commentators tied population to natural history's growing interest in examining humans as a species, and to questions of how concerned states should be about tracking and promoting population growth. France was in the midst of a massive pronatalist project begun by Louis XIV, and essayists engaged in heated debates about why France had become supposedly depopulated and what to do about it, with Montesquieu writing a series of letters on "la dépopulation" and its causes in his *Persian Letters*.[27] Contrary to Botero, Montesquieu identified colonialism as a *cause* of depopulation, rather than its cure, and in his 1748 book *Spirit of the Laws* he portrayed the relationship between nations as a reproductive competition.[28] For Montesquieu, French laws have to intervene to encourage fertility and keep population growth at pace with its rates in climates more favorable to reproduction. In certain climates, Montesquieu argues, "nature has done everything; the legislator, therefore, has nothing to do."[29] In these places, "peoples multiply and increase greatly. Among them it would be a great discomfort to live in celibacy; it is not a discomfort to have many children. The contrary occurs when the nation is formed."[30] Montesquieu critiqued modern state formation by claiming it was causing demographic stagnation, and he used warmer non-European spaces—like Turkey or the colonial Caribbean—as evidence. At the same time, he approached the subject of population growth through its opposite—"la dépopulation"—urging pronatalist intervention by stoking fears of drastic population decline.

English philosophers were infected with a similar population fever in the eighteenth century, as mercantilists equated fertility

with wealth. Depopulation fears featured prominently in this discourse too: just as Montesquieu had taken up the theme of decline in France in order to argue for measures to increase growth,
other commentators insisted that Europe's population had fallen
from a previous state of abundance. David Hume intervened with
a detailed refutation of the widely held assumption that the world
had been well-populated in antiquity, only to suffer massive depopulation during the Middle Ages, from which it was still trying
to recover. In one of his longest essays, "Of the Populousness of
Ancient Nations," Hume mocks a 1753 essay by a member of
the Philosophical Society of Edinburgh, Robert Wallace, and attempts to turn the tide of population thinking away from the
idea of reclamation of a past abundance. Hume insists that writers
should stop framing the discourse in terms of an anxious desire
to recover from depopulation, and instead focus on social management that promotes growth. Hume reads histories of ancient
empires and concludes that the population of antiquity could not
have been as great as that of his contemporary world, making a
claim similar to Montesquieu's—namely, that improper government causes the numbers of people to dwindle: "[A]ll extensive governments, especially absolute monarchies, are pernicious
to population, and contain a secret vice and poison, which destroy the effect of all these promising appearances."[31] At this key
mid-eighteenth-century moment, the memory of the extinction-
threatening medieval plagues had begun to fade, and the nostalgic
tone of much population theory ceded in favor of the question
of management.

Building on Hume, Malthus suggested that the population catastrophe that political theorists needed to worry about
was the one that loomed in the future, rather than in the past.
Frances Ferguson describes how, far from being the first to warn
of population disasters, Malthus "was considerably revaluing a
topic that had long been invested with a sense of crisis."[32] As
a result of Malthus's influential focus on limits, what had been a
discourse of reclamation from some earlier, more abundant past

turned into a discourse of anxiety over unrestrained growth. Malthus claimed that human reproduction occurred at a stable rate that could be calculated in abstraction from its social and environmental contexts. Malthus called on states to "check" the frightening and unrestrained power of human fertility that continually "goes on doubling itself," out of compassion for the people who would suffer if they were merely left to nature. By the time Malthus wrote, the new United States of America had already completed its first constitutionally required census, and Britain was about to pass the landmark 1800 Census Bill, nearly two centuries after Bodin's treatise calling for states to count their subjects. Yet for all this development in discourses about population as a science or political arithmetic as a state policy, depopulation remained ever-present in discussions of human numbers in their positivity. Whether the census itself felt like a cataclysmic event, as in the case of the Anglo-Saxons after the Norman conquest, or whether essayists like Montesquieu insisted that states needed urgently to develop policies to forestall ongoing depopulation, or whether Malthusian famine loomed if leaders did not reign in masses of frighteningly fecund human bodies, threats of a massive wasting of human life continued to accompany calls to assign human groups a number.

While philosophers debated the purpose of state censuses and built the scaffolding for these "normative frameworks," early modern English Protestant readers turned to biblical stories of numbering for guidance. John Milton, in particular, interpreted the story of the "sin of David" as evidence that God prohibited states from counting their people. In *Paradise Regained* (1671), Milton chastises what he sees as a growing interest in political arithmetic by reminding readers of this story from the Book of Samuel.[33] Milton depicts Satan trying to appeal to Jesus's pride in the wilderness, just as Satan had tempted David to number Israel. Jesus tells Satan that he remembers what happened as a result, and so this tactic will not work on him:

> Where was it then
> For *Israel*, for *David*, or his Throne,
> When thou stood'st up his Tempter to the pride
> Of numb'ring *Israel,* which cost the lives
> Of threescore and ten thousand *Israelites*
> By three days' Pestilence? Such was thy zeal
> To *Israel* then, the same that now to me.[34]

For Milton, the biblical sin of David shows how attempts to count a realm's inhabitants are a pernicious overreach of state power. Moreover, these numberings directly cause depopulation: "numb'ring *Israel* . . . cost the lives" of tens of thousands of people. Instead of portraying census counts as events that happen in response to a prior cataclysmic destruction, Milton retells the sin-of-David episode as a story in which numbering people purely out of "pride" invites depopulation by an angry God. For Milton, the sin of David again conceptually intertwines cataclysm with the act of numbering populations.

Milton's critique of political arithmetic in post-Restoration England shows how persistent warnings of the "sin of David" could be. Bodin had taken pains to dismantle the power of this particular biblical critique when he called for states to count people nearly a century earlier. He had to change the popular interpretation of this story in order to wash censuses clean of their association with the threat of retributory pestilence. Bodin argues in *Six Books* that David's sin did not consist of taking a census; rather, his sin had been to exclude women, children, and others from his count of fighting men:

> [M]any ignorant divines abuse themselves, in thinking that *David* was grievously reprehended by God, and punished, for that he commaunded his people should bee numbered; . . . But in my opinion herein was the greater offence, that the prince . . . did not number all his people, but those onely that were able to beare armes. (*SB*, 638–639)

For Bodin, David's error was not in the act of numbering, but rather, in not numbering enough of the population. Censuses should not be solely focused on counting potential laborers or soldiers, but rather, should attempt to number the population as a whole.

Although many English commentators on population read and agreed with Bodin, invocations of the sin of David in protest of English state-sanctioned counting efforts continued in force throughout the seventeenth century, as Milton's epic shows, and far into the eighteenth century as well. As late as 1771, an English magazine article laments that mentions of the sin of David helped thwart a Parliamentary effort to begin collecting mortality data for the whole of England. The article describes how the increased availability of mortality statistics "would furnish the most perfect basis yet extant for political calculations, respecting insurances on lives, and other circumstances of apparent utility," but when an addendum to the bill was introduced "for numbering the people of both sexes and all ages before the act took place . . . nothing but the *sin of David was heard of*, till the bill was laid aside."[35] The article presents invocations of the "sin of David" at this late date dismissively, yet shows that they still held enough power in England to contribute to the tabling of proposed census legislation well into the era when political arithmetic reigned in political theory.[36]

The impressive longevity of the "sin of David" as an anti-census trope points to a larger mystification and fear surrounding the imposition of official counts on social groups. Before this fear could be conquered at home with the British Census Bill of 1800, English imperial policymakers used colonial spaces as testing grounds for experiments in political arithmetic. Before John Graunt published one of the foundational works of English demography, *Natural and Political Observations Made upon the Bills of Mortality*, in 1665, his collaborator Petty had already completed the extensive Down Survey of Ireland in 1659. Similarly, the Lords of Trade in England demanded an extensive census of the sugar colony Barbados in 1680, a decade before Petty circulated his plan for uniting the wealth of the British Empire through careful accounting in *Political Arithmetick*. In the view of state policymakers, colonial spaces were laboratories for the use of accounting as a means of social control. The people meeting and migrating within these networks also found contact zones grappling with questions about what counting could do to separate, identify, and understand colonial bodies, but they invented their own ideas for how it could be done. These formulations of bodies that could be understood through numbers and visions of global humanity separated into populations were profoundly shaped by the experience of colonial migration, slavery, wars, trade, and displacement.

Accounting for Colonialism

While philosophical and poetic rhetoric in Europe aligned colonialism, cataclysm, and censuses, indigenous people in the Americas confronted viscerally the upheaval wrought by expanding trade and colonial incursion. As Powhatan's order shows, the Americas were not uncounted spaces awaiting the arrival of European methods of quantification; rather, colonial encounters produced acts of counting people from all sides. The anecdote in Smith's *Historie* is not unique; in 1612—the same year Bacon coined "population" and four years before Uttamatomakkin accompanied Pocahontas—a Jesuit in what is today Maine wrote to his superiors that he "suddenly discovered Six . . . canoes Coming towards us," and the twenty-four Wabanaki men inside them "went through a thousand maneuvers and ceremonies before accosting us . . . In short, they continued to Come and go; they reconnoitered; they carefully noted our numbers, our Cannon, our arms, everything."[37] Tense and potentially hostile early colonial interactions like this between a priest and a group of men in canoes elicited heightened attention to counting bodies. This enumerating tactic of war—as the Latin *poplo-* refers to—structured meetings between indigenous people and Europeans around the Americas.

The question of how, when, and for what purpose people would be counted was a colonial dialogue of mutual engagement.

The Americas were not simply receptacles for imported European counting methods; rather, colonialism fostered the taking of and experimenting with population counts. One of the major advancements in European population science may even have been born out of one mathematician's conversations with Algonquian speakers. Thomas Harriot was an English court mathematician who visited the ill-fated Roanoke colony in 1585–1586, and upon his return, innovated new algebraic formulations of zero as well as made the first known calculations, before Malthus, of the limits of world population.[38] Harriot passed these unpublished notes on to his student Sir Walter Raleigh, who then included discussions of world population in his widely read *History of the World*. Harriot completed an orthography of the Algonquian language after extensive conversations with the prominent Algonquians Manteo and Wanchese, and Michael Booth suggests that the novel grammatical formulations Harriot studied in Roanoke enabled him to see algebra in a new way upon his return. In this way, Booth argues, Harriot may have been "a conduit for the introduction of Native American thought into the conceptual substructure of modernity."[39] To take Booth's speculation a step further, Harriot's firsthand research in America, and his contemplation of the potential of settler colonialism, may have also led to his interest in global population science. We cannot know for sure how much Manteo, Wanchese, and their world were on Harriot's mind when he attempted to calculate the maximum number of people who could stand on the globe, but neither can we discount the possibility that interactions in the Americas contributed instrumentally to this scientific history.

If colonialism's role in Harriot's contribution to the scientific history of population thought is conjectural, we know for sure that censuses—along with fears of cataclysm and extinction—explicitly fill the pages of the most extensive alphabetic book by an indigenous writer from the early colonial period. Felipe Guaman Poma de Ayala's 1615–1616 text, *El primer nueva corónica y buen gobierno* (The First New Chronicle and Good Government) tells the story of Spanish conquest from the perspective of an Andean member of the Yarovilca ethnic group, who served as viceroys within the Inca empire in Peru.[40] The Incas were effective bureaucrats who employed *quipus*, a form of writing based on counting knots arranged on bundles of rope, in order to keep track of the people and possessions under their control. English readers knew about these textile census records through Samuel Purchas, who himself met Uttamatomakkin in London, even if they aligned them only with writing or mathematical instruments in general, and not counting people in particular.[41] Purchas included "Quippos in Stones or Threads, as in Peru" in his essay on "Discourse on the Diversity of Languages," and includes them as methods used by "Arithmeticians and Astronomers in the figures of their Arts,"[42] along with Egyptian hieroglyphs and Mexican pictographs. Moreover, Purchas's widely read collection of travel stories from 1625, *Hakluytus Posthumus or Purchas His Pilgrimes*, includes sixteenth-century Spanish writer Garcilaso de la Vega's description of an "oration" by the Incas about the first attempts to convert them to Christianity that "was kept by the tradition of Quipus (or Quippos) which are the knot-records of Cassamarca where the deede was done."[43] The Spanish considered this form of writing and census-taking threatening enough to have the Council of Lima order the destruction of all quipus in 1583, and modern museums did not begin collecting the extant fragile artifacts made of cotton until 1895.[44] As a result, no one today can fully interpret the texts that recorded some of the most expansive pre-Columbian censuses in the Americas.[45]

In a book-length letter to the Spanish king written in Spanish, Quechua, and Aymara and filled with illustrations, Guaman Poma retells Incan history, including the effectiveness of their census-taking, in order to argue for more Andean self-rule within the Spanish Empire. When trying to understand how Anglophone writers in Atlantic colonies experimented with methods of counting people as a response to colonial encounters—and thus cultivated new quantifiable forms of subjectivity in the process— Guaman Poma's writing about censuses illuminates the active role indigenous people played in this dialogue. Writing in response to colonialism fostered a proliferation of new ways of using quantification to understand social life, and Guaman Poma's book points to how writers like Smith or Harriot were not simply applying metropolitan methods abroad, but rather, were responding to colonial experiences. Guaman Poma's text arises from different political contexts and languages than those which organized the British Empire, but learning from the ways indigenous people responded to colonialism by counting bodies requires making hemispheric connections. [46] Transnational comparisons help to ameliorate the loss of records like Uttamatomakkin's stick or the results of the Wabanaki men's reconnaissance, and bring indigenous texts into conversation with, in this case, European population science.[47] Because of the paucity of indigenous voices in the historical record (a silencing that colonialism enforced), the archive presents only Smith's version of Uttamatomakkin's reconnaissance efforts; however, it also includes Guaman Poma's writing about orders to "number the people" from exactly the same year.

Guaman Poma wrote the lines of his chapter on the "General Inspection" in a form that resembles that of a *quipu*, thus illustrating how the census is inextricably bound up with the representative form in which Incans recorded it, as can been seen in Figures I.1 and I.2.[48] The chapter describes how the laws of the Incas "order that there be chief accountants" (GP, 185 [187]), and how the census divided people, including women and children, into ten *vecitas*, or age groupings: "Such inspections were done every six months, going from group to group according to the age of the women . . . In every extended family the people will keep an account of their children with *quipo* strings."[49] This constant monitoring, Guaman Poma claims, had social engineering and promoting population growth as its distinct goals. As part of a *vecita*, each person has a distinct relation to the kingdom, and is assigned a

FIGURE I.1 Andean quipu from the Khipu Database Project, khipukamayuq.fas. harvard.edu (Image courtesy Gary Urton).

particular obligation to it. Guaman Poma writes, "The ones that were able worked; the ones that could have a husband and give birth, multiplied" (GP, 222 [224]). Telling the story of the census, Guaman Poma contrasts Andean capacities for social engineering with the disarray Spanish rule has brought about at every turn: by counting *vecitas*, inspectors were able to redistribute resources to those who had little, such as orphans and the elderly. Without the census, however, Guaman Poma writes that previous programs like the abundant "charity for the sick old ladies in the kingdom" have been abandoned: "Under Christian doctrine, there is no one who would do the same for young boys and girls, and old women who can still work will not even bend over to do anything so they become poor. . . . [T]hus it turns the world upside-down" (GP, 220 [222]). For Guaman Poma, counting people works simultaneously as history, resistance, and political engagement.[50]

At the same time that the book draws on censuses to make sense of what Andeans lost as a result of conquest, it also remains

FIGURE I.2 "First General Inspection." From Don Felipe Guaman Poma de Ayala, *El primer nueva corónica y buen gobierno*, page 195 [197]. Copenhagen, Det Kongelige Bibliotek, gks 2232 4° (Courtesy of Det Kongelige Bibliotek/ The Royal Library of Denmark).

preoccupied with a form of cataclysm. Called *"pachacuti"* and loosely translated as "world-reversal" or "cataclysm," the *Nueva corónica* generally uses *pachacuti* as a synonym for a depopulating "disaster," such as a volcano eruption, plague, famine, or destructive storm.[51] Guaman Poma, who worked as an assistant to a Spanish priest, interweaves Incan history with the biblical story of Noah and the Flood, calling it *unu yacu pachacuti*, or "water-cataclysm" (GP, 51).[52] Guaman Poma's history of the Andean people repeats the idea that they are descended from ancient people who were dispersed by the Flood, connecting colonialism to a previous moment of catastrophic population loss and subsequent fertility.[53] When he first relates the story of Noah, he claims that the Flood was in part God's response to overpopulation: "The world was so filled with men that they no longer fit, and they no longer knew the Creator and Maker of men. So God ordered that the world be punished; everything created within it, for their sins, was punished by the waters of the flood" (GP, 16). After the dispersal of the Flood, the people of the Andes repopulated the earth: the "First generation of Indians . . . [were] the ones who came from Noah's ark after the Flood. After the people from Noah's ark multiplied by God's order, they spread throughout the world" (GP, 49). Andeans used the concept of *pachacuti*, or cataclysm, to interpret their experience of European invasion—certainly an upheaval of their experience of the world—while at the same time adapting it to make sense of the "mental furniture" the invaders brought with them, as Sabine MacCormack argues: "When thinking of *pachacuti* after the invasion," MacCormack states, "Andeans took cognizance of the Last Judgment, but they did so on their own terms."[54]

Writing stories about censuses and about depopulating cataclysms enabled Guaman Poma to confront the dramatic changes and losses of colonial invasion "on [his] own terms." The *Nueva corónica* embraces the blending of beliefs, writing methods, and languages inherent to colonialism in order to manipulate discourses about population in a self-affirming way.[55] It shows how

a writer located far from the center of imperial power could turn
to population counts as a representative tactic to respond to colonial upheaval. In the century and a half before Malthus, English
writers who visited and settled in American colonies stepped
into a discursive field of human accounting that Guaman Poma,
Powhatan, and the Wabanakis had already established. The history of how modern citizens came to understand themselves as
quantifiable therefore cannot be told as one solely of exportation
from east to west, but rather includes the adaptation of ideas about
population by the colonial objects of state accounts who turned
themselves into subjects. Counting bodies was not—or was not
only—a top-down political imposition, but could also foster horizontal connections when those being counted were counting
as well. Through acts of representative creativity like Guaman
Poma's, colonial writers marshaled the concept of people as data
in order to tell their own unique stories.

Naturalizing an Enumerable Self

While recognizing cross-colonial connections and the ongoing
presence of indigenous voices, *Counting Bodies* focuses primarily on writing and printing in the British Atlantic colonies that
experimented with new ideas about population before this field
of inquiry was established as a science. It tells the story of how
enumerating people on a regular basis came to seem natural and
normal, and therefore it presents case studies that illuminate moments within a broader epistemological shift largely driven by
colonialism. Each case study, like that of Guaman Poma, highlights
a particular and idiosyncratic step toward conceiving of the self as
a number within a larger quantifiable whole. Taken together, the
case studies open a window into a vibrant early colonial creative
field of experimentation with how to apply accounting methods
to social life. Rather than attempting a history of discourse—
and certainly this line of inquiry is indebted to Michel Foucault's
work on the history of population thought[56]—I investigate the

complexities of texts from different moments in place and time in order to offer what Bruno Latour calls "a more realistic account of science-in-the-making," a breaking down of differences between the "social world" and "objective reality."[57] This breaking down involves a dissolution of the perception that there was a linear march from Bodin toward quotidian statistics, replacing it with the recognition that there were instead laterally reaching nodes of a rhizome, each node unique and brimming with possibilities for new ways to count human bodies.[58]

The first chapter, "Poetics of the Ark Ashore," traces the effects and transformations of Jean Bodin's population theory as it filtered into the consciousness of the first generation of English Puritan migrants to New England. I show how poetry can and did conceptually realign social relationships according to ideas about population in the way that we have otherwise only credited to self-consciously theoretical or political texts. In the process, I argue that the relationship between early population thought and colonialism fundamentally shaped the Puritan antecedents of American literature. Like William Bradford, the chronicler of Plymouth colony, America's first English poet Anne Bradstreet developed forms of writing that adapted influential early population theories to lived experience in the colonies. Whereas Bradford carefully designed an intergenerational census that highlighted Puritan success, Bradstreet transformed French poet Guillaume du Bartas's renderings of colonial population to infuse representations of numbered bodies with affective and reproductive concerns.

After considering New England, the second chapter turns to the Caribbean to show that population discourse did not solely emerge from settler colonies. In "Measuring Caribbean Aesthetics," I show how slavery fostered new forms of human accounting, and reveal the storytelling inherent in the tables, lists, and budgets that marked the early decades of the Atlantic slave trade. The most extensive account of seventeenth-century English Caribbean sugar cultivation, Richard Ligon's *True and Exact History of the Island of Barbados*, combines late-Renaissance aesthetic theories of measuring bodies with the emerging economy of extracting profits from indentured and enslaved labor to take a narrative census of a chaotic island. Ligon combines natural history, anecdotal storytelling, and plantation accounts to provide a snapshot of Barbados and its inhabitants decades before the first imperial census of the island. Ligon's human accounting responds to the unprecedented turbulence of the radically new social environment of Caribbean colonialism, showing how enumerating bodies can make the violent and dangerous seem beautiful and controlled. Ligon's peculiar mixture of aesthetics and body counts was far different from the methods used within imperial political arithmetic, but he formed it out of intimate experience, as a way to disavow instability and intensify the allure of investment in an exotic island.

While the book's first half illuminates writings by early colonial migrants who turned to conceptions of population to understand their presence in the New World, the second half emphasizes the ongoing way in which population counts mediated inter-colonial interactions. The third chapter, "Counting in King Philip's War," argues that keeping track of population numbers was central to the ways in which second-generation Anglo-Americans wrote about wars of territorial expansion. In it, I show how English colonial settlers used population counts as a weapon against indigenous people, drawing on the authority of numerical language to efface indigenous claims to both land and perspectives on history. Against Increase Mather's triumphalist account of the war, Puritan Mary Rowlandson's narrative of her experience as a captive vividly portrays both the necessity and the impossibility of waging a colonial war between cultures by counting either side. In the context of wartime hostage-taking, Rowlandson's attempts at early human accounting show how women and children pose a very real threat to framing war as a numerical competition. Unlike adult men, their bodies render them particularly vulnerable to becoming adopted as members of the other side.

Continuing with an investigation of how entrenched thinking about people in terms of population became a form of colonial self-conception, the fourth chapter, "The Death and Life of Colonial Mortality Bills," traces the forms of human accounting that appeared in the earliest colonial newspapers across North American port cities. Applying the methods of the literary critic to materials that have until now been primarily the province of historians and historical demographers, I look for the stories about subjectivity told by these frequently printed tables to argue that colonial death statistics paved the way toward public acceptance of the state practice of counting life. The tallies of local deaths that appeared in newspapers across Anglo-American cities in the early eighteenth century portrayed colonial bodies as currency in an Atlantic colonial circuit of information, connecting settler communities with metropolitan culture in a way that refutes arguments that the North American climate is inhospitable to human reproduction. Yet paradoxically, these assertions about reproductive potential are based on counts of burials, because deaths are easier to count than births. Borrowing a tool from postcolonial theory, Achille Mbmebe's concept of "necropolitics" helps elucidate the role death plays in the negotiation of race and community in these early colonial cities. The tables themselves—called bills of mortality—present an ordered and segregated vision of colonial social life that neutralizes the threat of mixture between the different kinds of people living and dying in Philadelphia, Charleston, New York, or Boston. Benjamin Franklin, especially, focused his early efforts as a printer on burial data, and Malthus's later use of Franklin's calculations of colonial population—calculations about the regeneration of life that were based on recorded numbers of death—shows the centrality of colonial print culture to the development of population science.

The epilogue, "Mourning the Figure of Three-Fifths," traces the resonances of cataclysm and colonial accountings of race at the turn of the nineteenth century, when population became both an organizing principle of the new US government and a term increasing in circulation after Malthus published his influential work. I read the US Constitution's clause counting slaves as "three-fifths" of a person in dialogue with Thomas Jefferson's *Notes on the State of Virginia* and the American reprints of William Cowper's series of poems on the annual bills of mortality as late forms of human accounting. These texts show how unresolved problems from earlier population discourse continue to linger in a later era, while at the same time they signal a profound realignment of the role of counting people in everyday life.

Describing how to engage productively with scientific discourse, Latour insists on blurring the distinction between "the ontological questions on the one hand and the epistemological questions on the other." Latour argues that "something has been lost" within a critical approach that "depends on a clear distinction between what is real and what is constructed, what is out there in the nature of things and what is there in the representation we make of them."[59] Walter Mignolo and Diana Taylor have explicitly linked this type of critique of "what is real" with colonialism, a political activity that meant "that the dominant views of languages, of recording the past, and of charting territories become synonymous with the real by obstructing possible alternatives."[60] *Counting Bodies* shows that the ways writers, performers, and printers represent bodies numerically shapes what kind of matter those bodies are, and most importantly, that there is more than one way to do that shaping. Answers to ontological questions have profound consequences: if a human body counts as one, and not as an inseparable part of a group, or of an ecosystem, how can societies recognize rights beyond those of the individual? How do we understand the agency of assemblages, as Jane Bennett has discussed, or of geological phenomena?[61] If a nation's founding document counts certain bodies as only three-fifths of a person, what kind of work must be done to *re*count them as whole individuals within that society? Historicizing the notions of countable bodies that emerged at the end of the eighteenth century and recognizing their colonial origins renders these questions both visible and urgent.

CHAPTER 1

Poetics of the Ark Ashore

In the seventeenth century, the counting of human bodies fostered different ways of viewing intimate relationships, social stratifications, and colonial potential. It was an imaginatively productive activity, encouraging the development of new ways of conceiving of the connections between people both in domestic spaces and on the world stage. Because counting intervened in the most private of bonds, explorations of counting people in poetic and personal writings are just as worthy of scrutiny as is the state science of political arithmetic. The work of seventeenth-century New England poet Anne Bradstreet shows how encounters with emerging ideas about people as populations provided fertile ground for reimagining both political and domestic relationships through poetry. By detailing the ways Bradstreet intervened creatively into the questions population science asks about community, membership, and reproduction, I argue for a more complex and varied understanding of the power dynamics involved in the making and shaping of scientific meaning. Bradstreet's writing shows that new ideas about the implications of numbering bodies can emerge from a vantage point that combines colonial and domestic spaces with affective and reproductive concerns.

Along with Puritan leader John Winthrop, Anne Bradstreet migrated to Salem, Massachusetts, in 1630 at the age of eighteen with her husband and parents on the ship *Arbella*. Educated by her father Thomas Dudley and given access to a wide range of reading materials thanks to her father's support and her membership in one of early New England's most influential families, Bradstreet wrote poetry throughout her life and circulated it among family and friends. In 1650, *The Tenth Muse Lately Sprung Up in America* was published in London, inaugurating Bradstreet as the first published American poet of English-language verse. She later claimed that her brother-in-law published it without her permission, and the debate over the accuracy of this claim reflects the tensions surrounding female publication at a time of transition from the practice of sharing manuscripts among a coterie to the printing and mass distribution of books—especially in the Massachusetts Bay Colony, where church leaders had excommunicated her sister Sarah three years before *The Tenth Muse* appeared.[1] In 1682, Bradstreet's family published a posthumous second edition of *The Tenth Muse*, adding her later poems, including "The Author to Her Book," which makes the claim about the book having been "snatched ... by friends" to the printer.[2] Bradstreet's legacy as the first Anglo-American poet was powerfully influential from the start: Edward Taylor, the eighteenth-century Puritan poet of religious meditations, kept a copy of *The Tenth Muse* in his library, and in the late twentieth century, the poet Adrienne Rich wrote an introduction to a new edition of Bradstreet's complete works which claimed Bradstreet as an origin for American feminist writing.[3]

The mantle of "America's first English poet" has not been an easy one for Bradstreet's writing to bear. The weight of Bradstreet's extraordinary biography, compounded by the fact that some of her most famous poems are intensely personal, increases the gravitational pull toward searching for the poet inside the poetry. While

Bradstreet was praised in her lifetime primarily for epic poems on ancient history and natural philosophy, Rich dismissed these poems as imitative of male writers, and instead celebrated her personal lyrics about marital love, mourning, and domestic trials. These lyrics include poems like Bradstreet's 1659 "In Reference to Her Children," which links a reflection on mothering work with an act of counting: "I had eight birds hatched in one nest / Four cocks there were, and hens the rest. / I nursed them up with pain and care, / No cost, nor labour did I spare" (ll. 3–6).[4] Following Rich's division, critics have rarely considered Bradstreet's epics and lyrics together as complementary forms comprising coherent conceptual responses to questions that reappear across Bradstreet's writing. For example, Ivy Schweitzer highlights Bradstreet's male family members' commandeering of a woman's publication by describing the long poems as appearing "in a state of incompleteness that no poet ... would have permitted for publication."[5] Our modern inability to integrate Bradstreet's lyrics and epics as worthy of study with the same conceptual tools reflects the inability to resolve the debate as to whether she chose printed book publication: the most fruitful analysis lies in combining both viewpoints in an approach to her work. The epics in *Tenth Muse* engage with Renaissance debates about the body and complicate philosophical assumptions about femininity[6]—subjects that constitute the arena in which the personal concerns of the lyrics contend. Even if, as Schweitzer contends, Bradstreet's longer poems were intended only to be drafts, not completed works ready to be shared, they nevertheless reflect a particular engagement with history and natural philosophy that persists, albeit in different forms, across her lyrics. By refusing to separate the concerns motivating a lyric like "In Reference to Her Children," from, for example, the interest in colonial conquest that appears in Bradstreet's monarchical epics, I show that Bradstreet's portrayal of motherhood grapples with the particularly colonial difficulties of migration and sustaining connection in the absence of physical proximity. Bradstreet's census of her children goes on to lament how each "bird" takes flight: the first "left me quite" (l. 10), the second was "blown by southern gales" (l. 19), another "to the academy flew" (l. 29). She thus presents a vision of family only tenuously attached to a particular place, but connected instead through the memory of the mother who raised them: "In shady woods I'll sit and sing, / And things that past to mind I'll bring" (ll. 71–72). In one example of the problems to which Bradstreet returns throughout her writing, this seemingly simple lyric describes how the affectively charged, absent presence of a mother bonds family members in the face of stretching colonial networks that threaten to divide them. Bradstreet's writing returns, across all these forms, to the problems of membership within a community, of success across generations, and of determining the limits of individuality inside intimate relationships.

These problems Bradstreet describes regarding the cultural work of motherhood are also the central concerns of population science; indeed, the books from her father's library which Bradstreet drew upon for her own writing were filled with ideas about the need for, and implications of, counting people across time and across the globe. Bradstreet read extensively among writers influenced by early theories of world population, including Sir Walter Raleigh, whose 1614 *Historie of the World*, upon which Bradstreet based her own historical epics, considered the decline of population in classical times, as well as the French Huguenot poet Guillaume du Bartas, whose biblical epic about the creation of the world was deeply influenced by Jean Bodin, the influential early advocate of state censuses. Du Bartas's 1578 epic poem was translated into English by Josuah Sylvester in 1605 as *His Divine Weeks*, just a year before English translations of two early works of population science by Bodin and Giovanni Botero began circulating in London. Bradstreet wrote an ode to her "great, dear, sweet Du Bartas" (l. 3) in 1641, and friends repeatedly compare her to him in the prefatory poems of *The Tenth Muse*.

Early theorists of population science politicized intimate realms of family life when they advocated for regular state counts of women and children as well as men. Censuses that encompass every kind of body, not just those of potential soldiers, assign public significance to individuals who otherwise would be rendered visible to the state only through their relation to others, such as a husband, father, or master. Seventeenth-century political arithmetic added women, children, and the elderly or disabled to the total. Population counts throw open the doors of the home, and in the process they subject the individual building blocks of a family network to inspection.

However, population science goes farther than merely representing bodies that are usually excluded from discourses about economics and state power. From its earliest iterations, population thought has consistently examined the conditions of reproduction. Botero insisted that "planting" people in colonies would ensure the greater "increase" of families at home, and Montesquieu lamented the colonies' drain of metropolitan virility at the height of French natalist politics. Questions of how quickly people reproduce, and how that ability compares to that of members of outside groups, propelled discussions of how to keep censuses. In 1685, thirteen years after Bradstreet's death in Massachusetts, British Royal adviser and surveyor William Petty noted the urgent state interest in discovering how long indigenous women in New England breastfed their children, as a way to compare their population growth rates with those of imperial subjects: "At what age have young women usually their first child? and after what age do they beare none? . . . How long do their children suck? And what food do they give them in the first yeare, besides the mother's milk? . . . How many Children have the most fruitfull women, and at what distances?"[7] Women do not merely become visible, along with their children, through censuses and the population discourse that surrounds them; their sexuality, their labor, and their mothering work comes under state scrutiny as well. The state shines a light into the domestic realm and imbues pregnancy, nursing, and childrearing with an altered political dimension. When the globe becomes divided into counted, monitored, and competing populations, relations between nations come down to relations between husband and wife and between mother and child.

More than any other early modern poetry in the colonial Anglophone Atlantic world, the body of work produced by Puritan poet Anne Bradstreet calls attention to the collapse of distinctions between the personal and the political.[8] I uncover Bradstreet's open engagement with ideas about the global implications of population and fertility rather than her subversions of this discourse, while at the same time I present her as uniquely positioned to contribute a reproductively female perspective to these early debates. Bradstreet labored as a wife and mother in a settler colony, an environment which politicizes reproduction and places women's bodies at the center of inquiries into colonial population. Through her writing, Bradstreet responds to emerging discourses about population that altered the political significance of her own body's reproductive capacity.

Bradstreet's poetry about her "four cocks, and hens the rest," or, more famously, of her "little babes, my dear remains" (l. 24) in "Before the Birth of One of Her Children," explores the stark contrast between disappearance and fertility delineated by population discourse. Less famously, Bradstreet's epic "Four Monarchies" tells the story of an ancient battle waged within colonial population dynamics. In this confrontation, named the battle of "Arbela" and thus resonating with Bradstreet's own colonial experience of arriving in America on the ship *Arbella*, an outnumbered legion claims victory over a far greater number of barbarians by linking the cultural work of shaping character to imperial success. Read together, Bradstreet's epics, lyrics, and prose consider the question of what makes a person a member of a community, which is a central concern of population science. Bradstreet's writing explores the limitations of viewing people in terms of populations by exploring the ways affect, displacement, and motherhood impact simple counts.

Bradstreet's poetry demonstrates how emotional connections and the labor of shaping character—the central preoccupations of the cultural work of motherhood—cause imprecisions and potential fluctuations in the enumeration of generations. From their beginnings, discussions of population vacillate between the nodes of cataclysm and regeneration, with each one inconceivable without the other. In Bradstreet's writing, the labor of mothering becomes the site of death, pain, and cataclysm upon which regeneration depends. These representations of motherhood shift the large-scale abstract concerns of population science to a much more intimate sphere, one which includes affective bonds in considerations of who counts and how they might be counted. Whereas a writer like Du Bartas draws upon the figure of Noah, as Guaman Poma did, to portray the conceptual ties between colonial destruction and population, Bradstreet's portrayal of mothering work replaces Noah as the representative field through which to understand the proximity between mortality and reproduction. Across Bradstreet's writings, mothering labor becomes a two-stage process of producing new life, and then shaping that life—a means of intervening in the world to protect against the destructive forces that loom alongside reproduction. Bradstreet explores the difference between the production of mere numbers of humans and the raising, "with pain and care," of desirable kinds of people. Unlike a population count, which represents human life as static and easily categorized, Bradstreet's writings focus on the instability of life after birth and the need for representative tools, such as lists, to intervene and repeatedly order the world. Like a colonial mother, written records that organize worldly phenomena work to shape mere life into a coherent community, transforming potential catastrophe into vibrant population. A list counting and ordering humanity is an abstract reminder of communal bonds across space and time—a reminder that must be continually updated—and in Bradstreet's writing, the memory of a mother serves a similar enduring purpose.

Enumerating Colonial Success

The same year that Bradstreet's *Tenth Muse* first appeared in print, William Bradford took a second census of the original *Mayflower* passengers, thirty years after their arrival in Plymouth Colony, in his history *Of Plymouth Plantation*. Both 1650 texts portray families and generations on a world stage. Bradford's census and Bradstreet's poetry are contemporaneous texts using different forms to understand similar problems. Both texts ask questions about how to measure the success of a colony through reproduction, how to represent family and communal relationships, and how to distinguish a member of a group from an outsider in the context of colonial migration.

Bradford took the initial census of the passengers on the *Mayflower* in 1620, a decade before Bradstreet sailed to Massachusetts. Bradford appears to have read Bodin's writings, and he paid careful attention to the losses and gains of this original group over three decades.[9] Bradford's second census of these families in Plymouth Colony, taken in 1650, points to the representational problems the first generation of New England Puritans faced in assessing the rise and fall of their own numbers. The colonists in Plymouth endured catastrophic losses of life in the early years of the settlement, and Bradford's second census simultaneously acknowledges these deaths while refusing to count them numerically.[10] "I have thought it not unworthy my paines to take a veiw of the decreasings & increasings of these persons," Bradford writes, "and such changs as hath pased over them & theirs, in this thirty years."[11] Separated into two columns (one on the left for listing the numbers of each household, and one on the right for describing the household in narrative form), those households whose members have died by 1650 without leaving progeny are represented in the left-hand column only by a blank space, not the number zero, as illustrated in Figure 1.1. For example, no numbers appear in the ledger next to the words, "Mr. Martin, he & all his, dyed in the first infection not long after the arivall" (452). In his history, Bradford could have chosen to take a census only of the living

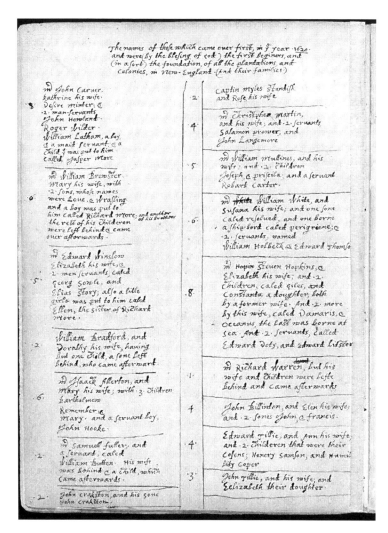

FIGURE 1.1 Bradford's 1650 census (Courtesy State Library of Massachusetts).

inhabitants of Plymouth Colony thirty years after its founding, excluding completely those families who left behind no survivors. However, his strategy of using the left column to enumerate only the living, while acknowledging both the dead and the living in prose in the narrative space on the right, firmly ties the measurement of the community's population to the original colonial endeavor. Through narrative, the generational chain of the colonists remains unbroken, and through numbers, only the success of those generations may be measured. Bradstreet was a member of a different community of New England Puritans, but her writing also considers these questions of measuring generations. Moreover, she complicates this discourse by describing the work of motherhood as the labor of producing those numbers in the left-hand column.

Bradstreet's epics acknowledge her interest in theories of the body and ideas about the rise and fall of populations, while her lyrics explore the tensions inherent in raising a family upon which God will bestow favor. Illustrating a connection similar to that between Bradstreet's epic and lyric poetry, Bradford's comparative censuses represent each individual family's ability to produce offspring as reflective of the success of the colony as a whole. The narrative column focuses on the household, but the numerical column ties that household to the larger story of the community. For example, the first entry of the second census notes the number "15," and then tells the story of the Carvers:

> Mr. Carver and his wife dyed the first year; he in ye spring, she in ye somer; also, his man Roger and ye little boy Jasper dyed before either of them, of ye commone infection. Desire Minter returned to her freinds, & proved not very well, and dyed in England. His servant boy Latham, after more then 20. years stay in the country, went into England, and from thence to the Bahamy Ilands in ye West Indies, and ther, with some others, was starved for want of food. His maid servant maried, & dyed a year or tow after, here in this place.
>
> His servant, John Howland, maried the doughter of John Tillie, Elizabeth, and they are both now living, and have 10. children, now all living; and their eldest daughter hath 4. children. And ther 2. daughter, 1. all living; and other of their children mariagable. So 15. are come of them. (450)

Whereas in Bradford's 1620 accounting of the passengers, the Carver family and servants are listed as totaling "8," thirty years later that number has been replaced by "15," even though the narrative column describes how almost all of them died or left in the first years of the colony. The numbers transform the loss of "ye common infection" into a decisive gain for the entire Carver household, not just for the one servant who survived. Thanks to the children that "are come of them," the column of numbers tells a story of a second generation of colonists who have nearly doubled the numbers with which they began.

The numerical columns of Bradford's comparative census portray a colonial view of population that contrasts abundant increase, as in the case with the Carver household, with unrecorded absence, like that of the Martins. In the representative logic of the left-hand column of numbers, a family that has not reproduced simply disappears. All of the families to whom Bradford accords a number in the 1650 accounting have increased their numbers from the first census, even if only one servant survived and had progeny.[12] In this way, Bradford's comparative census denies the possibility of population decline or even of stability. The only direction for the numbers in the left-hand column to go is up; Bradford includes no number zero, and no family that was not completely eradicated is counted as having fewer members than lived in 1620. At least within the logic of the numerical left-hand column, Bradford presents the original *Mayflower* passengers as having only two options: disappear or increase.

Over a decade after Bradford represented colonial population with his second census, and in a different part of New England, Bradstreet wrote elegies for lost grandchildren that reflect her own fears about the fecundity of the second generation she labored to create. In another elegy, Bradstreet praises her own mother, Dorothy Dudley, for living long enough to see the lasting fruits of her mothering work: "Of all her children, children lived to see" (l. 19). Like a mortality table counting her family's losses, the increasing intensity of the three successive elegies Bradstreet writes between 1665 and 1669 suggests a mounting fear that reproduction is failing. When the third of Bradstreeet's daughter-in-law Mercy's children dies almost as soon as he is born, Bradstreet must also face the possibility that she may not live to see children "of all her children," as her own mother did: "No sooner came, but gone, and fall'n asleep, / Acquaintance short, yet parting caused us weep; / Three flowers, two scarcely blown, the last i' th' bud, / Cropt by th'Almighty's hand; yet is He good" (ll. 5–8). In this elegy for her grandson Simon, Bradstreet counts backward from three, to two, to the last, counting down toward smaller numbers rather than representing an increase in number across generations. The metric stress on "is" in "is He good" makes this declarative statement sound like a question, and the lines that follow, which a biographer describes as "very angry,"[13] repeat the contraction "let's" three times as though Bradstreet is half-heartedly reconstituting a beleaguered group in response to a catastrophic succession of losses: "With dreadful awe before Him let's be mute, / Such was His will, but why, let's not dispute, / With humble hearts and mouths put in the dust, / Let's say He's merciful as well as just" (ll. 9–12). Bradstreet cautions against speaking twice —"let's be mute" and "let's not dispute"—before ending the short poem with an injunction to praise God. But the praise she gives refers to his judgment of the community: he is "merciful" and "just" in his choice of taking Mercy's offspring, and his actions are a proper reflection of what the "mouths put in the dust" deserve.

Like Bradford comparing his census of the first generation of *Mayflower* migrants with a census of their descendants, Bradstreet's elegies portray the struggling second generation of her colonial family as a measure of the "humble hearts" around them. Taken together, the elegies Bradstreet writes for her own mother, these three grandchildren, and finally for their mother Mercy, reflect the stark contrast between the numerical absence and abundant increase in Bradford's human accounting. Bradstreet's elegies narrate the complete destruction of her daughter-in-law Mercy's family, like Bradford tells the story of the Carvers. Unlike Bradford in the second census, however, Bradstreet in her poetry mourns the dead. Her affective bonds with each "dear babe" prevent them from going unrecorded, as they would have in Bradford's column of numbers: "Farewell sweet babe," Bradstreet writes of her granddaughter Elizabeth, "the pleasure of mine eye" (l. 7). The dead appear numerically, as well, in Bradstreet's elegies. Not only does she count backward, after Simon's death, from "Three flowers, two scarcely blown," to "the last i' th' bud," but also she enumerates each death in the title of her elegies with the date and the exact age of the dead, recorded in years, months, and days. For Bradstreet, numbers serve to account for and measure each lost life, insisting on its presence in the past. For Bradford, counting human numbers is relevant only when pointing toward the future.

Du Bartas's Noah and the Fertile Ark Ashore

Although Bradstreet and Bradford were both seventeenth-century New England Puritans influenced, to varying degrees, by Bodin's advocacy of state censuses, they wrote for very different purposes. Bradstreet wrote for an intimate circle of friends and family; Bradford wrote to give a small political community narrative shape. Early British imperial political arithmetic, however, points toward the subject of the bodies of women like Mercy Bradstreet and Dorothy Dudley, and of the mothering labor involved in both nurturing and, if necessary, mourning children. A century before Petty demanded to know the age at which indigenous women weaned their children, Bodin's career had linked anxious interest in women's unregulated power within intimate social spheres to the desire to count people. Though his much-debated theories of state power, the body, and censuses influenced many political philosophers, Bodin was best known in the seventeenth century for his 1580 On the Demon-mania of Witches. Historians have attributed witch-prosecution fevers throughout Europe in the ensuing decades in part to this book, which Bodin wrote after he advocated state censuses in his treatise on commonwealths. In this later work, Bodin insists on the vitality and prevalence of pernicious female power, following up his embrace of human accounting with an inquiry into the potential threat women pose to social order.[14] Concerns about women's social roles thus attended scientific thought about population from the beginning. This discourse connects Bradford's and Bradstreet's concerns, and shows how each writer presents a different lens through which to view the subject of colonial population.

Bradstreet developed her poetic approach to considering generational increase partly as a response to Du Bartas's interpretation of the biblical precedent for settler colonialism. Guillaume de Salluste, Seigneur Du Bartas finished *Les Colonies*, the section of his epic that considered how to understand the New World through a reading of Genesis, in 1584, and based it on his reading of Bodin's work. Before Milton, Du Bartas was the poet of choice for English Protestants like Bradstreet, though he is little-read today. Especially in the section *Les Colonies*, Du Bartas and his English translator Sylvester promoted ideas about human reproduction as a colonizing force. As a way to incorporate the Americas in a narrative of biblical history, Du Bartas suggested that the Americas were, like Ararat, first peopled by a European boat gone astray. New England readers like Bradstreet encountered a vivid portrayal of the interconnectedness of progeny, colonial success, and biblical precedent in Du Bartas's epic.

Les Colonies begins with an imperative to trace the origins of all inhabited places: "Yea, sing the Worlds so divers populations; / And of least Cities showe the first Foundations."[15] *The Colonies* separates place and genealogical connection from the outset; privileging the "populations," in the sense of centers of human habitation, and "first foundations" of cities over discussions of ancient races or titles. With this move, the poem can concern itself with the ways that different people come to inhabit different places, creating a vision of humans as having been migratory since the beginning of time, rather than attached to fixed locations.

Occupants of a territory follow one another in their possession of a place, like stewards:

> Sith it befals not alwayes, that his seed
> Who builds a Town, doth in the same succeed:
> And (to conclude) sith vnder Heav'n, no Race
> Perpetually possesseth any place:
> But, as all Tenants at the High Lords will,
> We hold a Field, a Forrest, or a Hill. (*DW*, 270)

Here Du Bartas naturalizes colonization by concluding that no one race has a right to their land in perpetuity. This then makes peripheral landscapes volatile places; a "Field, a Forrest, or a Hill" is always contested ground, even for those who descend from the town's original builder.

To render this instability a more familiar and less threatening prospect, Du Bartas turns to the biblical story of Noah. When Guaman Poma invoked Noah, as I have shown, it was to draw a parallel between the cataclysmic Flood and colonization, and to write a shared history for Andean and European peoples. Despite coming from a very different location and literary tradition, Du Bartas draws on Noah to do something similar. For Du Bartas, Noah's story encapsulates both the exhilarating promise of populating a place anew, and the history of drastic mortality that makes the comprehension of human numbers in aggregate possible. The figure of Noah also allows Du Bartas to embrace migration and write about humanity as "doomed to wander."[16] This conception of humans as nomadic rather than tied "perpetually" to any particular location places a heavy emphasis on perpetuation, or the continuation of a race's line. Noah's family's fecundity offers a precedent for the possibilities for European fertility in new Ararats. This is very different from Guaman Poma, who interpreted the Flood as punishment for the world becoming too full of people—in that contemporaneous Andean text, the cataclysm was a population-checking measure. For the Huguenot Du Bartas, by contrast, the story presents colonization as a fortunate opportunity and the Flood as an incitement to fantastic reproduction. In *Les Colonies*, we see Noah's "happy Spawn, in sundry Colonies / Crossing from Sea to Sea, from Land to Land, / All the green-mantled nether Globe hath mann'd" (DW, 272–273). Sylvester's translation rhymes "seed" with "succeed" early on, and then "land" and "mann'd" to tie together populousness with the right to rule. The lucky "spawn" are scattered and yet still unified by both the "Globe" and by their common ancestor, Noah. This "manning" takes place, however, in the aftermath of cataclysm, if not violent conflict. When Bradstreet read Du Bartas's vision of the biblical precedent for colonial reproduction, she encountered a vision that presents raising large numbers of children as an essential colonial task of both rectifying and justifying the foundational suffering that occurred in the past.

As a survivor of the Flood whose family must repopulate the world, Noah simultaneously embodies the memory of mortal cataclysm and the promise of boundless fertility, and Du Bartas uses him to imagine the New World as a land recovering from a catastrophe. Just as Noah landed providentially on the hill that would become the known world, some stray seafarers may have landed in America and then filled it with people:

> Why! think ye (fond) those people fell from Heav'n
> All-ready-made . . .
> Or that they grew out of the fruitfull Earth,
> As Toad-stools, Turneps, Leeks, and Beets haue birth?..
> That spacious Coast, now call'd *America* ,
> Was not so soon peopled as *Africa* . . .
> But the rich buildings rare magnificence,
> Th'infinit Treasures, various gouernments,
> Showe that long since (although at sundry times)
> 'T had Colonies (although from sundry Climes):
> Whether the violence of tempestuous weather
> Som broken Vessels haue inforced thither;
> Whether som desperat, dire extremity

Of Plague, War, Famin; or th'Authority
Of som braue *Typhis* (in adventure tost)
Brought weary Carvels on that *Indian* Coast. (DW, 276)

A great storm, flood, "plague, war, [or] famine," washed men up
on America's shores, according to Du Bartas, and filled them with
people. And as this land was colonized once, so can it be colonized
and repopulated again. The crossing of the sea, and the confrontation with a foreign world, is itself a cataclysm like Noah's Flood,
which creates the opportunity for filling a space with new generations. Like population discourse, and like Bradstreet's movement
in her writing between epics and lyrics, Noah's story blurs the
distinction between cosmic and domestic concerns. In Du Bartas's
telling, the precedent of Noah's family on Ararat turns successful
reproduction into the test of whether colonialism can truly work.
There is no autochthony in the world—indigenous people did
not "grow up" from "toad-stools"—and this divorce of the human
capacity to reproduce from the land that sustains that labor frames
territorial competitions in terms of fertility. Pondering how one
stray ship could have peopled the New World, Du Bartas asks:

Have not our Daies a certain Father know'n,
Who, with the fruit of his own body grow'n,
Peopled a Village of a hundred Fires,
And issue-blest (the Crown of Old Desires)
In his own life-time, his own off-spring saw
To wed each other without breach of Law? (DW, 277)

Du Bartas makes it sound easy: a father lives long enough to see
his offspring, the products of his own desire, "people a village,"
and marry each other as distant cousins. This is a very different
vision of how Noah's family might have repopulated the world
than Guaman Poma gives: in that text, the world is repopulated
because of God's order to do so. Du Bartas focuses much more
on embodied human sexuality, divorced from a divine com-
mand: the population comes from "the fruit of his own body."

Seamlessly portable, innately reproducible, and territorially in-different, Du Bartas's colonizing populations are responsible for determining political control of a "village," a hill, or a continent, with their sexual desires alone. Overwhelming fertility—the capacity to "people a village of a hundred fires"—here restores the casualties wrought by cataclysm. Du Bartas recalls how Noah was able to do this without needing to draw upon any other line of descent, and imagines human reproduction itself as a colonizing force.

Then at the moment when Du Bartas's poem considers the sexual desire driving this political force, it turns toward cataloging the differences of various peoples. Sex and climate are the variables that introduce difference into a world population that springs from the same source, and a description of desire is followed by the urge to obsessively classify:

> And, but in season, *Venus* lists to enter.
> And, the cold, resting (vnder th' *Artick* Star)
> Still Master of the Field in champian War,
> Makes Heat retire into the Bodies-Tower:
> Which, there vnited, gives them much more powr.
>
> O! see how full of Wonders strange is Nature:
> Sith in each *Climat* , not alone in stature,
> Strength, hair and colour, that men differ doo,
> But in their humours and their manners too.
> Whether that, Custom into Nature change:
> Whether that, Youth to th'Elds example range:
> Or divers Laws of divers Kingdoms, vary-vs:
> Or th'influence of Heav'nly bodies, cary-vs.
>
> The Northern-man is fair, the Southern foul;
> That's white, this black; that smiles, and this
>   doth scoul (JS, 278–279).

The poem here asks the question of how to account for human difference, how to begin classification if, since Noah, humans have been perennially migratory and spring from the same source. Beyond "fair" or "foul," groups can also differ in their capacity for fertility. When the poem discusses "heat" and "cold," Du Bartas is referring to an early milieu-theory of climate, which posits that the cold of temperate climates forces northern bodies to retain heat, and thus sexual passion. The theory represents heated European bodies as potent both militarily and sexually.[17] Custom, parenting, laws, and divine intervention might all introduce variation in the post-diluvian world, but throughout *Les Colonies* the power rests in the group who can, like Noah, produce a maximum amount of progeny. In this biblical epic, Du Bartas fills an imaginative gap within thinking about colonial populations by casting humans as essentially migratory creatures equipped with reproductive capacities that make that migration succeed. Bradstreet found in Du Bartas's epic a compelling representation of the biblical foundations for colonialism, and the promise of new settlements maintained primarily by human fertility.

Cataclysm and Regeneration in Bradstreet's Poetry

When Bradstreet responded to writing by Du Bartas and others on bodies, nations, and families in her own poetry, she both embraced their ideas and shifted the focus of the conversation toward the affective bonds and mothering labor that cultivate bodies for the world. Moreover, Bradstreet reframes discussions about heat, humors, and the globe that Noah "hath mann'd" as a *querelle des femmes*, or literary quarrel about women: she personifies these forces and replaces teleology with competing desires. This allows Bradstreet to present the possibility of creating catalogs of the world's people as simultaneously enticing and mystifying. Rather than imparting unquestionably authoritative information, counts and catalogs inevitably frustrate the readers' desire for them to be comprehensive and complete. This complex, and alternately alluring and intimidating, representation of the task of classifying and listing people and their environments captures the conceptual entanglement of depopulation and population in Bradstreet's century. In *The Four Elements*, Bradstreet creates a poetic list of the world's peoples, as Du Bartas does when he announces he will "sing the world's divers populations." However, unlike Du Bartas, Bradstreet presents the Earth speaking in the first person about what she contains:

> To tell you of my countries and my regions,
> Soon would they pass not hundreds but legions:
> My cities famous, rich, and populous,
> Whose numbers now are grown innumerous. (ll. 155–158)

Bradstreet's Earth is teeming, but she is also coy—she holds information that the reader desires, but cannot necessarily access. Bradstreet has her brag to her sisters, the other elements Fire, Water, and Air, about her incalculability—her resistance to being recorded with a specific number. Bradstreet's Earth remains just beyond the reach of quantification, despite the desires for profit that send men in search of her commodities. She brags about a few of the animal species she contains, including unicorns and hyenas:

> Thousands in woods & plains, both wild & tame,
> But here or there, I list now none to name;
> No, though the fawning Dog did urge me sore,
> In his behalf to speak a word the more,
> Whose trust and valour I might here commend;
> But time's too short and precious so to spend.
> But hark you wealthy merchants, who for prize
> Send forth our well-manned ships where sun doth rise,
> After three years when men and meat is spent,
> My rich commodities pay double rent. (l. 192)

Earth gives the impression that it is possible to make a complete list of the species, wealth, and people she contains, but she is unwilling to share that list. The poem draws upon multiple meanings of the word "list" when Earth demurs with "I list now none to name," both the "list" that means desiring and the "list" that means registering. Species like the "fawning dog" long to be listed, to be named and counted in their thousands. The *OED* records the first use of the word "list" to mean a catalog or registry in Sir Walter Raleigh *History of the World*, one of Bradstreet's major sources for encountering early population discourse.[18] By personifying the Earth as a woman vying for a suitor, Bradstreet sexualizes the quantifying, archival impulse. The creation of lists thus carries both reproductive potential and affective power. This female Earth serves not only as a space where quantification is opaque, but also one in which numbers can be almost magically manipulated—by sending ships forth across her spaces, she can create profit, or "double rent," across her body.

Bradstreet's Earth's capacity to manipulate quantification extends, however, into inscrutably dispatching catastrophe. Not only a "womb" ready to people any available space, Bradstreet's Earth also serves ominously as a "tomb":

> Now I must show mine adverse quality,
> And how I oft work mans mortality: . . .
> The Corn and Hay do fall before th're mown,
> And buds from fruitful trees as soon as blown;
> Then dearth prevails, that nature to suffice
> The mother on her tender infant flies;
> Thy husband knows no wife, nor father sons,
> But to all outrages their hunger runs . . .
> Because in the abyss of my dark womb
> Your cities and yourselves I oft intomb.
>   (ll. 223–224, 229–234, 243–244)

Bradstreet's seemingly conventional "womb/tomb" rhyme encapsulates the difficulties of conceptualizing human numbers in their positivity. Disaster renders population visible, and so the meanings of womb and tomb blend into one another through rhyme, just as the meaning of population once blended with that of depopulation. Bradstreet also describes how Earth's fickle capacity for both populating and depopulating directly attacks the family, separating mothers from infants, and husbands from wives. We can see here how Bradstreet connects ideas about natural devastation with her personal loss of her grandson—she would later elegize her grandson Simon as "the last i' th' bud," and write that the children who died before him were "scarcely blown." The concern in her earlier epic with "buds from fruitful trees as soon as blown" shows her prevailing concern with the precariousness of migratory reproduction. Her epics depict how the act of mothering itself, replacing Du Bartas's character Noah, becomes the nexus of catastrophe and regeneration on a global scale. Bradstreet focuses very little on the figure of Noah or the story of the Flood in her work, unlike Guaman Poma or Du Bartas, likely avoiding the dangers of performing biblical interpretations as a female. In Noah's place, Bradstreet focuses instead on maternal power. Motherhood becomes a site, like Bradstreet's character *Earth*, that creates grief even as it creates life. The inherent losses involved in mothering labor become Bradstreet's response to the stark contrast between fertility and disappearance described by early writers on colonial population like Bradford. Bradstreet's many poetic representations of motherhood are both varied and complex, and they do not cohere into any one clear vision of women's reproductive labor. Exploring these multiple visions shows how Bradstreet fills the void in population discourse about what happens between successive generations.

Bradstreet's only poem directly addressing colonial politics uses the frame of motherhood to understand empire, turning global networks into intimate relations. A daughter comforts her troubled mother in "A Dialogue Between Old England and New," with Bradstreet imagining New England as a child who can be a source of redemption for her mother country during the English civil war. Echoing how Bodin noted that colonial migration could cleanse, and therefore strengthen, a commonwealth's people, and how Botero represented colonies as places in which to plant populations and increase the empire's fertility, Bradstreet portrays New England as a young reproductive woman who can restore her weary mother to health. The poem begins and ends with the daughter's voice, and imagines that the children England has sent away are the antidote to its civil strife. The health of one generation is reflected in the other: both mother and daughter insist on a genealogical connection that makes them part of the same body—not separate individuals. New England reassures Old England, "You are my mother nurse, and I your flesh" (l. 216), and Old England wonders if she and her daughter can feel the same pain: "Thou a child, a limb, and dost not feel / My fainting weak'ned body now to reel?" (ll. 18–19). Old England fears that war will bring the agents of depopulation: "For wants, sure some I feel, but more I fear, / And for the pestilence, who knows how near; / Famine and plague, two sisters of the sword, / Destruction to a land doth soon afford" (ll. 88–91). The mother confesses her fears of experiencing Germany's problems: "I saw her people famished, nobles slain, / Her fruitful land, a barren heath remain" (ll. 144–145). Bradstreet's imperial mother turns to her colonial daughter when she fears population loss.

The bodily bond between mother and daughter assuages Old England's fears of mass starvation and the spread of epidemics, and New England ends the poem insisting that Old England look toward a future in which redemption is assured: "Oh Abraham's seed, lift up your heads on high, / For sure the day of your redemption's nigh" (ll. 286–287). Bradstreet imagines bearing the "seed" in the conquest of threats to Christianity as the balm for a ravaged nation—and directly ties this hope to imperial endeavors abroad: after New England presents herself as her mother's comfort, she encourages Old England to "with brandished swards to Turkey go / . . . And do to Gog as thou has done to Rome" (ll. 282, 285). Fears of depopulation in the mother country are soothed by the promise of reproductive colonies, of scattered "seed," uniting members of a community in the present, as well as placing them within a prophetic historical continuum. This poetic representation of motherhood ameliorates population catastrophes and offers the promise of fertile population growth, making intimate and familial the distance across the Atlantic between England and America.

Given Bradstreet's investment in the idea that the abundance of successive generations can ameliorate the concerns of their parents (a preoccupation Bradford shared), Bradstreet's elegies for her grandchildren and daughter-in-law explore a crisis of more than faith. Considering how the promise of New England relieved the pains of her mother Old England in "A Dialogue," the deaths of members of the generations Bradstreet had hoped to leave behind challenge the promise that her own colonial family will prove redemptively populous. Bradstreet's elegies are carefully controlled negotiations of mourning that record the specter of English death. These elegies contend with the difficult subject of the death of English children, events which threaten a Du Bartian faith in English ability to colonize through population. In the way that Max Cavitch describes Puritan elegies as "fundamentally devoted . . . to [projecting] a future that would transcend elegiac salvos of resentment," Bradstreet's elegies here attempt to transform the mortality they commemorate into a vision of a reproductive future that triumphs over generational decline.[19] Bradstreet emphasizes the memory of affection, as she does elsewhere in her poetry, as the intimate bond that connects family members across the distance between life and death, just as it connected mother and daughter across an ocean in "A Dialogue Between Old England and New."

In the elegy for her mother, Bradstreet writes that like Old England, her mother found an earthly redemption by leaving an abundance of descendants to remember her. Like Noah, or like Du Bartas's imaginary father, who lived to see a village peopled with "the fruit of his own body grow'n," Bradstreet praises her mother Dorothy Dudley for living to see multiple generations prosper and carry on her memory—as Bradstreet does in the act of writing her elegy:

Here lies,
A worthy matron of unspotted life,
A loving mother and obedient wife ...
Of all her children, children lived to see,
Then dying, left a blessed memory. (ll. 6–8, 19–20)

The poem repeats "children" twice in a row, creating a sense of abundance within the line that emphasizes the importance of "[living] to see" successive generations prosper. Moreover, the parallel structure of the couplet's second line pairs the mention of grandchildren with the "blessed memory" that restores Dudley's presence after "dying." Given the emphasis on successful progeny in this elegy, Bradstreet's subsequent elegy to a granddaughter Elizabeth is both a commemoration of an individual death and a commentary on Bradstreet's own legacy. The 1665 elegy for Elizabeth portrays an infant's death as a disruption of the natural order that can only be ascribed to a mysterious intercession by God's hand:

By nature trees do rot when they are grown ...
But plants new set to be eradicate,
And buds new blown to have so short a date
Is by his hand alone that guides nature and fate. (ll. 13, 17–19)

The child's death is an inexplicable interruption, forcing Bradstreet to do the memorializing instead of leaving behind a "blessed memory" through her descendants. Elizabeth was to Bradstreet "the pleasure of mine eye / ... [a] fair flower that for a space was lent," a special luxury whose death Bradstreet will "bewail" (ll. 7, 8, 10). Bradstreet's elegies explore the role of memory and loss within the affective bonds of motherhood across generations, emphasizing both the precariousness of reproduction and the powerful potential of abundant fertility.

Bradstreet's successive elegies for grandchildren who died in their infancy emphasize further the precariousness of the mothering labor that occurs between birth and a child's entry into adulthood. A later elegy to the granddaughter who died earlier the same year as Simon, mentioned above, mocks the notion that the birth of children can be taken for granted: "More fool then I to look on that was lent / As if mine own, when thus impermanent" (ll. 18–19).

The subsequent 1669 elegy to Simon communicates an exhausted despair in the face of the idea that any memory of affection can restore a form of presence after the loss involved in death. Instead, in the next life, God will "return and make up all our losses, / And smile again after our bitter crosses" (ll. 13–14). Bradstreet's elegies memorialize her dead progeny using the language of lending, losses, and making whole—imagining the lives of new generations of her family as a kind of personal account between herself and God. They portray successful reproduction as a kind of ongoing system of credit in which debts are never fully repaid, but can be called in at any moment.

Bradstreet's elegy to her daughter-in-law Mercy, also written in 1669, shows how the life and death of successive generations of family reflects on the credit to earlier ones. Unlike the figure of Old England, or Dorothy Dudley, this elegy portrays the poet as bereft of the comfort of knowing that children and grandchildren will serve as a restorative comfort:

> And live I still to see relations gone,
> And yet survive to sound this wailing tone;
> Ah, woe is me, to write thy funeral song,
> Who might in reason yet have lived long,
> I saw the branches lopped the tree now fall,
> I stood so nigh, it crushed me down withal.
> My bruised heart lies sobbing at the root,
> That thou, dear son, hath lost both tree and fruit. (ll. 6–13)

Even though it ends with a mention of the son who has just been made a widower, the elegy returns most often to the pain of the poet—layering multiple "I"s with "me" and "my"—focusing on the ways that this young woman's death affects a member of the older generation who mourns her. The poem positions Bradstreet as "at the root" of a tree whose "branches" have been "lopped," connecting multiple generations of family with one image.

Within the elegy form itself, Bradstreet's poetry contrasts numerical exactitude with descriptions of uncertainty and inscrutability. Each elegy title carefully counts the age of the dead and the date of death: her mother died "December 27, 1643, and of Her Age, 61"; Mercy died "Sept. 6, 1669, In the 28 Year of Her Age"; Anne was "Three Years and Seven Months Old" and Simon was "But a Month, and One Day Old." This is in keeping with the diaristic quality of her personal poems: marking the dates of her husband and sons' various travels, and, in her meditations, recalling the trajectory of her life. The elegies open with time as a fully known quantity, placing exact ages and dates in the title, but then the lines of the poem open up to mystery and doubt. In the elegy to Simon, Bradstreet's persona seems to be calming a dispute with her readers: "Such was His will, but why, let's not dispute, / With humble hearts and mouths put in the dust, / Let's say he's merciful as well as just" (ll. 10–12). The barely quelled debate in the body of the poem underscores the irrefutability of the carefully calculated information offered in the poem's title—Simon's name, date of death, and age ("but a month"). Unlike Bradford, who refuses to count the dead, Bradstreet carefully enumerates each life lost. The numerical disappearance of the dead colonists in Bradford's second census subordinates individual life for the sake of measuring the community's growth, while Bradstreet's numbers insist on intimate, affective bonds between individuals that last beyond death.

Grief and loss appear throughout Bradstreet's writings about mother–child relationships, even when she writes of the living. Like the separation in her elegies between the numerical titles of dates and ages, and the much more complex lyrical affect of the lines that follow, Bradstreet describes motherhood as divided between the mere fact that she has produced children, and the ongoing labor of molding, shaping, and blending her identities with theirs. Bradstreet's writing develops this contradiction between representations of relationships as fixed and as constantly mutating in descriptions of how a mother labors toward two births of her children: one physical, one spiritual.

In her testimony "To My Dear Children," Bradstreet meditates on her labor as a mother, and describes it as a labor that can never be finished. At first, she was incomplete without her children, but even after they are born and grown, her labor continues:

> It pleased God to keep me a long time without a child, which was a great grief to me and cost me many prayers and tears before I obtained one, and after him gave me many more of whom I now take the care, that as I have brought you into the world, and with great pains, weakness, cares, and fears brought you to this, I now travail in birth again of you till Christ be formed in you. (AB, 241)

As a childless wife, she grieves; and as a mother, her labor pains continue indefinitely. She quotes from Galatians (4:19) to describe the work of being born into Christ as a mother's ongoing "travail," and separates the idea of a physical birth from a spiritual one—both of which are equally her responsibility. Here Bradstreet imagines motherhood dualistically, as both the production of life, as well as a perpetual ongoing effort to "form Christ" in her children. At no point in this process is Bradstreet ever an individual independent from her children: she is incomplete before they are born, and incomplete even long after they are adults. Moreover, imagining two births for every individual opens possibilities for when and how others outside the intimate family can intervene to shape new life. The focus on the labor that continues after birth points toward the potential for a human number to switch categories or fall away from the community that originally claimed it as one of their own.

Bradstreet's poetry focuses on the unreliability and innumerability of humans' reproductive capacity. It is never quite knowable, never quite as reassuringly powerful as Du Bartas's old man, who lives to see the village he peopled with "a hundred fires." Also, Bradstreet does not represent families as stable and secure—there is no second census moment, or "hundred fires" moment, where she describes her work turning her children into *her* children as completed, or as having proven a particular success or accomplished a reclamation of some kind. With this focus on the instability and fragility involved in reproductive labor, Bradstreet acknowledges that the lines between population groups must always be insisted upon, rather than taken for granted, since the sources of difference for Bradstreet are inscrutable too.

In Bradstreet's writings, motherhood is the labor of understanding and shaping the differences between people. In "Meditations Divine and Moral," Anne Bradstreet offers this advice on childrearing: "Diverse children have their different natures: some are like flesh which nothing but salt will keep from putrefaction, some again like tender fruits that are best preserved with sugar. Those parents are wise that can fit their nurture according to their nature" (AB, 273–274). In the same way that merchants preserve commodities for a sea voyage, mothers have to handle children differently as they make their way to becoming individuals who will retain their essential qualities when transported to different locations. This meditation is both a commonplace aphorism of colonial motherhood and a description of the particular aspects of childrearing work on which colonialism puts pressure: the threat posed by human diversity and the difficulty of preserving those varying natures from "putrefaction." As Bradstreet's poems repeatedly show, the end result of Anglo-colonial motherhood is a family of children scattered across the Atlantic world. Crossing a diversity of spaces, colonial children encounter a diversity of climates, languages, ecologies, nations, and cultures. Bradstreet's depictions of motherhood repeatedly acknowledge this threat of change and consider the methods of preserving connections in response.

Shaping Population Across Generations

Bradstreet's epics offer an example of the risks involved in assuming mothering labor ends at birth, that is, in the mere production of human bodies. When Bradstreet adapts Raleigh's contemplations about ancient populations from his *History of the World* into her own monarchical poems, she questions whether collective strength lies in sheer numbers of men or in the particular quality of those men. This question occurs in a depiction of a confrontation between Alexander the Great and the Persian king Darius, in the sole instance in Bradstreet's epics when a smaller number of particularly honorable men overcome a horde of barbarians. The battle was named the Arbela, nearly the same as *Arbella*, the name of the ship that carried Bradstreet and John Winthrop away from their homeland. The battle's name and its uniqueness in describing the victory of outnumbered forces endows it with a particularly colonial resonance within Bradstreet's monarchical poems. In this episode, Bradstreet considers the problems presented by colonial population dynamics when one small, incursive force must overpower a larger number of men.

Highlighting the peculiar importance of Bradstreet's writing of the battle of Arbela, the rest of the monarchical poems in *Tenth Muse* explicitly ascribe victory to the party with the highest number of forces. These poems consistently refer to the relative numbers of ancient armies, and these counts point toward population discourse, given that the Latin root of the word "population," still being wrangled into English, refers to an army.[20] One Persian army is consumed by an overwhelming force: "heaps on heaps such multitudes they laid, / Their arms grew weary by their slaughters made" (ll. 1429–1430); another manages to hold off the Greeks by sheer accumulation: "His foot was seventeen hundred thousand strong, / Eight hundred thousand horse, to these belong / His camels, beasts, for carriage numberless, / For truth's ashamed, how many to express" (ll. 986–989).

Alexander's forces overcome geographic hurdles to defeat the Persians, and characteristically here, Bradstreet's poems specifically count the army's numbers: "Thirty-two thousand made up his foot force, To which were joined five thousand goodly horse" (ll. 1657–1658). After the battle, the final tally of the numbers point clearly to Alexander: the Greeks followed the Persians in retreat, "and twenty thousand of their lives bereave / . . . This victory did Alexander gain, / With loss of thirty-four of his there slain" (ll. 1681, 1683 1684). Bradstreet's adaptations of ancient history directly engage with the relative power of armed quantities, almost invariably equating larger numbers with greater strength, and disregarding training or human diversity.

But Bradstreet's version of Alexander's conquest over Darius is special, and especially colonial.[21] Darius's army outnumbered Alexander's by hundreds of thousands of men in this massive confrontation, known alternately as the Battle of Gaugamela or the Battle of Arbela. At its conclusion, Bradstreet's poem identifies the location: "At Arbela this victory was gained / Together with the town also obtained" for Alexander (ll. 1969–1970). The ship *Arbella* had been named after Lady Arabella Johnson, a prominent Puritan and passenger on the ship who died shortly after arriving in New England. When writing her monarchical poems, Bradstreet must have been keenly aware of the resonance between the name of the surprising and decisive battle of Arbela and the name of the principal ship that launched her colony in America.

In the battle of Arbela, in Bradstreet's retelling, the power to shape men's characters matters more than any other kind of strength. Armies are reflections of their leaders, Bradstreet writes of Darius: "But as the king, so is the multitude, / And now of valour both are destitute" (ll. 1903–1904). Darius trusts in the advantage of the sheer multitude, but the poem explores the difference between men who can be counted as men, and men who possess ineffable qualities that could make their smaller numbers actually matter more. The poem pities Darius for having mere numbers of men, rather than men of quality:

> Yet he (poor prince) another host doth muster,
> Of Persians, Scythians, Indians in a cluster;
> Men but in shape and name, of valour none
> Most fit, to blunt the swords of Macedon. . . .
> Yet [he] had some hope that on the spacious plain,
> His numbers might the victory obtain. (ll. 1905–1908, 1913–1914)

Bradstreet layers different kinds of racial otherness ("Persians, Scythians, Indians") to depict an image of "men but in shape and name," men as waste, whose bodies are not filled with the spirit and honor that can enable them to hold their land. When describing this upset victory where an army of 250,000 is pitted against Alexander's 45,000, she is careful to note that the numbers slain that day are in dispute: "Forty-five thousand Alexander had, / But is not known what slaughter here was made. Some write th' other had a million, some more" (ll. 1965–1967). Bradstreet acknowledges that ancient historians debate exactly how Alexander won. But her poem expresses hope that at least once in a long succession of contests between aggregated groups on a battlefield, the kind of men brought to the fore will matter more than the number of them—that cultivation of a certain *kind* of man will matter more than careless gathering of them. This is the battle of Arbela, perhaps similar to the battle of the *Arbella*: the struggle to beat historical odds by claiming a new land with "valour" rather than "numbers." Alexander refuses to engage in a surprise night attack to gain an advantage for his outnumbered forces, even sleeping late the next morning: "But he disdained to steal a victory; / The sun should witness of his valour be / And careless in his bed, next morn he lies, / By captains twice is called before he'll rise" (ll. 1957–1960). He calmly trusts in the superiority of his men over Darius's hordes— hordes that have none of the interior qualities that will make them victors. Bradstreet's poetic rendering of the battle of Arbela shows how the power of leadership, communal cohesion, and essential character can—at least once—triumph over the power of mere numbers of humans.

Though written in lyric rather than epic form, Bradstreet's poems about motherhood similarly contemplate the labor involved in shaping either "men but in shape and name" or men of valor in a contested colonial space. Bradstreet's testimony to her children alludes to two kinds of birth for every individual: a physical creation of a body, and the cultivation of the spirit within that body "till Christ be formed in" it. Colonialism threatens the unity of this two-tiered process of producing populations because it scatters families across the globe, testing whether "valour," Christian spirit, or other qualities can survive within an individual after he or she is extracted from the group that originally cultivated her or his character. If "as the king, so is the multitude," then Bradstreet's lyrics ask what happens when a member of the multitude travels far from the king. Bradstreet's work includes many occasional poems marking the travel of family members, honoring their leave-takings and arrivals, describing the pain of separation, and celebrating the arrival of letters from a missing loved one. Travel interrupts the intimacy of the kind of mothering and caretaking work that can extend past infancy: the labor of shaping the spirit within the human shape. When emotional intimacy outside of physical proximity does the work of securing connections and continuing to affirm membership in a particular group, in Bradstreet's lyrics kinship takes on a death-in-life quality. The act of mourning the loss of someone's physical presence, in these travel poems, takes the place of the intimate reproductive labor that keeps character and connection alive.

The lyrics "Upon My Son Samuel His Going for England" from 1657 and "On My Son's Return Out of England" from 1661 both describe the danger of traveling by pointing out the precariousness of social connection when the traveler ventures away from home. The first poem dismisses the potential of strangers to care for Samuel, praying for divine help on his journey because "mortal helps are brittle dust" (l. 12). Addressing God in prayer, the lyric honoring Samuel's return acknowledges the threat violent strangers pose to a traveler: "From dangers

great Thou didst him free / Of pirates who were near at hand"
(ll. 11–12). However, this poem expresses gratitude that Samuel
instead met with strangers who treated him kindly: "In country
strange Thou didst provide, / And friends raised him in every
place, / And courtesies of sundry sorts / From such as 'fore ne'er
saw his face" (ll. 15–18). On the way back "To th' land of his nativity"—not only to the land of his birth, but also to the mother
who gave birth to him and who writes this lyric—Samuel hap-
pily met with unfamiliar people who "raised him" and extended
him "courtesies," standing in the place of family. Transatlantic
travel rends the social connections that keep people both physically and spiritually or emotionally safe, and these lyrics credit
God's provision of strangers who take the place of family with
restoring the traveler to "th' land of his nativity." Political arithmetic as practiced by policymakers like William Petty similarly
represents the movement of people like Samuel in the service of
favorable population ratios, but Bradstreet's descriptions of travel
emphasize the importance of social support to retain the connection to a territorial homeland in the midst of migration.

Membership in social groups becomes a ghostly, absent presence that sustains connection across the Atlantic. Writing itself
preserves the bond that sustains motherly caretaking work past infancy, and ensures that people maintain their membership in social
groups as they venture far beyond the people who shaped their
character. The preface to Bradstreet's "Meditations Divine and
Moral" addresses Bradstreet's son Simon, acknowledging that the
son asked for a piece of writing to keep his mother's presence alive
after her death. The preface begins by asserting that parents live on
after death in the lives of their children: "Parents perpetuate their
lives in their posterity and their manners" (AB, 271). However, the
preface states that the son has requested a written object to sym-
bolize this after-death connection: "You once desired me to leave
something for you in writing that you might look upon, when
you should see me no more" (AB, 271). In the absence of physical presence, writing takes the place to sustain the transmission of
"manners" to posterity.

Bradstreet's poems portray writing as a stand-in for absent motherly connection that perpetuates the work of raising and shaping children. The poem with which I began this chapter, "In Reference to Her Children," describes how the difficulty of raising children increases rather than decreases with time:

> Great was my pain when I you bred,
> Great was my care when I you fed,
> Long did I keep you soft and warm,
> And with my wings kept off all harm,
> My cares are more and fears than ever,
> My throbs such now as 'fore were never. (ll. 57–62)

The repetition of "great" at the beginning of the first two lines of this poetic sentence, describing the pain and care of mothering, is mirrored by the "ever" and "never" rhymes of the final couplet, insisting that mothering labor increases with time, rather than achieves completion. The poem portrays familial connection as active, ongoing, anxious, and painful, especially once children no longer live near enough for their mother to be able to "[keep] off all harm." In place of this protective proximity, the poem prescribes language and memory as a way to sustain intimate connection:

> When each of you shall in your nest
> Among your young ones take your rest,
> In chirping language, oft them tell,
> You had a dam that loved you well,
> That did what could be done for young,
> And nursed you up till you were strong,
> And 'fore she once would let you fly,
> She showed you joy and misery:
> Taught what was good, and what was ill,
> What would save life, and what would kill.
> Thus gone, amongst you I may live,
> And dead, yet speak, and counsel give:
> Farewell, my birds, farewell adieu,
> I happy am, if well with you. (ll. 83–96)

Not only is mothering in this poem the labor of nursing, but also it is a source of protective moral education: it teaches children the difference between killing and saving life, and between "good" and "ill." By sharing memories of the education these adult children received with their own "young ones," the mother in this poem can be "dead, yet speak, and counsel give." "Chirping language" and the ability to "oft them tell" sustains the protection and moral knowledge that originally bonded the family together across generations.

Bradstreet's portrayal of mothering work ties generations together, with grandchildren reflecting the long-ago labor of grandparents. At the same time, this labor is perpetually ongoing, even increasing with time, and never completed; it only transforms into language—into the ability to "speak" and "counsel"—after death. This spoken memory of connection, or a written version (as her son requested of her), insulates this social group from becoming merely "men but in shape and name." The protective moral education of mothering creates powerful bonds that diffuse high moral character throughout each member of the group—bonds that can, through language, last beyond death. The problem with this view of the essential role of mothering in sustaining the character of family members across generations is that it is tenuous once those members scatter across the globe, far away from the original "nest." This poem describes the mother's concerns after the scattering of her children as highly anxious "throbs," worse than the pain of labor. The continuity of social connection without physical proximity is by no means assured: it takes an enormous amount of effort, memory, and above all, writing. As Bradstreet's poetry moves between representations of children as limbs of their parents' bodies and as isolated individuals adrift in a hostile world, poems about motherhood become elegies for the living. They describe colonial motherhood as a process of simultaneously securing the perpetuation of a colonial community by tying generations together, and mourning the instability of those connections. Mothering work is therefore as ghostly and tenuous as it is essential and ongoing.

The poems repeatedly describe writing, and lists in particular, as the means of sustaining the labor that both edifies and unifies social groups. Lists are essential unifying tools for Bradstreet's poems, and "In Reference to Her Children" begins with a list counting the "eight birds hatched in one nest / Four cocks there were, and hens the rest." Lists create unity and imbue similarity to disparate elements in representational form, making them an ideal stand-in for a motherly presence. In the same way that lists both separate and align different kinds of things, on paper at least, the ever-present, but often not physically present, work of mothering protects adult children from becoming "men but in shape and name."

When Bradstreet's son Simon asked his mother to write him something to remember her by, Bradstreet produced an enumerated list. The seventy-seven "Meditations Divine and Moral" she left for him enumerate aphorisms and life lessons that might continue to shape Simon's character, and that of his own children, beyond her death. Mothering work itself becomes an enumerated list: it transforms into a written representation of social connection made orderly through numbers. The lessons vary from comparing life on earth to a sailing ship on its way to a heavenly port, to comparing ungrateful Christians to children who are "hardly weaned; although the teat be rubbed with wormwood or mustard, they will either wipe it off, or else suck down sweet and bitter together," as in Meditation 38. In this unifying, enumerated list, Meditation 26 emphasizes the importance of political unity to protect against enemies: "A sore finger may disquiet the whole body, but an ulcer within destroys it; so an enemy without may disturb a commonwealth, but dissentions within overthrow it." The form of the numbered list unifies each of these disparate thoughts, which otherwise follow no pattern, into one image that the son Simon can "look upon, when you should see me no more," finding a mother in a list of lessons. Writing, and especially the list, enables the mothering work of shaping people to continue beyond separations of distance and death.

Powerful Lists

Bradstreet's representation of the character-stabilizing function of writing and lists recalls Du Bartas's Bodin-inspired emphasis on the political significance of lists that create a unified representation out of variety. The particular ways Bradstreet describes Du Bartas's influence on her poetry call attention to the blending of parent-child relationships, science, and politics. For Bradstreet, Du Bartas is a figure who combines intimate education with scholarly endeavor. In the 1641 poem "In Honour of Du Bartas," Bradstreet depicts her writing as a conversation between a mother and a child who has seen the wonder of Du Bartas, but does not have the skill to describe it. Bradstreet's muse "sees the riches of some famous fair . . . but understanding lacks," and then "At night turns to his mother's cot again, / And tells her tales (his full heart over-glad) / Of all the glorious sights his eyes have had; / But finds too soon his want of eloquence" (ll. 21, 22, 29–32). Similarly, in the "Prologue," Bradstreet demeans her capacity to emulate Du Bartas: "A Bartas can do what a Bartas will / But simple I according to my skill" (ll. 13–14), claiming that "To sing of wars, of captains, and of kings, / Of cities founded, commonwealths begun, / For my mean pen are too superior things" (l. 3). Yet Bradstreet goes on to do just that: she does sing of "wars, of captains, and of kings" in her monarchical epics. The self-demeaning rhetorical move of the "Prologue" points to the unreliability of the poetic voice in "In Honor of Du Bartas" that claims she is "weak brained" relative to Du Bartas's talents, namely, "Thy art in natural philosophy, / . . . Thy piercing skill in high astronomy, / And curious insight in a-natomy, / Thy physic, music, and state policy" (ll. 38, 40–42). Just as the "Prologue" announces that Bradstreet will indeed write world-historical epics by claiming her pen is too "mean" to do so, the ode to Du Bartas informs the reader that this poet is keenly interested in science and politics by identifying herself as too "weak brained" to understand them. The 1641 ode begins its conclusion with a second mothering metaphor, following the one comparing

Bradstreet's muse to a star-struck child prattling to his mother. In this metaphor, however, Du Bartas is the mother: the poem addresses its honored subject as "O pregnant brain, O comprehension vast" (l. 75). In addition to Dorothy Dudley, Du Bartas is a list-making mother for Bradstreet, one whose motherly conversations encompass not only morality, but also the science of understanding the world and its people. Just as population science uses censuses and record-keeping to order the raw material of human reproduction into social classifications, Bradstreet's lists that stand in for mothers continue shaping and educating people well beyond childhood.

Bradstreet's poetry shows her interest in Du Bartas's attempts to craft a unity for disparate elements within a world system. In a poem in honor of her father, she writes that she wishes to describe "How divers natures make one unity. / Something of all (though mean) I did intend / But feared you'ld judge Du Bartas was my friend" (ll. 35–37). This poem describes her writing in general as a space that brings order and coherence to otherwise disordered "natures." Elsewhere, Bradstreet's poems are constantly dividing and cataloguing in search of this "one unity." On the title page of Bradstreet's 1650 *Tenth Muse* (which appeared as a result of her brother-in-law taking her manuscript to London of his own volition), the title page is itself a catalog of its contents, as shown in Figure 1.2.

The book itself is a list of poems bringing together different philosophical phenomena into four epics and organizing the generations of three monarchical linages in coherent poetic narratives. In the epic describing the Four Constitutions (like "The Four Elements," "The Four Constitutions" is a *querelle des femmes*), Phlegm makes peace with the other constitutions by pointing back to how, once collected on the page, each of the four plays a role to serve a greater purpose: "Two hot, two moist, two cold, two dry here be, / A golden ring, the posy UNITY" (ll. 604–605). Phlegm then looks back to the earlier poem describing the elements to join those competing sisters:

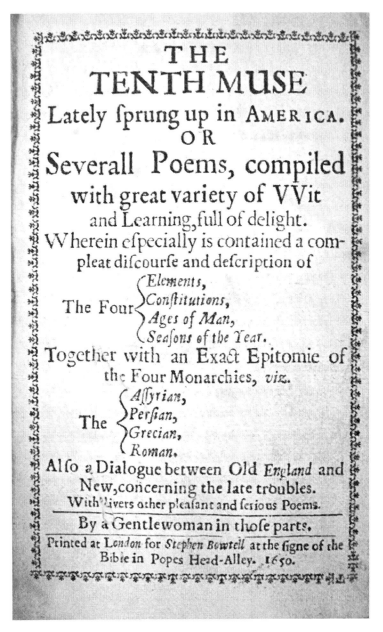

FIGURE 1.2 Title page to 1650 edition of *The Tenth Muse* (Courtesy Clements Library, University of Michigan).

> Nor jars or scoffs, let none hereafter see,
> But all admire our perfect amity;
> Nor be discerned, here's water, earth, air, fire,
> But here's a compact body, whole entire. (ll. 606–609)

The poems on natural philosophy all work toward the goal of carefully composing one work that can both delineate differences between phenomena and also subordinate these differences to the writing that encompasses them. The four constitutions are separated, counted, and then unified through Bradstreet's pen, just as they are unified, though separately identifiable, in an individual human body. Bradstreet's epics identify disparate phenomena, set them to war with one another, and then appeal to the power of representation to encompass and make sense of their interrelatedness.

Bradstreet's Du Bartian poems seeking "perfect amity" of opposing phenomena through representation repeatedly thematize the interconnectedness of cataclysm and regeneration inherent in population discourse. The Earth sang of the world's populations in her female voice in "The Four Elements," and in the concluding section of this epic, the figure of Air desires that she be seen capable of catastrophic depopulation. Just as the Earth is both a "womb" and a "tomb," Air brings both lifesaving renewal and wasting disease:

> As my fresh air preserves all things in life,
> So when corrupt, mortality is rife:
> Then fevers, purples, pox, and pestilence,
> With diverse moe, work deadly consequence;
> Whereof such multitudes have died and fled,
> The living scarce had power to bury dead;
> Yea so contagious countries have me known
> That birds have not 'scaped death as they have flown,
> Of murrain, cattle numberless did fall,
> Men feared destruction epidemical. (ll. 457–466)

Although fresh air is necessary for "all things in life," Air describes her capacity for a population catastrophe, a "destruction epidemical" brought by her "corrupt" winds that bring disease and famine so "contagious" that "the living scarce had power to bury dead." When Air describes her cataclysmic potential, she gives up counting: "numberless cattle" succumb to her fearsome strength, and "multitudes have died and fled" because of her deadly work. The selfsame force that preserves also has the capacity to destroy, and this fickle power makes, as Air goes on to describe, "mighty monarchs fear their fates / By death or great mutation of their states" (ll. 485–486). In this epic, Bradstreet explores how changes in the number and the resources of a people ("mutation of . . . states") follow from the numerical chaos wrought by natural catastrophe. "The Four Elements" concludes when Air neutralizes the cataclysmic potential she just described by confining it within the form of a poem that clearly delineates and separates these four awesome powers: "I have said less than did my sisters three, / . . . But dare not go beyond my element" (ll. 487, 490). Like in the description of Darius's men versus Alexander's, Bradstreet's explorations of population and depopulation focus on the potential of the same type of forces to be alternately beneficial or malicious, depending on how they are either shaped or contained. And like the way that Bradstreet's numbered list of meditations can continue to mother Simon and shape his moral character long after his physical mother has died, written records, especially categorized or numbered lists, do the work of directing potentially deleterious forces toward good. The "whole, entire" and "compact body" that can contain all four elements exists in juxtaposition to the states that "mutate" because of depopulation, and to the actual mortal bodies made vulnerable by the elements. Only the imaginative record, the poem exposing and containing the different depopulating and populating elements, can create a "body" that will endure.

Despite describing the central role of a categorizing and unifying representation for organizing characters on a world stage, Bradstreet develops the idea across her poetry that a written record that unifies disparate facets is always only ephemeral. Even as she participates in trying to imagine the world as a unity whose many different aspects are recordable, she recognizes that this representation is fleeting, and exists only in writing. Just as mothering is never complete, even after children have children themselves, or after a mother dies, a written representation that orders an otherwise chaotic world is never final or complete. Similarly, Bradford had to return to his original census and take it again to measure how a later generation had improved upon the first, showing how the work of measuring the health or success of a colonial community is ongoing.

Bradstreet directly addresses the problem of unfinished work in shaping a colonial family in "Before the Birth of One of Her Children," a poem which more than any other entwines a "womb" and a "tomb." In this lyric, the pregnant poet wishes a tearful pre-emptive farewell to her husband in anticipation of her possible death in childbirth. On this occasion, in which the prospect of population on an individual scale entails a grave risk of a concomitant loss of life, the poem contemplates how all human ties are transitory: "No ties so strong, no friends so dear and sweet, / But with death's parting blow are sure to meet. / The sentence past is most irrevocable, / A common thing, yet oh, inevitable" (ll. 5–8). In a post-diluvian world where human society is doomed to migrate, Bradstreet renders parting as both "common" and "inevitable"—indeed, even birth is a parting. Alluding to her vulnerability in childbirth, Bradstreet tells her husband to keep her memory fresh, and to "Kiss this paper for thy love's dear sake" (l. 29). For Bradstreet, the paper record is a remedy for broken physical connection—working as a substitute for "[lying] in thine arms" (l. 22). The paper becomes a crucial tie between the speaker and those she loves, at a moment when her physical condition is about to be drastically altered. Her connection with her children becomes increasingly symbolic, a representation rather than an ongoing practice, once they are born into a transatlantic system that disperses families across colonial spheres.

Bradstreet's poetry explores the discourse about population in the settler colonial society she helped to build, and focuses on the links between cataclysm and regeneration. This focus on the fragility of the distinction between valor and treachery, and between safety and insecurity, opens up questions about how the potential diversity within human nature can be controlled and categorized after birth—questions that, in Bradstreet's poetry, inevitably return to motherly labor and the representation of that social role. Her choice of forms—lyric poetry and prose works about domestic and spiritual life, as well as historical epics—and her focus on illuminating and complicating mother-child relationships reflects the nature of population concerns in her particular early colonial experience, one very different from, for example, Guaman Poma's or contemporaneous Barbados, as I will show in subsequent chapters. Like the Battle of Arbela, the ongoing colonial battle of the passengers of the *Arbella*, in Bradstreet's terms, will be decided by how well each generation can influence the generation it leaves behind.

CHAPTER 2

Measuring Caribbean Aesthetics

In the seventeenth century, the island of Barbados was more populous than any other colony in English North America save for Virginia and Massachusetts; it was also indisputably the richest colony.[1] Ships arrived carrying slaves kidnapped from Africa to work the plantations; and ships left carrying sugar, an expensive but highly transportable commodity. Although bustling with people and extraordinarily wealthy, Barbados was a starkly unequal society, even by seventeenth-century standards. Those first planters who could consolidate massive tracts of land and multiple refinery mills became so rich and powerful that half of their dynasties remained intact on Barbados over a century later.[2]

Yet this source of tremendous wealth for a few British planters remained, for the most part, a way station for both the owners and the laborers who passed through it, with high death rates undergirding a social structure that moved both goods and people around the Atlantic.[3] Slave mortality was especially dire: according to one Barbadian large-scale planter's calculation in 1689, he had to purchase six slaves a year to replenish his slave labor force of one hundred.[4] But little was done to foster any kind of quality of life on Barbados in the seventeenth century. There were few roads, fewer churches and schools, and enough epidemics to attest to poor living conditions for white, Indian, and black inhabitants alike.[5] This was a social experiment—if we cannot call it a society—different in nearly every way from Willam Bradford's Plymouth or Anne Bradstreet's Salem. As historian Richard S. Dunn puts it, Barbados before 1700 "was the richest and yet in human terms the least successful colony in English America."[6] The island brimmed with the tension between spectacular monetary success and dismal social failure.

This tension may have been precisely what the Crown sought to examine and control with the massive census it demanded of Governor Jonathan Atkins in 1680, constituting "the most comprehensive surviving census of any English colony in the seventeenth century." In order to keep his job, Governor Atkins sent "a richer store of information than any North American census before the 1770's."[7] This store of information included a detailed map; ship, military, and church records; and alphabetical lists of the names of 2,639 landholders and 405 householders in each parish, including accounts of every acre, slave, and servant in their charge (as can be seen in Figure 2.1).[8] Bookkeeping techniques facilitate the international trade in sugar and slaves, and Governor Atkins applies these same methods to the surveillance of the people caught up in these exchanges. To render visible, to draw connections, to restore balance: the extraordinarily comprehensive 1680 census tried to address all these goals with the language of accounting.

Unfortunately, hopes that this form of census could solve sociopolitical problems were disappointed on both sides of the Atlantic. Despite its unusual breadth, the Crown remained suspicious of Governor Atkins' veracity upon receiving his box of data, and promptly replaced him. The incident shows how the census could serve as a volatile point of contention between England and its colonies in the seventeenth century, an attempt to regulate imperial relationships that might merely foreground the mistrust and instability it was intended to address. If the island of Barbados

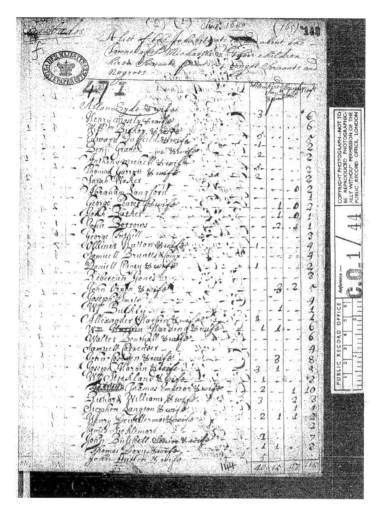

FIGURE 2.1 Page of a parish register sent in the 1680 Barbados Census (Colonial Office Group, Class 1, Piece 44, 142-379, Public Record Office, UK National Archives).

could not travel to the metropole for scrutiny, then the box of data could travel in its stead. Censuses collapsed space, if not to bring the colonies under intimate surveillance, then to present Charles II with a scapegoat, such as Governor Atkins, when that intimate knowledge eluded his grasp.

Before the census, the most comprehensive description of the world of seventeenth-century English sugar cultivation in Barbados (and indeed, in all of the Caribbean) was Richard Ligon's *True and Exact History of the Island of Barbados*. The motley form of this travelogue reflects the chaotic colonial experience that produced it, just as Bradstreet's metric feet reflect the orderly settlement to which the Puritans aspired. Ligon, a gentleman without a fortune, had to flee England in 1647. He was a royalist during the civil war, and he found himself "a stranger in my owne Country,"[9] so he boarded the first ship he could to the West Indies. Upon returning to England, he would again turn to Barbados when he found himself in trouble, this time writing an account of his travels while languishing in a debtor's prison after a failed investment scheme.[10] First published in 1657, Ligon's unique *History* attempts many of the same tasks as the later census: visibility, balance, and connection across distance. It is an accounting handbook for prospective sugar planters; a travel narrative filled with stories later writers would retell and transform; a foundational natural history of an island's resources; and a portrait of a strikingly new social landscape at the moment when planters began to replace white servitude with African slave labor.[11]

Yet this account is also, for Ligon, a book about art. Ligon begins the book with a letter reminding his patron of how interested he had been in Ligon's watercolors of the island: "You were ... pleased, to cast your eyes upon some pieces of Limning, which I had done since my return." The book includes elaborate engravings of local flora—plates so expensive to produce that they may have delayed publication[12]—and at one point, Ligon prefaces his description of a Barbadian scene with, "I will speak as an artist" (*HB*, 82). Ligon's *History* explores the intersection of aesthetic ideals and mathematical reckoning. With this unique blend of art and measurement, the narrative intervenes in a still-heterogeneous discourse on how to view people as countable numbers, by blending new forms of representation, such as accounting, with aesthetic preoccupations with proportion, harmony, and beauty. Much like

Bradstreet's poems provide a helpful contrast to Bradford's census as stories about counting colonial population, Ligon's focus on artful proportion and profitable planning stands in relief to the later official accounting. The 1680 census would attempt to bring Barbados under control through counting parts and comparing them with the whole in a similar way—even to the point of basing the map of the island Governor Atkins included in the box of data on the map Ligon included in his *History* over two decades earlier (see fig. 2.2).[13] However, the census elides the focus on aesthetics that, for Ligon, was the purpose of human accounting.

Ligon's map attests to the violence inherent in the efforts to control human life on Barbados. Though it was highly derivative from earlier sources, the most significant contribution Ligon made to Barbadian cartography are his cartouches, including one

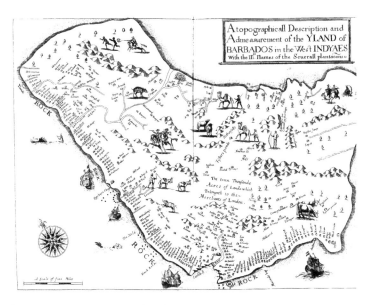

FIGURE 2.2 Ligon, "A topographicall Description and Admeasurement of the ISLAND of BARBADOS in the WEST INDIES," *A True and Exact History* (RB 139768, The Huntington Library, San Marino, California).

at the top left, visible in Figure 2.2, of a white man on a horse chasing two Africans.[14] By drawing this striking scene of movement, power, violence, and inequality in numbers, Ligon presents his *History* as a narrative that will combine economics and natural history with the human stories that routinely are left out of these other forms of representation. The cartouche shows how attuned Ligon was to the threats abounding in this unprecedented island environment. Ligon's drawings of island plants also required him to be cognizant of the interplay between appreciation of beauty and recognition of death. As Karen Kupperman notes with regard to these descriptions of flora—work that Royal Society member Sir Hans Sloane would later draw heavily upon in his landmark early-eighteenth-century natural history of the Caribbean— "[A]ll that beauty sometimes camouflaged death. Some of these fabulous plants were deadly poison if one did not know how to use them properly."[15] Just as Ligon is proud of his watercolors of island plants—using his skills as an "artist" to render a threatening natural environment pleasing—his representations of the extraordinarily turbulent social life of 1640s Barbados also draw upon aesthetic tools to make the violent and dangerous seem beautiful and controlled.

Although Ligon wrote before the comprehensive 1680 census, before William Petty's 1690 treatise *Political Arithmetick*, and even before John Graunt's early analysis of population statistics in the bills of mortality, he wrote well *after* two highly influential forms of counting and measuring human life were underway. The first is the active and expanding slave trade, an economy that demanded without question that numbers be applied to human bodies. Long before England instituted regular censuses or tracked healthy bodies in London, slave ships used accounting practices to track slave bodies across the Atlantic. When Ligon arrived in Barbados, English planters' investment in this new experiment in ways of talking and writing numerically about people was just beginning. But Ligon also employs ideas about measuring humans that have their origins in aesthetics. Repeatedly in his history, Ligon invokes artists such as Andrea del Sarto and Albrecht Dürer when he writes about the African slaves he encounters. Over the course of the previous century, Renaissance artists in the vein of Leonardo da Vinci had advocated applying numerical measurement to the human body in an effort to represent ideal forms. At a time when higher level mathematics was still not widely taught, geometry was associated with a certain kind of Northern Italian aesthetic, just as accounting methods were the peculiar language of merchants.[16] Active in the sixteenth century, Dürer was widely known in Ligon's time for his theories of bodily proportion, advocating, along the same lines as da Vinci, the application of numerical measurement to visual art. This approach to representation, influential during the Renaissance but still circulating by means of engravings Ligon would have encountered, emphasizes the harmony of parts to a whole and the use proto-scientific forms of inquiry to showcase natural beauty. Ligon mixes these lingering aesthetic theories with accounting methods, and together these approaches work to make Barbados, and the strange entities in it, seem both attractive and incorporable within a world system. In Ligon's *History*, Dürer's ideas about anthropometry (that is, the application of mathematical skill to human diversity) combine with accounting language to render beautiful the unprecedented social landscape created by sugar colonialism.

The budgets and lists for prospective plantation owners that Ligon includes in his *History* are not separate endeavors from his Dürer-inspired descriptions of servant bodies or his elegant renderings of dangerous plants. Ligon's ideal plantation budget is itself an aesthetic object, placing bodies in harmonious relationships that are as appealing as the economic results they might produce. Like Ligon's storytelling and natural history, the numerical abstractions of a budget also render an ideal plantation where sugar cultivation, profits, and carefully arranged labor hierarchies all contribute to the beauty of the whole. The budget fashions a harmonious social order out of a motley aggregate, a representation whose goal is not verisimilitude in representing an actual

Barbadian planter's holdings, but rather engineering social order out of tremendous disorder through the application of mathematically arranged proportions. For Ligon, the presentation of internal consistency through attention to proportions and an appreciation of beauty takes precedence over fidelity to a verifiable reality.

Ligon's focus on beauty and proportion shows how his version of colonial human accounting differs from that of another early tale of sex and population on an island: Henry Neville's fictional *Isle of Pines* from 1668. Neville's mercantilist focus on women's reproductive potential contrasts with Ligon's more complex representations of island women, figures who cannot always be perfectly quantified. By blending mathematically structured aesthetics with plantation economics, Ligon's unique early vision of human accounting leaves room for the possibility of an uncountable remainder in any attempt to quantify a volatile colonial society. These problems with counting appear particularly in Ligon's attempts to represent laboring women. The struggle to represent these female figures numerically points toward the central difficulty of social life in the early years of sugar colonialism: namely, how to reproduce labor in a place so utterly hostile to human life. In this way, we can see that Ligon and Bradstreet share a similarity beyond being two English writers who published books about life in the colonies within a decade of each other, despite their vast differences of place and form. Like the Puritan poet, Ligon focuses on articulating particularly colonial forms of reproduction by measuring bodies numerically—this time in relation to sugar slavery rather than settler colonialism.

Myra Jehlen has described reading Ligon as an act of confronting a "clash of two ordinarinesses"—or, as a process of finding contemporary readers' sense of the "ordinary" totally alienated by Ligon's banal presentation of slavery.[17] But Ligon also shows how what is ordinary to us—that is, the enumerating of human bodies like any other commodity—was in his time still an unfamiliar, and at times unwieldy, method for making sense of social life.

Moreover, he shows us that far from being in opposition, book-keeping and the beautiful can be gracefully intertwined.

Slave Bookkeeping

Ligon's *True and Exact History* describes a Caribbean sugar planta-tion as a beautiful system ordered into elegant proportions through the application of mathematical calculation. From the beginning of the travel narrative, a poem by Ligon's cousin George Walshe mentions amounts in sterling in order to promise that the *History* will show readers that "*3000l.* will clear / No lesse then *7000l.* a year."[18] These profits are not from "a jugling Chymick sense, / But drawn from reason and experience"—a rational ability Ligon demonstrates through his mathematical aptitude. When Walshe promises that Ligon will show men how to turn three thousand pounds into seven thousand, and when Ligon transforms plan-tation ownership into a series of calculations, they are engaging in the relatively new discourse of bookkeeping, markets, and investments. [19]

　　The full title of the *History* promises an accuracy of "propor-tions" and "shapes" in this architectural manual for sugar profits: *A True and Exact History of the Island of Barbados: with a mapp of the island, as also the principall trees and plants there, set forth in their due pro-portions and shapes, drawne out by their severall and respective scales: to-gether with the ingenio that makes the sugar, with the plots of the severall houses, roomes, and other places that are used in the whole processe of sugar-making.* Ligon is obsessed with scale, proportion, and calculation in his history, presenting himself as a skilled manipulator of numbers who can interpret the island. Ligon combines drawings set metic-ulously to scale and extensive tables listing necessary commodities and their cost with his prose in the *History*. Though he is interested in describing human shapes and quoting from artists who have done so, he himself does not draw human figures: as Kay Dian Kriz explains with regard to Sloane's *Voyage to . . . Jamaica*, natural histories did not generally include studies of humans until much later.[20] When Ligon examines one particular Barbadian tree, the Palmetto Royal, he includes its precise measurements, describing in both his narrative and in his figures how the proportions of each tree adhere to this scale (see fig. 2.3). Ligon admires precise proportion, and in describing the qualities of Barbados, he counts and measures obsessively. He takes the size of the island, the maximum

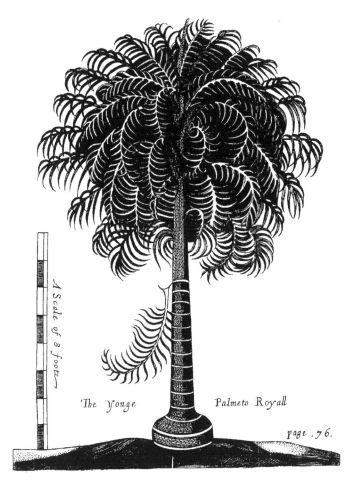

FIGURE 2.3 Richard Ligon, "The Yonge Palmeto Royall," *A True and Exact History* (RB 139768, The Huntington Library, San Marino, California).

weight that various animals can carry, the height of the trees, and even enumerates the ways his body responded to the environment: he gives the precise number of "stooles and vomits that five kernals from an island plant" induced in him (*HB*, 67). The *History* ends with—and seems to lead toward—a comprehensive budget that a reader might use to plan his own sugar venture (see fig. 2.4).

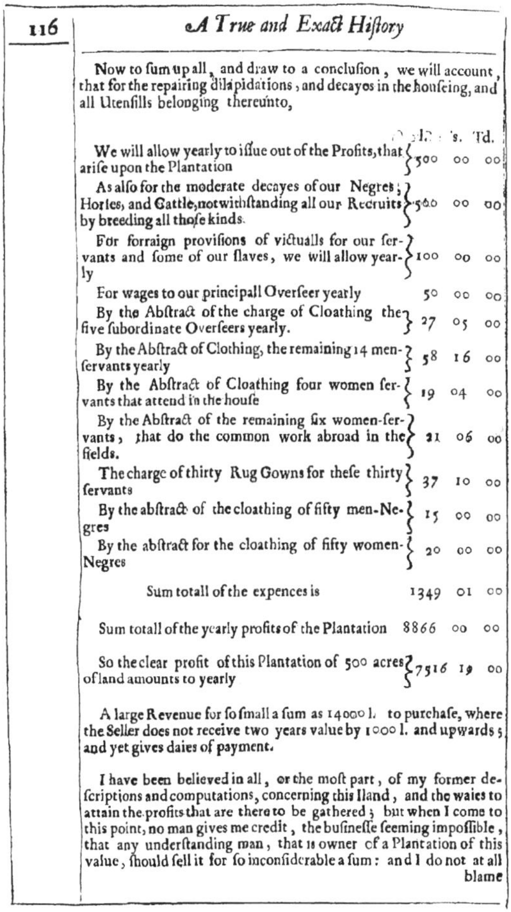

116	*A True and Exact History*

Now to fum up all, and draw to a conclufion, we will account, that for the repairing dilapidations, and decayes in the houfeing, and all Utenfills belonging thereunto,

	's.	Td.
We will allow yearly to iffue out of the Profits, that arife upon the Plantation	500	00	00
As alfo for the moderate decayes of our Negres; Horfes, and Cattle, notwithftanding all our Recruits by breeding all thofe kinds.	500	00	00
For forraign provifions of victualls for our fervants and fome of our flaves, we will allow yearly	100	00	00
For wages to our principall Overfeer yearly	50	00	00
By the Abftract of the charge of Cloathing the five fubordinate Overfeers yearly.	27	05	00
By the Abftract of Clothing, the remaining 14 men-fervants yearly	58	16	00
By the Abftract of Cloathing four women fervants that attend in the houfe	19	04	00
By the Abftract of the remaining fix women-fervants, that do the common work abroad in the fields.	21	06	00
The charge of thirty Rug Gowns for thefe thirty fervants	37	10	00
By the abftract of the cloathing of fifty men-Negres	15	00	00
By the abftract for the cloathing of fifty women-Negres	20	00	00
Sum totall of the expences is	1349	01	00
Sum totall of the yearly profits of the Plantation	8866	00	00
So the clear profit of this Plantation of 500 acres of land amounts to yearly	7516	19	00

A large Revenue for fo fmall a fum as 14000 l. to purchafe, where the Seller does not receive two years value by 1000 l. and upwards; and yet gives daies of payment.

I have been believed in all, or the moft part, of my former defcriptions and computations, concerning this Iland, and the waies to attain the profits that are thereto be gathered; but when I come to this point, no man gives me credit, the bufineffe feeming impoffible, that any underftanding man, that is owner of a Plantation of this value, fhould fell it for fo inconfiderable a fum: and I do not at all blame

FIGURE 2.4 Ligon, *A True and Exact History*, 116 (RB 139768, The Huntington Library, San Marino, California).

Everything is enumerated here, from clothing for the male and female servants to spirits and candles.

But Ligon does more than count: he calculates. He carefully lays out instructions for constructing a sugar ingenio, or mill, and for dividing land between the necessary parts of a plantation, all in order to project possibilities for future production. In one passage, he begins methodically with the assertion that Barbados has 392 square miles of land, and proceeds to subtract the amount of land required to raise animals and other provisions, leaving 262 square miles each containing 640 acres of land: "So then, we multiply 262. by 640. and the product will amount unto 167680" (*HB*, 94). These calculations immediately turn to bookkeeping and profit: "So here, we make our computation upon the place, and say, . . . if 10 acres of Canes will produce 375 l. what shall 55072. which is the number of acres contained upon the 2/5 of the land, allotted for Sugar Plantations, upon which the Canes must grow: and by the Rule of 3. we finde, that it amounts to 2665200. in sixteen months" (*HB*, 95). Tantalizing his readers with the language of the market—such as "we multiply" and "we make our computation upon the place"—and seeming to account for errors with moves like subtracting an estimated number of acres that men uninterested in trade will farm, Ligon can end with authoritative pronouncements assuring his readers of island profits: "Now you see what a vast Revenew this little spot of ground can produce in 22 months time" (*HB*, 96). Assuming the voice of a bookkeeper, Ligon renders Barbados a space in which everything from the territory to the behaviors of its inhabitants is calculable and can be extrapolated in ways that, for a careful mathematician, will ensure sizable profit.

Geometrically precise ratios, proportions, and scales help Ligon to represent Barbados as a template for similar planting endeavors elsewhere, creating the sense that a plantation is a transportable system, both economically and socially. He assures his readers that his careful study of one plantation in Barbados will be useful to those interested in running their own elsewhere: "I had time enough to improve my selfe, in the knowledge of the management of a Plantation of this bulk; and therefore, you may give the more credit in what I am to say, concerning the profit and value of this Plantation, which I intend as a Scale, for those that go upon the like; or to varie it to greater or lesse proportions, at their pleasure" (*HB*, 23). Ligon wants his careful attention to numerical details on the island to represent a system whose proportions remain intact even as they are enlarged or reduced. For him, a useful representation is one that maintains its internal proportions as it is moved or manipulated for different ends. The aesthetic Ligon seems to value most when he writes about Barbados is a geometric one, which is filled with perfect and therefore manipulable scales, whether applied to island fauna or a plantation's layout.[21]

Despite Ligon's interest in numerical skill, he much prefers performing calculations to actually compiling raw data. His preferred work is intellectual, and he spares himself the trials of a land surveyor traversing a treacherous island in the Caribbean heat. He complains that knowledge of the scale of Barbados has not yet been capable of surviving the passage to England: one surveyor "once took an exact plot of the whole Iland" (*HB*, 276) and sent it to England, but the account then disappeared. So Ligon attempts to recreate the lost data by finding the original surveyor. The surveyor tries to remember what he wrote down in the missing record while Ligon interrogates him: "I desired then to know, how many miles the broadest, and how few the narrowest parts might be. He told me, that he guest, the broadest place could not be above seventeen miles, nor the narrowest under twelve; and that the length, he was assured, was twenty eight miles" (*HB*, 26). Recognizing that these numbers are based only on conjecture, Ligon uses them anyway, and busies himself with geometry. Although "it was a hard matter to conclude upon any certainties," Ligon sets out to calculate the size of the island: "I will be as modest as I can in my computation; and take but 14. which is lesse then the Medium, and multiply 14. which is supposed to be the breadth, by 28. which is assured to be the length, and they make

392 square miles in the Iland. Beyond this, my enquiries could not reach, and therefore was compell'd to make my estimate upon this bare Supposition" (*HB*, 26). The surveyor, who has actually walked the length of the island, is presented here as a source of figures—as he attempts to recall the length of the "broadest place" and "the narrowest"—and Ligon as the mathematician.

Though Ligon insists that all he produces is "an estimate" based upon a "Supposition," he is nonetheless satisfied enough with his "modest" guess of 392 square miles to offer that figure to his readers without further investigation. The process of imagining the scale of Barbados—a process based on educated guesses, mediums, and multiplication—seems more important than the fidelity of the numbers produced to a territorial reality. Verisimilitude does not appear to be relevant to Ligon, given that he admits his number is a guess. What he does appear to be interested in is the use of mathematical skill to render an imaginative portrait of Barbados in its entirety. The geometric blends with the aesthetic; similarly, the surveyor and cartographer resemble the philosopher and artist. Mathematics is a medium that Ligon can manipulate, not necessarily a realm of numerical facts constrained by its proven relation to objective reality.

This story about scale begins with a mea culpa: "The length and breadth of this Iland, I must deliver to you only upon trust; for I could not go my selfe about it, being full of other businesse" (*HB*, 26). Discovering the precise scale of the island is not as important to Ligon as his "other businesse" there, signaling Ligon's interest in presenting his readers with something more than data.

Ligon bases much of his role as storyteller and commentator on an interest in counting, scales, and proportions that at times appears more aesthetic than instrumental. But as his cousin Walshe promised, there are also pages filled with numbers that are concerned explicitly with how to make a profit off of sugar. While Ligon might struggle to describe the entire territory of Barbados with precise numbers, he counts every last person, animal, and scrap of clothing when he turns his attention to an ideal single plantation. Here is a moment when the merchant's eye is difficult to distinguish from that of an artist in the vein of da Vinci or Dürer, especially since both rely on calculation. A plantation owner would likely keep account books of his property, but an artist with an interest in proportion would similarly be drawn to considering how parts relate to a whole within an ideal form. The *History* moves swiftly between counting objects and humans, and measuring acres of land or quantities of construction supplies. Ligon begins his model budget by laying out a careful plan for how to get the most out of the "one thousand pound" allotted for clothing the various kinds of laboring bodies on a plantation (*HB*, 109). For "men and women Negres," he suggests spending "100 l. in Linnen Cloth, as Canvas and Kentings, which you may buy here in London, of French Marchants, at reasonable rates; and you may hire poor Journy-men Taylers, here in the Citty, that will for very small wages, make that Canvas into drawers, and Petticoats" (*HB*, 109). He follows this by describing what clothing to make for the white servants, and then only at the end does he advise a prospective planter to shop for himself and his own family, allotting a hundred pounds for fine clothing for a planter's family, and twenty-five for hats—more than the cost of the clothing for all the servants.

Comparing the narrative of expenses with the budget table reveals gaps between the two forms, allowing this narrative to be a place where categories shift and blend, and where one line in a ledger can take up a disproportionate share of concern. In the narrative, the slaves' bodies are simultaneously the first and last priority—purchasing heaps of cheap material for their clothing is the first task Ligon recommends, yet it also constitutes the smallest expense. When this list appears in the form of a table of accounts, however, the allotment for slaves' clothing appears at the bottom (see fig. 2.5). The ledger also sets up an opposition between profit and the material conditions of bodies on the plantation—each item on the list chips away at the overall possibility of profit from an initial investment, and when taken together, labor collectively mounts the primary obstacle. According to the ledger, the five male Christian overseers will each need "Six pair of Linnen or Irish stokings," and "Three *Monmouth* caps"; the women servants will each need "three petticoats" and "three wastcoats"; and all the Christian servants will need blankets "to cast about them when they come home hot and wearied, from their work." Following the careful detailing of the different ranks of Christian servants—thirty in all—the budget includes only two lines for all clothing needs of the hundred African slaves: "Now for the Negres . . . The fifty men shall be allowed yearly but three pair of Canvas drawers a piece . . . The women shall be allowed but two petticoats a piece yearly" (*HB*, 115). Although Ligon plans for an equal number of male and female slaves, the women's clothing will cost more, leading to a total cost of of 20*l.*, as opposed to the 15*l.* projected for the men. Overall, the ledger's careful observance of clothing and its costs inscribes a hierarchy of degradation, beginning with the relatively well-clothed male overseers and ending with the slaves dressed in rags. The care Ligon takes to note the higher expense of a slave woman's petticoat is the only miniscule exception to this otherwise linear narrative of steep social descent.

As he moves between the prose and the ledger in the *History*, Ligon translates the work of bookkeeping into the creation of a social aesthetic. By attending to the clothing costs associated with bodies, rather than the bodies themselves, Ligon's budget fashions an orderly hierarchical arrangement out of a system that requires Christians, Africans, indigenous people, men, and women to intermingle. In order to observe this translation, we first have to understand how numbers were more of a rhetorical tool than evidence of a verifiable reality for an early modern bookkeeper like Ligon. As Mary Poovey has described, bookkeeping "helped confer cultural authority on numbers," rather than the other way around. Numbers gradually took on an aura of fact by means of the way bookkeeping employed "the precision of arithmetic," rather than eloquence, to serve "as the instrument that produced both truth and virtue."[22] Merchants showed that they were trustworthy by proving their ability to perform arithmetic in a consistent way, *not* by having any kind of auditor-observer compare their books with their actual activities. Ligon uses arithmetic for a similarly abstract purpose in his conversation with the surveyor; and again, with the ledger for clothing, Ligon uses numbers and calculation to arrange the social hierarchy of a plantation. He may produce a prospective planter's shopping list in the process, but aesthetics dovetailed with utility in seventeenth-century mathematics and the bookkeeping practices that employed it.

Early modern accounting handbooks prescribed a gradual transition away from narrative and toward lists across of series of books. First a merchant would journal his transactions; then those transactions would be recorded in list form; and finally a bookkeeper would prepare a ledger of credits and debits. With this method, a merchant elevated his status and veracity by displaying his ability to be consistent across each book, rather than by proving the original book's relation to what actually transpired. Using arithmetic, anyone inspecting the books could check this consistency—an activity that stands in for the impossibility of checking the authenticity of the merchant's initial record of a transaction in the journal.[23] Ligon employs standard bookkeeping practices in the *History*, describing the clothing needs of servants and slaves in narrative form, and then translating those original observations into a ledger in which the text is shortened. And like in a standard accounting ledger, Ligon sums up the total cost of clothing for each individual group, just as a bookkeeper would sum up the credits and debits at the end of each page. This enables the reader to check Ligon's arithmetic and thereby determine whether Ligon is consistent at least with respect to himself. Like a good early modern bookkeeper, Ligon fashions a system that is unified by the practice of arithmetic and the form of assigning numbers to narrative descriptions. Ligon makes himself appear trustworthy, and the workings of a plantation appear neat, unified, and therefore beautiful. This aesthetic—Ligon as bookkeeper/artist, and the plantation as harmonized system—makes an investment in sugar appear attractive in a multidimensional sense, blending frugality with geometric beauty.

Like Governor Atkins's later 1680 census, Ligon's ledger attempts to assert tremendous power over a large number of people, translating bookkeeping methods into a hierarchical social system.

On the page, the "Account of Expenses issuing out yearly for Cloathing" forms a rough pyramid of male servants, female servants, and the heterogeneous slaves undergirding them all.

Using the tools of a merchant taking inventory, Ligon marks class differences by separating servants on either side of the page, and separating races by noting the cost of rug-gowns for Christian servants. The management of a sugar plantation—and by extension, the management of a colony dominated by this economy of imported labor—depends upon this seemingly simple application of bookkeeping to human life. Showing how the design of the budget seamlessly folds into human accounting, Ligon comments on the extremely high death rate for island inhabitants in the process of describing the clothing requirements of servants: "Black Ribbon for mourning, is much worn there, by reason their mortality is greater; and therefore upon that commodity I would bestow twenty pound" (*HB*, 110). Investment in sugar, Ligon suggests here, requires attention to significant mortality rates and rituals of mourning in the form of preparing the advance purchase of "Black Ribbon."[24]

Unlike in his narrative prose, Ligon's ledger erases any distinction between "Negroes and Horses." Ligon estimates the cost of illness or death of both, and notes that this number does not take into account the benefit the owner can recoup by "breeding all those kinds" (see fig. 2.4). The methods of the bookkeeper erase the distinction between the bodies of slaves and those of laboring non-human animals on Barbados. In the budget, the reductionist flattening of complex and contentious human interactions into enumerated lines conveys the image of an elegantly arranged plantation social system. By contrast, Ligon counts everything in sight in his narrative prose, using numbers to conflate quantities of space, animals, and people. In providing his readers with the proportions of an exemplary plantation, he details the holdings of one "eminent planter of the Iland" whose plantation contains "500 Acres of Land, with a faire dwelling house, an Ingenio plac't in a roome of 400 foot square; . . . a Garding house; of 100 foot long, and 40 foot broad; . . . Houses for *Negroes* and *Indian* slaves, with 96 *Negroes*, and three *Indian* women, with their Children; 28 Christians, 45 Cattle for worke, 8 Milch Cowes, a dosen Horses and Mares, 16 Affingoes" (*HB*, 22). Precise counts of measurement like "500 Acres" and "400 foot square" flow seamlessly into counts of people, like "96 *Negroes*, and three *Indian* women." Space, humans, and animals all become visible through the same measuring eye, as when Ligon moves immediately from "28 Christians" to "45 Cattle." There is no arrangement here, no arithmetic, and no hierarchy—the slaves come before the Christians, and all kinds of people appear between quantities of land and animals. Whereas the ledger and the conversation with the ledger points to Ligon's mathematical ability, this list points to the inherent quantifiability of every aspect of a plantation. It implies that numbers can identify and sort any type of quantity: land, structures, animals, or people.

The more Ligon tries to enumerate the human bodies on Barbados, however, the more he faces the difficulty of representing different classes of people as separate from one another, and of making sure this representation does not appear to threaten the power relationships on the island. Ligon's index lists his consideration of "The number and nature of the inhabitants" alongside "the Scituation of the Iland," "Commodities exported and imported," and "What materials grow on the Iland, fit to build with," as though he were preparing a complete census. But his attempt at describing the inhabitants resembles his conversation with the surveyor. Like mapping territory, taking a colonial census proves at first difficult, but then becomes possible, thanks to Ligon's skills in compiling and manipulating information from others. Ligon admits that the constant movement that characterizes an island dominated by Atlantic trade hinders his efforts: "It were somewhat difficult, to give you an exact account, of the number of persons upon the Iland; there being such store of shipping that brings passengers dayly to the place." In order to grasp the total number, Ligon again eschews any actual counting on his own, instead relying on hearsay: "[I]t has been conjectur'd, by those that are long acquainted, and best seen in the knowledge of the Iland, that there are not lesse then 50 thousand soules, besides Negroes; and some of them who began upon small fortunes, are now risen to very great and vast estates" (HB, 43). Fifty thousand is a gross overestimate—historians dispute how trustworthy early Barbadian tax documents are, but place the number of whites on Barbados in 1640 at between 8700 and 10,000, and even by 1660 it was only up to 22,000.[25] Though Ligon only alludes to the subject here with his "besides Negroes," when he visited Barbados the colony was in the midst of fateful demographic changes. White population growth entered a permanent slowdown—numbers of whites have never been higher on Barbados than they were at the time of the Restoration, according to Dunn—and just after 1660 the slave population became a majority.[26] Ligon's offhand exaggeration from vague sources suggests carefulness around this sensitive topic more than carelessness, as though he intended to assuage prescient fears held by those "long acquainted" with the island that the conspicuous ratcheting up of the slave trade would soon leave whites outnumbered.

At this racially charged moment, Ligon's count of inhabitants presents the island as a place where social control is possible. Like the earlier estimate of the island's territory, Ligon's point is not that his numbers are correct, but that quantification can make Barbados knowable. Ligon then uses counting to present himself as a trustworthy eyewitness to life on Barbados by being consistent unto himself. Ligon's overestimate of the island's population is followed immediately by a justification of the developing institution of slavery. Ligon claims that the enlightened self-interest of investors ensures better treatment for slaves than for indentured servants: "The slaves and their posterity, being subject to their Masters for ever, are kept and preserv'd with greater care then the servants, who are theirs but for five yeers, according to the law of the Iland. So that for the time, the servants have the worser lives, for they are put to very hard labour, ill lodging, and their dyet very sleight" (*HB*, 43). In this demography (beginning with "The Iland is divided into three sorts of men, viz. Masters, Servants, and slaves"), Ligon imagines the characteristics of slaves, masters, and indentured servants as proportional to one another, united in balanced harmony by the profit-driven plantation system. Ligon places the distinctive feature of slavery into a dependent clause—"being subject to their Masters for ever." Ligon's bookkeeping vision portrays a plantation as an enumerated whole whose overarching goal of profit protects even the most powerless group of people. In keeping with the focus on art, it emphasizes the proportion and internal consistency of an ideal plantation in order to render this labor system appealing.

Numeracy and Power

The problem with a real plantation, unlike an ideal one, is how to control the labor force that makes sugar profits possible. When describing the differences between servants, slaves, and masters, Ligon repeatedly emphasizes masters' superior capacity of numeracy. When considering cultural differences between Africans and Europeans, Ligon echoes John Smith belittling Uttamatomakkin, in his identification of numeracy as the primary gap between racial groups. While Europeans perform figures with Arabic numerals, Ligon asserts in his narrative that Africans do not have a system of recording numbers, even though they are able to count. He ignores the possibility that, like Guaman Poma, Africans have access to methods of counting unknown to him, and that access to these methods might have been severely curtailed by the violence they endured at the hands of slaveowners. According to Ligon, the slaves measure their ages and other lengths of time by counting the moon, but have to rely solely on their memory of how many months have past: "they are resolved to remember, they account by the Moon; as, so many Moons since one of these, and so many Moons since another; and this account they keep as long as they can: But if any of them live long, their Arithmetick failes them, and then they are at a dead fault." For Ligon, racial difference here lies not in raw intellect, but in the use of sophisticated systems of representation like writing and mathematics. "For what can poor people do," Ligon asks in relation to African slaves on Barbados, "that are without Letters and Numbers, which is the soul of all businesse that is acted by Mortalls, upon the Globe of this World?" (*HB*, 52). "Letters and Numbers" together make up the undergirding "soul" of all global commerce, and the people with power over these means of representation can "do" vastly more than the "poor" Africans. Ligon elevates bookkeeping here to a tool for global commerce, and by extension, power over illiterate and innumerate peoples.

This tool of global conquest works, for Ligon, in suppressing revolt as well. Africans' lack of numeracy relates to their inability, Ligon suggests, to recognize their numerical advantage over whites and to organize themselves behind a leader who could challenge their servitude. Ligon avoids assigning a particular number to the slave population, but he addresses the specter of revolt head-on, and even repeats gross exaggerations of the number of slaves: "It has been accounted a strange thing, that the Negres, being more then double the numbers of the Christians that are there, and they accounted a bloody people . . . that these should not commit some horrid massacre upon the Christians, thereby to enfranchise themselves, and become Masters of the Iland" (*HB*, 46). Even as he grossly overestimates the racial disparity at the time, Ligon rearranges the conjectured data so that that the slave population does not represent an aggregate number at all, but instead is hopelessly subdivided and incapable of amassing a near-majority. Other than the legal prohibition against slaves holding weapons, and, Ligon claims, their "subjected" spirits as a result of enslavement, "there is a third reason, which stops all designes" of rebellion: "They are fetch'd from severall parts of *Africa,* who speake severall languages, and by that means, one of them understands not another: For, some of them are fetch'd from *Guinny* and *Binny,* some from *Cutchew,* some from *Angola,* and some from the River of *Gambra*" (*HB*, 46). Africans' numbers may be large, but they are poorly arranged, he proposes. There is no hierarchy to organize these numbers into a monolithic challenge to white numbers, according to Ligon; no way to sum these groups together without denying what Ligon would like to see as their inherent separateness. Just as he did not walk the island to determine its size, Ligon does not attempt to enumerate these groups. Instead, he uses speculative arithmetic to display the qualities he most values: hierarchy, harmony, and proportion. Ligon applies human accounting in a way that serves his overarching vision of a beautiful and controlled plantation system, claiming that the African slave labor upon which sugar planters are increasingly relying is hopelessly subdivided into innumerable distinct ethnic groups. Ligon represents the slave population on Barbados as a quantity that is not as unified as it looks on a ledger with Arabic numerals adding up the total number of slaves, because "one of them understands not another"—because Africans' own representative systems are not intelligible to one another.

In retrospect, Ligon may have observed correctly the communication difficulties between newly arrived slaves, but underestimated the amount of time it would take to overcome these hurdles. Slaves rose up against white plantation owners repeatedly throughout the seventeenth and eighteenth centuries, and as historian Richard Dunn points out, they staged a major revolt ten years after Ligon left Barbados. The leader was a man whom planters said must "have been a 'Prince' in his own country, where he had led great armies to victory."[27] Slaveowners both exploited and feared the African legacy of their slaves; they speculated whether their slaves' experience living under African kings would divide them, or would provide them with a leader who could unify their otherwise randomly assembled numbers.

The act of recognizing numbers of people is itself a powerful force in this violent and unstable new social system. Ligon describes a revolt among the white Christian servants that occurred shortly before he arrived, and counting intervenes at the end of this story to signal the removal of the threat. As noted earlier, in 1647 Ligon witnessed a moment of transition on Barbados between a labor force consisting primarily of European indentured servants and one that would come to consist almost entirely of African slaves. When Ligon looks back to the prior revolt, he describes an era when the exploitation of white "Christian servants" was the primary engine of sugar cultivation on Barbados. He takes care to voice objections to how sugar planters subject servants to "worser lives" than the slaves, and avers, "Truly, I have seen such cruelty there done to Servants, as I did not think one Christian could have done to another" (*HB*, 44). Ligon directly attributes the threat of revolt among servants to the planters' poor treatment of this segment of the labor force: "[S]ome cruell Masters will provoke their Servants so, by extream ill usage, and often and cruell beating them, as they grow desperate, and so joyne together to revenge themselves upon them" (*HB*, 45). Unlike the slaves—whom Ligon claims cannot recognize the potential power of their united numbers because of African ethnic divisions—starvation, overwork, and beatings foster the conditions under which Christian servants may "joyne together" their numbers into a force that undermines the power of plantation owners.

As Ligon tells it, an exact body count of people signals the defeat of the servant's revolt. While in the planning stages, Ligon does not say how many of the servants are rebellious: "Their sufferings being grown to a great height, & their daily complainings to one another (of the intolerable burdens they labour'd under) being spread throughout the Iland; at the last, some amongst them, whose spirits were not able to endure such slavery, resolved to break through it, or die in the act" (*HB*, 45). "Some" of the servants cannot endure the sufferings of exploited labor that amount to "such slavery" (an odd choice of words, given that Ligon earlier compared the life of African slaves favorably to that of servants)—though at this point in the telling, this "some" is unclear. Ligon describes how one servant with knowledge of the plot alerted a Master, and as a result, "eighteen of the principall men in the conspiracy, and they the first leaders and contrivers of the plot, were put to death, for example to the rest" (HB, 46). Eighteen executions result in a definitive mortality count that clarifies and eradicates the threat of the "some amongst them" who had dared to "joyne together to revenge themselves" against the planters' brutality. When Ligon describes a serious threat to the labor system that fuels sugar profits, he tells a story that begins with vaguely defined multiplicity and ends with a body count signaling the restoration of the plantation owners' power.

In contrast with the story of the servant's revolt, Ligon turns to the non-human world to consider the possibility that a mighty non-hierarchical agency could arise from an assemblage of otherwise uncountable and impotent creatures. Masters on Barbados may have the power of numeracy, but by studying Barbadian ants, Ligon obliquely returns to the problem of laborers' growing power of sheer numbers. An avid naturalist, Ligon tells a detailed story about the ant colonies he observes during his stay that focuses on how they use the strength inherent in their overwhelming numbers. He tells of an experiment (and encourages his readers to test it) wherein ants who cannot reach a quantity of sugar floating in a glass of water will drown themselves until their corpses create a pile that enables the ants behind them to crawl over it to the floating goal. These "abundant" and "busie Creatures . . . make a bridge of their own bodies, for their friends to passe on; neglecting their lives for the good of the publique; for before they make an end, they will make way for the rest, and become Masters of the Prize" (HB, 64).[28] Ligon focuses closely on the ants' primary strength, their multitudes: when they see sugar they want, they instantly "come in thousands, and tenne thousands, and in an instant, fetch it all away" (HB, 64). Here, sugar is the prize, and Ligon's story of servants who sought to revolt so that they could become "Masters of the Iland" implies that both Africans and English alike could be the ants that seek it. In the same way that laborers vastly outnumber plantation owners on Barbados, ants are ubiquitous: "If I should say, they are here or there, I should do them wrong; for they are every where" (*HB*, 63). Unlike the carefully ordered numbers of humans on a plantation as represented by Ligon's ledgers, the ants crawl in their multitudes beyond any barriers attempting to contain them; they are not constrained within a particular place within a larger system, but instead "are every where."

Even as Ligon presents knowledge of counting and plantation management as a source of power that ensures masters' control over servants and slaves on Barbados, he meditates on the potential power of innumerable aggregates when he turns to the natural world. In contemplating a swarm of ants, Ligon imagines a kind of natural agency that does not require an outside organizing force to become mobilized. Without a specific leader, the ants are able to perform breathtaking feats: the ants cannot kill cockroaches, their "mortall enemies," but they are able to avidly carry off the body of a dead cockroach even though "his body is bigger then a hundred of them," because the laboring ants "never pull contrary waies" (*HB*, 63). The ants are so numerous that they could not possibly be counted, and so ubiquitous and unvaried that they could not be organized by subdividing them into different groups. Yet they act as an amorphous aggregate to achieve their goals.[29] Upon seeing Barbados, Ligon compared the political organizations of men with the balance of the native ecosystem—and advocated that ecology provides the better model: "[T]ruly these vegetatives, may teach both the sensible and reasonable Creatures, what it is that makes up wealth, beauty, and all harmony in that Leviathan, a well governed Common-wealth" (*HB*, 20, 21). Given his willingness to ponder and sympathize with the condition of laborers on Barbados, and to examine forms of numeracy, Ligon's natural history provides a safe avenue for exploring—albeit indirectly—whether slaves and servants were capable of such orderly subordination to their own common good against the cockroaches who preyed upon them. The story of the revolt tells a tale of perfidy, and island rumors insist that Africans are divided by Old-World allegiances, but the tale of Ligon as awestruck by the ants poses a question about the limits of control by top-down powers like the act of counting. Unity, harmony, will, and agency can also be mustered from within, and Ligon hoped, in the case of the English during the interregnum, that they would be. In the process of his meditation on what an uncounted assemblage can do, he leaves open the possibility that laborers were capable of overpowering competitors in their own way. As Kriz argues regarding Sloane's *Voyage to . . . Jamaica*, the people, plants, and animals that Ligon writes about ultimately "proved remarkably resilient to a reordering of knowledge that attempted to stabilize and naturalize a network of power relationships" in the text.[30] Ligon creates a framework of taxonomic and enumerate disparity that appears to "stabilize and naturalize" an incredibly volatile social environment, yet he also includes stories and observations that question the totalizing power of these classificatory tools.

Romances of Population

Ligon compares forms of numeracy in another portion of text as well, when he describes how Africans and the English count births in different ways. In a story involving the slave Macow, Ligon claims that for the English, the birth of twins is a welcome event—and certainly a planter who will enslave the children of slaves would welcome this reproduction of labor. But Ligon claims that Africans believe that a wife's pair of children is a reflection of morality, in that two children signal her two lovers: "[I]f any of their Wives have two Children at a birth, they conclude her false to his Bed, and so no more adoe but hang her." When Macow saw that his wife had given birth to twins, he set out to find a rope: "But the Overseer finding what he was about to do, enformed the Master of it, who sent for *Macow*, to disswade him from this cruell act, of murdering his Wife, and used all perswasions that possibly he could, to let him see, that such double births are in Nature, and that divers presidents were to be found amongst us of the like" (*HB*, 47). The master tries to teach Macow that "double births are in Nature," even though Macow does not share the view that higher rates of reproduction are always better: "[W]e rather praised our Wives, for their fertility," the master explains, "than blamed them for their falsenesse" (*HB*, 47). In this exchange, Ligon depicts the English as capable of correcting the Africans' views about the social implications of slave women's fertility.

The master goes to great lengths to preserve the source of his slaves' increased numbers—the woman's body—and threatens to kill Macow when he refuses to be dissuaded from murder: "[T]he Master perceived . . . that the ignorance of the man, should take away the life of the woman, who was innocent of the crime her Husband condemned her for, told him plainly, that if he hang'd her, he himselfe should be hang'd by her, upon the same bough" (*HB*, 47). "Ignorance" comes to mean adhering to an interpretation of the meaning of fertility that is different from the belief that slave numbers are always a credit to a plantation's wealth. Tellingly, this life-or-death conflict between opposing senses of the significance of human numbers takes place from beginning to end over the body of a reproductive woman. Lying behind Ligon's binary of a master and slave's population views is the actual woman, whose labor of being "brought to bed of two Children" initiated the conflict between the two men. She does not appear on the scene, except when the master foretells how Macow will hang beside her "upon the same bough" if he kills her. The anecdote about Macow, the twins, and the political economy of sugar-planting signals how Ligon represents laboring women—women who simultaneously produce changes in population numbers and property values—as contact zones where beliefs about human population collide.

Ligon's stories about women on Barbados might at first seem separate from his political theorizing, but they enable Ligon to contemplate harmonious dramas of order, fascinating conflicts over what human numbers might mean, beautiful visions of immeasurable beings—or, indeed, all of these. Besides the frequent references to Ligon's natural history work that appeared in Sloane's *Voyage to . . . Jamaica* (first published in 1707), Ligon's *History* had a vibrant eighteenth-century afterlife because of an anecdote it includes about the slave Yarico, an Indian woman betrayed by her English lover, which exploded into a cultural phenomenon through essays, poems, and plays.[31] Sir Richard Steele, as his *Spectator* persona, writes in 1711 that he "was the other Day amusing myself with Ligon's Account of Barbadoes," and relates "[o]ut of that honest Traveller, in his fifty fifth page, the History of Inkle and Yarico." In *The Spectator's* version, Yarico witnesses a young Englishman named Thomas Inkle escaping from a band of Indians. Like Pocahontas saving John Smith, Yarico rescues Inkle: she "rushed from a Thicket" and "grew immediately enamoured of him, and consequently solicitous for his Preservation." She lovingly holds him in her arms for protection inside a cave, and "[i]n this manner did the Lovers pass away their Time, till they had learn'd a Language of their own," which enables Inkle to promise his lover "how happy he should be to have her in his Country, where she should be Cloathed in such Silks as his Wastecoat was made of, and be carried in Houses drawn by Horses." But once Yarico sees an English ship, and calls out to it to take the couple away, Inkle "began seriously . . . to weigh with himself how many Days Interest of his Mony he had lost during his Stay with *Yarico* . . . Upon which Considerations, the prudent and frugal young Man sold *Yarico* to a Barbadian Merchant," even though Yarico is pregnant with his child. The story ends with an ironic condemnation of the costs of mercantile thinking: Inkle "only made use of that Information [that Yarico was with child], to rise in his Demands upon the Purchaser."[32] Over a half-century after Ligon's story first appeared, Inkle and Yarico's love becomes a cautionary tale about the effects of thinking like a cold-hearted accountant.

In the original version of the tale, however, Ligon focus on Yarico's relationship to reproductive labor. In the *History*, Yarico first appears when Ligon briefly mentions her kindness in saving him from the terrible chigoes, a local insect: "I have had tenne taken out of my feet in a morning, by the most unfortunate Yarico an Indian woman." We do not learn why she is "unfortunate" until later on. "Indian women have the best skill to take them out," Ligon gratefully writes, since chigoes "will do more mischiefe then the Ants, and if they were as numerous as harmefull, there were no induring of them." Unlike the ants who come in innumerable quantities, these tiny beasts torture by laying eggs: "This vermine will get thorough your Stocken, and in a pore of your skinne, in some part of your feet, commonly under the nayl of your toes, and there make a habitation to lay his off spring . . . which will cause you to go very lame, and put you to much smarting paine" (HB, 65). If the ants call to mind ingenuity and the possibility of an order without numbers, the source of the chigoes' threat is a frightening fertility. Sad Yarico appears at the moment when tiny beasts underfoot torture Ligon with their threatening capacity to reproduce—thus Ligon remembers her story of interracial love when he recalls the pain of pests laying eggs in the wrong places.

Placed within its context in the History, Ligon's version of Yarico's story seems inspired by an interest in slave women's fertility. Ligon begins his story of Yarico by describing how an Indian slave woman gave birth to the child she had by a Christian servant. Though the History is unclear, other readers of Ligon's narrative have assumed this woman is Yarico, since he refers to Yarico as "this Indian Maid" in the paragraph after describing his Indian slave's exceptional birth: "We had a woman, a slave in the house . . . [who] chanc'd to be with child . . . and [when] her time was come to be delivered . . . walk'd down to a Wood, in which was a Pond of water . . . and in three hours time came home, with her Childe in her armes, a lusty Boy, frolick and lively" (HB, 54–55). Perhaps the "lusty Boy" was indeed the son Yarico had by the Christian "youth," Thomas Inkle, who "forgot the kindnesse of the poor maid" in hiding him "from her Countrymen (the Indians) in a Cave" and "sold her for a slave" (HB, 55). Even if

Ligon merely associated the two women's stories in his mind, it is telling that he is interested first in the reproductive capacity of the woman "who was of excellent shape and colour . . . small brests, with the nipls of a porphyrie colour . . . [and who] would not be woo'd by any means to weare Cloaths" (*HB*, 54). Only after he describes how this naked and alluring woman is modestly "loath to fall in labour before the men" and removes herself to give birth alone in the woods does he tell the equally brief story of "poor *Yarico* [who] for her love, lost her liberty" (*HB*, 55). In this way, Ligon links the original story that inspired *The Spectator*, Dryden, and a century's worth of poetry and drama with the common belief that Indian women are free from Eve's burden of painful childbirth, as well as with the potential of reproducing slave labor that this freedom involves.[33] Ligon borrowed from and repeated stories of alluring foreign women that had been circulating for centuries around the Atlantic—stories like the woman who gives birth by water with surprising ease, or the woman who betrays her people to protect her white lover.[34] When Ligon describes these familiar reproductive figures in the context of his interest in measuring people numerically, however, he explores the beauty of proportion and the limits of mathematical thinking. He uses these figures to contribute to aesthetic theories or ideas about hierarchical order, not—or not solely—to describe methods of increasing efficiency or profits. Whereas *The Spectator* could give Inkle a name and fault his bookkeeping mindset for rendering him insensible to romance, Ligon ascribes no cause to Yarico's betrayal: "But the youth, when he came ashoar in the *Barbadoes, forgot the kindnesse of the poor maid*" (*HB*, 55) is all he writes. Bookkeeping, for Ligon, was not at odds with romance, or art, or social harmony. Ligon was never as interested in producing raw data as he was with using accounting to render an alluring portrait of sugar planting, and the same expansive interpretation of numbers, measurements, and proportion apply to Ligon's depiction of the slave women whose reproductive labor increases profits for their masters.

The Spectator's reinvention of the Inkle and Yarico story offers one contrast to Ligon's particular alignment of reproduction and accounting, but Henry Neville's novella *Isle of Pines*, appearing in 1668 and therefore more closely contemporary with the *History*, highlights the uniqueness of Ligon's system of counting beautiful slave women.[35] Like Ligon, Neville does not set monetary concerns in opposition to sexual desire, as the *Spectator* does. However, Neville—an active political theorist—leaves no room for interpretive space between numbers and the actual bodies numbers are put in the service of counting. Whereas for Ligon, counting and measurement are aesthetic tools with which to approach and appreciate novel and beautiful forms, Neville applies numbers to island bodies as a means of ideal control and irrevocable categorization.

Neville's odd text is an epoch away from Ligon in terms of the development of population thinking.[36] Indeed, the two texts are in some ways worlds apart:[37] Neville never left Europe, and thus probably never had an indigenous slave woman remove dozens of insects from his feet, as Ligon did. Moreover, in the eleven years between the appearance of Ligon's *History* and Neville's novella, British sugar planters thoroughly invested in the newly won prize of Jamaica, and the restored English monarch Charles II consolidated and streamlined control over the sprawling empire Oliver Cromwell had expanded in the previous decade. [38] Numerical accountings of English wealth abroad quickly became a serious matter of official state interest. During this critical time in the Empire, mathematical guesswork like Ligon's was succumbing to increased faith in the capacity of bookkeepers to inventory human bodies.

Neville's story is still clearly a part of an experimental phase in population writing, however. It recalls the story of Inkle and Yarico because it it begins with a shipwreck and a lone Englishman's sexual encounters on a strange island. Similar to Ligon's *History*, Neville's fantasy connects accounting practices and colonialism: the Englishman who washes ashore and who populates the island with his progeny, George Pine, is a ship "Book-keeper" (*IP*, 11). Neville describes the plentiful sex Pine has with the four women who survived the shipwreck—the captain's daughter, two white servants, and a black slave—and the factions that develop among the children and grandchildren of these first four unions. Pine the bookkeeper keeps a faithful written record of all these sexual transactions, including a census of the numbers of people born to each of his consorts and their descendents. By the time of his death, Pine counts that he has populated the isle with 1,789 people.

With George Pine, Neville revives the long association between population discourse and discussions of the Biblical figure of Noah, like that which appeared in the work of both Guaman Poma and Du Bartas, as I have shown.[39] Neville's story closely resembles that of Noah's "happy Spawn" in Du Bartas's *Les Colonies*, and starkly contrasts with Guaman Poma by abjuring any judgment of the cause of the shipwreck, as well as any lamentation afterward for the tragic event. Just as one father's family populates the world after the great flood in Genesis, Pine's fantastic reproductive capacity occurs in the aftermath of a catastrophe: namely, the shipwreck that kills everyone aboard save for Pine and the four women. Diversity and classification are an essential part of Neville's fantasy of population: the tribe of the "English" are descended from Pine's former master's daughter; the Trevors and Sparks are descended from servant women. The Phills are descended from Philippa, whom Pine calls a "*Blackamoor*" or "*Negro* female slave," though as a testament to the incongruity of race as a category in this period, Pine describes Philippa's first child as "a fine white Girl"; and all the Phills are "as comly as any of the rest" of the children from his other three wives.[40] By the time the colony is discovered by Dutch visitors, long after Pine's death, the Phils have attempted a rebellion which resulted in the creation of a harsh legal system on the island, and the Dutch leave just as another of Philippa's descendents leads an insurrection to challenge it.

The novella *Isle of Pines* is an equation: through reproduction, Pine turns himself plus four women into a grand total of 1,789 perfectly enumerated people before he dies. Just as Ligon uses accounting techniques to describe a plantation economy, Pine the fictional bookkeeper keeps impeccable records: when the Dutch visitors discover the island generations after Pine's death, the leading heir from the English tribe presents them with his ancestor's carefully preserved account of his life. Despite the many layers of translation Pine's narrative undergoes (from English to Dutch back to English, via a French ship at one point), the population counts remain clear in each language as they ascend from five at first, to "forty seven" (*IP*, 15), to "five hundred sixty five," to the progenitor's final count, in Arabic numerals that need no translation, of 1,789 (*IP*, 16).

The women labor as producers of these impressive numbers, and Pine writes down how many children result from each of his wives' births, beginning a demography that sets the stage for the later conflict between the tribes of English, Trevor, Sparks, and Phils: "My first Wife brought me thirteen children, my second seven, my Masters Daughter fifteen, and the *Negro* twelve" (*IP*, 15). Prior to Pine's first count of his children, sex and reproduction work to differentiate the four women according to their social class. One of the servant women, who because of the order in which he later names them is presumably Elizabeth Trevor—a distinctively Welsh name—is "something fat" (*IP*, 15), and therefore has trouble with labor. Pine also uses sex to separate Philippa from the others: they copulate only at night, and never when she is already pregnant. Unlike the Welsh maid, Philippa is extremely fertile: Pine says she becomes pregnant "commonly . . . at the first time I lay with her" and in labor—recalling Yarico's quiet unassisted birth—has "no pain at all" (*IP*, 15). Despite this, Philippa ranks third in total number of children, being "the first that left bearing" (*IP*, 15).[41] When Pine, outliving all four wives, takes the deathbed census that includes over four generations and writes his narrative, he introduces the names of the four clans for the first time (in fact, this is the first time his white wives are named at all). His two final acts are actually the first general commands we hear of on the island, besides the customs he develops regarding sex and marrying his children off: he "summoned them to come to me, that I might number them, which I did"; then he "gave this Narration . . . to my eldest Son . . . commanding him to keep it" (*IP*, 16). Pine's legacy is his bookkeeping; he writes a memorial of the transactions he makes with his body on the island, and then calculates the value that these exchanges produce. Rather than describing the values of commodities as he might have done on a ship, Pine turns bodies into inventory.

Social strife ensues once the regular censuses cease. No one keeps track of how many Pines there are after the ancestral book-keeper dies, and the population appears not to have reproduced much after this point either: upon arrival, the Dutch ship reports seeing an island filled with "about 2000 English people" (*IP*, 6), or only about a dozen more than filled the island when George Pine died several generations earlier. By the time foreigners appear, the Isle of Pine is engulfed in a level of permanent unrest that was entirely absent when the original Pine presided over his nearly two thousand offspring—conflict that arises largely over sexual practices. Pine's successors face a tension between the Christian precepts of the Bible and the sexual misdeeds of the people, most egregiously the Phills. The Pine leaders respond to "whoredoms; incests, and adulteries"—crimes that the original Pine "was forced to do for necessity" but his descendents do "for wantonness"— with declarations of "wickedness," and agree that the perpetrators should be "severely punished," to the point of death (*IP*, 17). Pine addressed human sexuality by counting and classifying its repro-ductive products; his successors attempt to regulate it through legal pronouncements and the threat of retribution alone, only to face civil war repeatedly.

Like Ligon, Pine at first counts Africans as "beside" whites. Just after the shipwreck, at the moment when the survivors first confront the isle, Pine begins his bookkeeping of bodies: "we had opportunity to land our selves, (though almost drowned) in all four persons, besides the *Negro*" (*IP*, 12). The initial account marks Phillippa as a racial outsider from the rest of the community, just as the other islanders will set her heirs apart as troublemakers later on. However, as long as Pine is alive and including his "white" children by Phillippa in the total count of his progeny without qualification, the island remains peaceful. Other scholars have similarly investigated how Pine's early actions lead to the island's future troubles, claiming that Neville critiques his progenitor for neglecting to leave behind a constitution for his successors.[42] However, Neville is just as interested in what Pine *does* do as he is in what he neglects: Pine turns his Inkle-esque obsession with bookkeeping into a social order that uses numbers to interpolate bodies into a commonwealth. Later on, those bodies cannot seem to have sex peacefully or increase their population when they are not represented by numbers in an authoritative record of the commonwealth. Without an accounting, the commonwealth stagnates; but with these methods, it grows exponentially.

In Neville's friend James Harrington's book *Oceana*, the state similarly constitutes itself by meticulously monitoring and promoting reproduction.[43] Harrington advocated the careful application of tax laws to encourage marriage and Pine-like quantities of offspring: "But if a man have ten Children living, he shall pay no taxes; if he have five living, he shall pay but half taxes; if he have been married three years, or be above twenty-five years of age, and have no child or children lawfully begotten, he shall pay double taxes."[44] Like in Neville's fiction, people can be measured numerically with simple calculations in Harrington's pronatalist utopia. Five living children equals precisely half the taxes a man owes to the state. A man whose wife has been barren for three years pays a harsh penalty, though women are not mentioned here at all.

As I described earlier in the case of Macow's twins, Ligon staged a similar conversation about the value of fertility between a ruler and a subject (in this case, a master and a slave), and in that conversation, too, women's labor remains unacknowledged. In the writings of political mathematicians like Neville and Harrington, bodies can be equated with a certain amount of wealth. For Ligon, all calculations are as much about beauty and harmony as they are about reality—even calculations having to do with profits. When Ligon tells his readers about the cost of one slave woman's petticoat, or which servant men require a hat, he attends to the means by which bodies enter a social space, and draws upon accounting practices to structure this exchange. In a much less mediated exchange, the women in Neville's fiction are vessels through which men reproduce social status. These castaways turn bodies into numbers with machine-like efficiency, stamping each human product with a tribal distinction.[45]

Ligon's Barbadians appear more fleshy and complex than Neville's imaginary population producers. *The Spectator*'s story of Inkle and Yarico sets accounting and desiring in opposition, and *Isle of Pines* conflates the two, but Ligon does neither. When Ligon describes female beings, he embraces measurement as an enhancement to desire, and mathematics as a means of adoring the beauty of flora, plantations, and bodies. This is because Ligon, unlike Neville, was drawing upon a discourse about beauty and knowledge that considers both the possibilities and the limits of numerical measurement. The only thing stopping the complete enumeration of Pine is the loss of its clear original patriarch, not any problem with numbers or problems with the application of numbers to bodies. Validated by the late Renaissance artists he likes to cite, Ligon embraces numbers, and the counting and categorizing of people, as means of eliciting, displaying, and focusing desire. But he also, in so doing, accepts the inevitable gap between numerical measurement and the qualities he would like to measure.

Immeasurable Women

One of the island beings Ligon loves most is the Palmetto tree, and he conveys his admiration for the tree by measuring it. Ligon spends four pages describing the beauty of the Palmetto across its life cycle, and his love for the tree takes the form of measuring its size. "I believe there is not a more Royall or Magnificent tree growing on the earth, for beauty and largeness, not to be paralell'd," he writes, "but how to set her out in her true shape and colour, without a Pencill, would aske a better Pen then mine; yet I will deliver her dimensions as neer truth as I can, and for her beauty much will arise out of that" (*HB*, 75). Ligon promises the reader that the Palmetto's beauty will become apparent in his numerical representation of its "dimensions." Styling the Palmetto species as his lover, Ligon admits that this measurable quality— size—is the root of his admiration for the tree: "For if Xerxes strange Lydian love the Plantane tree, was lov'd for her age, why may not I love this for her largeness?" (*HB*, 75). Ligon thus begins his investigations into how large a Palmetto can possibly be. As with the survey, he begins by consulting old island inhabitants, "ancient Planters," who claim that when they first arrived, "they have seen some of them three hundred foot high." Ligon then begins his own guesswork: "[A]mongst those that I have seen growing, which I have guest to be two hundred foot high, the bodies of which I measured, and found to be but sixteen inches diameter." Finally, Ligon confirms the legend of a three-hundred-foot tree by finding an old fallen specimen, asking African slaves to chop it up, and then performing the mathematical calculation for figuring relative ratios, which he displays fully in the text (see fig. 2.6): "I measured the diameter of her stem, and found it to be 25 inches. Now if we go by the rule of Three, and say, If 16 inches diameter make 200 foot high, what shall 25 inches? And by this rule we shall prove her to be 312 foot high" (*HB*, 77). Math here confirms the truth already available within existing stories, rather than revealing new evidence.

Ligon's dissection of a dead tree may resemble natural philosophy (still an inchoate practice during his lifetime), but his use of arithmetic's "Rule of Three" here participates in two other contemporary discourses.[46] The first is bookkeeping: like a bookkeeper's

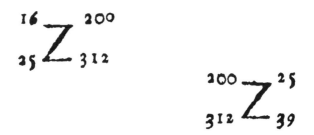

FIGURE 2.6 Ligon, *A True and Exact History*, 77 (RB 139768, The Huntington Library, San Marino, California).

prose account of a transaction in the memorial, Ligon begins with a hearsay record, and by gradually adding more and more numbers, turns the original narrative into a mathematical equation. The second is aesthetics. His interest in determining the trees proportions speaks specifically to the work of Albrecht Dürer, an artist he cites specifically when he evaluates whether the bodies he sees challenge or prove "Albert Dürers rules" (*HB*, 51).[47] Dürer famously grappled with the turn toward the application of geometry to art, advocated by Leonardo da Vinci and others, and wrote extensively about the benefits of precisely measuring proportions for the appreciation and representation of natural beauty. When Ligon measures diameter and calculates a tree's greatest known height using the Rule of Three, he is seeking the essence of the Palmetto in order to capture it in two dimensions (see fig. 2.7). For Ligon, measuring a tree for an explicitly natural philosophic investigation would have been a much more novel practice than doing so in order to draw it for aesthetic purposes, as artists had done for over a century.

By referring specifically to Dürer, Ligon invokes a complex and fraught debate within aesthetic theory about geometry, the branch of mathematics dealing with space and proportion. Philosophers such as Henry of Ghent associated geometry with melancholia, because the mathematician can so skillfully map out spaces around him that he loses the capacity to imagine spaces that cannot be measured. Geometry therefore became a science

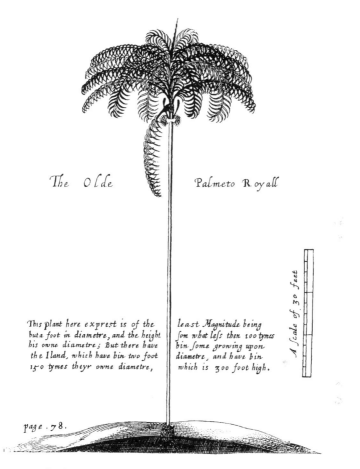

The   Olde   Palmeto Royall

This plant here exprest is of the
but a foot in diametre, and the height
his owne diametre; But there have
the Iland, which have bin two foot
150 tymes theyr owne diametre,

least Magnitude being
som what lefs then 100 tymes
bin some growing upon
diametre, and have bin
which is 300 foot high.

A Scale of 30 feet

page . 78.

FIGURE 2.7 Richard Ligon, "The Olde Palmeto Royall," *A True and Exact History*
(RB 139768, The Huntington Library, San Marino, California).

of reaching toward some impossible goal, of desiring to quantify
inherently limitless expanses.[48] Dürer explored this tension between the promise of mathematical theory and humans' lack of
divine knowledge in both his artistic and written work: "As for
geometry," he wrote, "it may prove the truth of some things; but
with respect to others we must resign ourselves to the opinion
and judgment of men."[49] When Ligon looks back to Dürer in

the midst of his plantation bookkeeping, he calls upon an artist known for exploring the tension between mathematical and metaphysical ways of knowing.

Dürer becomes useful to Ligon's narrative when it turns to describing the bodies of the African slaves laboring on Barbados. Just as Ligon sought to understand the Palmetto by measuring different specimens, he focuses on bodily proportions to study these strange new people: "I have been very strict, in observing the shapes of these people; and for the men, they are very well timber'd, that is, broad between the shoulders, full breasted, well filleted, and clean leg'd." Ligon concludes, through his observations, that the men's proportions "may hold good with Albert Dürers rules, who allowes twice the length of the head, to the breadth of the shoulders; and twice the length of the face, to the breadth of the hipps, and according to this rule these men are shap'd" (*HB*, 51). Ligon confirms that African men adhere to the proportions Dürer outlined for them in his writings when he studied various human subjects. Just as each class of people on a plantation exists in harmonious subjugation to the whole, each part of the body relates to each other part in composing a human unity.

Ligon refers here to Dürer's contributions to the Renaissance practice of anthropometry. As a blend of aesthetics and what we would retrospectively call scientific inquiry, anthropometry united mathematical skill with attention to human diversity—precisely what Ligon was attempting in studying the extraordinary collection of people assembled in the service of sugar plantations.[50] Dürer was known for his interest in studying the proportions of extraordinary people, and was especially attracted to abnormality. This attention to extreme shapes arose from the artist's belief that beauty arose in the midpoint between them: "Neither a pointed nor a flat head is considered beautiful," he wrote, "but a round one is, because it is the mean between the two others."[51] Dürer's willingness to depict unusual, rather than ideal, subjects led to his studies of non-Europeans, including one striking and detailed study of the head of an African man (as can be seen in Figure 2.8). Ligon insists that he, too, was "very strict, in observing the shapes" of the African men around

FIGURE 2.8 Albrecht Dürer, *Head Study of an African* (circa 1508), Albertina, Vienna (National Gallery of Art Library, Washington, DC).

him, and kept Dürer's ratio's in mind as he carefully examined them, confirming Dürer's postulations just as he had confirmed the old planter's tales of a three-hundred-foot-tall Palmetto tree. Dürer's mixture of measurement and aesthetics serves as Ligon's lens for scrutinizing the migrant male bodies around him on Barbados and harmonizing them with European forms of knowledge.

Ligon claims, however, that African women challenge these same European standards of the human form. When Ligon sees two young African women fetching water early in his journey on Cape Verde, he describes them as "creatures, of such shapes, as would have puzzelld Albert Dürer, the great Mr of Proportion, but to have imitated; and Tition, or Andrea de Sarta, for softnes of muscles, and Curiositie of Colouring, though with a studied diligence; and a love both to the partie and the worke" (*HB*, 16). Even the greatest masters of representation would be challenged to represent these sisters with fidelity, and Ligon admits, with regard to himself, that to "express all the perfections of Nature, and Parts, these Virgins were owners of, would aske a more skillfull pen, or pencill then mine." The teenage pair remain just beyond the reach of representation, no matter who attempts to capture their "colouring" or "muscles," because so much of the beauty that sets them apart from the others lies in their movement: "[T]hough all were excellent, their motions were the highest, and that is a beautie no painter can expresse" (*HB*, 16). Two laboring female bodies, entirely exceptional in form, and alluring not just for their particular attributes but primarily for the ineffable sum of their shared qualities, reveal the inadequacy of Ligon's studious diligence and careful record of the island. On the cusp of reproductive labor, at fifteen they are as "[i]nnocent, as [they are] youthfull," and as they move, bringing drinks for Ligon and his party, they "put themselves in the modestest postures that could be," movements that have not been taught to them but that Ligon is sure are "pure nature" (*HB*, 16). Ligon admires these women as he admired the Palmetto, but for some reason these similarly "natural" forms resist being loved through measurement in the same way as the tree.

If the young African virgins are such perfect embodiments of the human form that they lie just beyond the ability of even the greatest European artists to represent, then their opposite are bodies that similarly resist any aesthetic standards, requiring tools that Europeans do not possess in order to be represented.[52] Ligon finds such an example of a grotesque challenge to any existing understanding of human proportion in slave women who have finished childbearing. The water-fetching twin sisters, with all their virgin desirability, are on the verge of becoming mothers, yet as Ligon moves between writing about that pair and about female workers on Barbados, he vacillates between an image of inexpressible perfection and one of anomalous disproportion.

Ligon asserts that African women laboring to produce sugar profits on Barbados "puzzle" Dürer's rules of proportion: "[T]he same great Master of Proportions, allowes to each woman, twice the length of the face to the breadth of the shoulders, and twice the length of her own head to the breadth of the hipps. And in that, these women are faulty; for I have seen very few of them, whose hipps have been broader than their shoulders, unlesse they have been very fat" (*HB*, 51). Ligon identifies the women's bodies, not Dürer's rules, as "faulty," and points out that he has observed extreme specimens of this kind, ones who are "very fat." With these observations, Ligon participates in Dürer's endeavor to study extreme examples of one type in order to identify the norm, and positions himself as an observer of an oddity which even Dürer did not witness. Ligon described and drew the proportions of the Palmetto over the course of its lifetime, and he similarly attends to the way African women's bodies change with age. Though these women never adhere to the rules set by the "Master of Proportion," by the time they are middle-aged Ligon finds them grotesque:

The young Maides have ordinarily very large breasts, which stand strutting out so hard and firm, as no leaping, jumping, or stirring, will cause them to shake any more, then the brawnes of their armes. But when they come to be old, and have had

five or six Children, their breasts hang down below their na-
vells, so that when they stoop at their common work of weed-
ing, they hang almost down to the ground, that at a distance,
you would think they had six legs. (*HB*, 51)

Ligon betrays his reliance on European sources here by recycling stories about exotic women's breasts that describe them as either exceptionally firm or resembling another pair of legs, which had been circulating throughout Europe since the Middle Ages.[53] He also conflates
declining beauty with the loss of slave women's market value: once
they have come to be "old" and have completed their childbearing
labor, these women offer much less return on a master's investment.
Grotesque and ant-like, appearing at a distance to have "six legs," these
women repulse both potential buyers and potential admirers. African
women at this stage of life appear to stand outside of two globalizing
systems at once, simultaneously holding little value in the slave market
and little relation to Dürer's aesthetic anthropometry.

Ligon groups slaves and animals together in his plantation
ledger when he refers to problems with social reproduction, or
the losses to investment in slave, horse, and cattle labor "notwith-
standing all our Recruits by breeding all those kinds." When faced
with the task of describing the slave women of Barbados to his
English audience, he again embraces the comparison with animals. The seemingly six-legged older women look like insects,
and in another anecdote in his narrative, two planters attempt to
trade a similarly undesirable woman named Honor for a pig, thus
assuming the flesh of the two beings as comparable on the open
market. Ligon relates how one plantation owner tells his neighbor,
"I have great want of a woman servant; and would be glad to
make an exchange; If you will let me have some of your womans
flesh, you shall have some of my hoggs flesh" (*HB*, 59). Agreeing
that the two quantities can be measured with the same instruments of value and traded like any other commodity goods, the
neighbors decide on a price of "a groat a pound for the hogges
flesh, and sixe pence for the Womans flesh."

However, the deal goes sour when the slaveowner presents a woman with an anomalous figure. As I mentioned earlier, Ligon describes African women as having certain proportions except for those who are "very fat," and Honor is one of these extreme exceptions to the norm: "The scales were set up, and the Planter had a Maid that was extreame fat, lasie, and good for nothing. Her name was *Honor;* The man brought a great fat sow, and put it in one scale: and *Honor* was put in the other, but when he saw how much the Maid outwaycd his Sow: he broke off the bargaine, and would not go on" (*HB,* 59). The planter, unlike Honor's prospective buyer, recognizes that the value of a slave woman lies in her labor in both cultivation and reproduction, and this value is not as easily extractable as the meat in a hog's flesh. Honor is too extreme a specimen to enter into this commodity market of groats and pence for pounds of flesh. Her variation from the expected norm challenges two men's ability to agree on a fair comparison in price between hogs and women on Barbados, ending the possibility of an exchange. She deviates too much from an ideal form to be measured in this market system, and the men speculating over her body cannot agree on her worth.

Ligon describes both repulsive women and extraordinarily beautiful women as confounding a man's ability to measure on Barbados. Just as Honor's worthlessness confused the men who would have traded her, the twin virgins on Cape Verde who possess "a beautie no painter can expresse" render Ligon's numeracy useless. His equally enthralling love for the two "parallel Paragons" makes him unable to distinguish between them. In this confusion, this time Ligon himself is the human he compares to an animal:

I have heard it a question disputed, whether if a Horse, being plac'd at an equall distance, between two bottles of hay, equally good; and his appetite being equally fix'd upon either: Whether that Horse must not necessarily starve. . . . In this posture was I, with my two Mistresses; or rather, my two halves of one Mistresse: for, had they been conjoyned, and so made one, the poynt of my Love had met there; but, being divided, and my affection not forked, it was impossible to fix, but in one Centre. (*HB*, 17)

When Ligon tries to count the objects of his desire, first the young women are two; then they are "two halves" of one; next they are "conjoined"; and finally, they are united in one imaginary "Centre" that exists outside of either of them. This inability to count, or to divide his attention between the component parts of this assemblage of beauty, makes Ligon feel like a hungry yet immobilized horse. His desires simultaneously transfix and paralyze him, leading him to admire the twins like an aesthete, yet also rendering him as powerless as a beast of burden. Ligon could measure the Palmetto in order to express his love for it, but such is not the case with these twins. Indeed, he cannot even distinguish between them enough to count them as individuals. The Palmetto's beauty spurs him to measure it, yet he expresses his admiration of the twins only by abandoning any attempts to even determine whether they are truly one person or two.

This is why, for Ligon, aesthetic theories are essential for representing the contradictions of Barbados. The ethereal figure of one of Dürer's most famous engravings, *Melencolia I*, sighs in idleness toward a vision she cannot reach, thematizing the relation between mathematical endeavor and the inevitable disappointment of humans' limited capacity for understanding (see fig. 2.9).[54] In this engraving, Melancholia is surrounded by geometric instruments; as Erwin Panofsky argues, "equipped with the tools of art and science, yet brooding in idleness, she gives the impression of a creative being reduced to despair by an awareness of insurmountable barriers which separate her from a higher realm of thought."[55] Armed with the capacity to divide, to measure, and to calculate proportions, she nonetheless looks past her geometric tools toward an open space filled with flooded waters and devoid of Arabic numerals.[56] Her scales, ready for use, stand empty. This widely circulated engraving encapsulates the distinctiveness of Dürer's vision of the

FIGURE 2.9 Albrecht Dürer, *Melencolia I* (1514) (Harris Brisbane Dick Fund, 1943, The Metropolitan Museum of Art, New York, www.metmuseum.org).

fusion between art and geometry: ultimately the mathematician–artist will become conscious of a realm to which his numerical skills cannot be applied. Despite all the possible things left to be measured, consciousness of this immeasurable space leads to an idleness of perpetual longing. Ligon searches for and finds the limit to his capacity for numerical representation in the incomparable beauty and grotesqueness of laboring women around the Atlantic. These women are at the center of the key social problem of colonial resource extraction in the Caribbean: namely, the problem of the social reproduction of labor within a system marked by extraordinary levels of instability and death.

The African women Ligon describes elicit the sigh of melancholic admiration that marks the boundary between the enumerated account and the innumerable masses chronically left out. Political arithmetic, in Ligon's early rendering, creates a vision of the knowable world by always gesturing toward the specter of vast and immeasurable spaces beyond it. In this way, the exploitation of unaccountably fertile foreign populations becomes not only palatable, but also beautiful. Fashioning himself an artist, Ligon was perhaps looking for exceptional forms that might test, and ultimately overpower, his mathematical adeptness. "[Y]ou will think it strange, that a man of my age and gravity, should have so much to do with Beauty and Love," he admits. But he assures his readers that his studied observations come from a lifelong cultivation of artistic skill: "I have in my younger dayes, been much inclined to Painting, in which Art, colour, favour, and shape is exercised; and these Beauties, being a proper subject of all these perfections, (being in themselves perfect) I could not but consider them with a studied diligence" (*HB*, 17). Unlike the fictional George Pine, Ligon does not plan on fathering breathtaking numbers of children with the women he describes. Their reproductive contributions to Barbados are hard to quantify, and they alternate between appearing as intimate sensual partners, like Yarico when she picks insects from Ligon's feet, and as strangely animal-like creatures, like Honor when she sits on the scale opposite a hog. For Ligon, art, and not simply bookkeeping, offers the proper lens with which to study such creatures on Barbados. It is a melancholy task that interpolates bodies into a system of knowledge while still recognizing that at some point, calculation has its limits. The worth of some things, or people, or assemblages, might just be impossible to determine.

CHAPTER 3

Counting in King Philip's War

In her 1682 narrative of King Philip's War, *The Sovereignty and Goodness of God*, Mary Rowlandson remains certain of at least one thing regarding the Indians who hold her captive: there are a lot of them. They come in "great numbers,"[1] even a "vast number" (*SG*, 106), or perhaps "many hundreds" (*SG*, 79); they stand "as thick as the trees" (*SG*, 80) and seem to wield "a thousand hatchets" (*SG*, 80). Though when Rowlandson looks for food "there was nothing to be seen" (*SG*, 106), the Lord "strangely" (*SG*, 79, 105) provides for the Indians, and even while carrying their "old decrepit mothers" they are able to "[hold] the English army in play" (*SG*, 79). She cannot help "but be amazed at the numerous crew of Pagans that were on the Bank" (*SG*, 82) of a river opposite her, and arriving finally at an Indian settlement, Rowlandson is dumbfounded: "Oh the number of Pagans . . . that there came about me, that I may say as *David*, Psal 27. 13, *I had fainted, unless I had believed, &c*" (*SG*, 74). Rowlandson remembers only one time when the English army appeared "so numerous" as the group of Indians, but they quickly retreated to search for food. Though she can never pinpoint exactly how many Indians there are, it is not for lack of trying. Rowlandson likes to enumerate her experiences: her narrative is divided into sequentially numbered removes; she maintains updated body counts of the English around her; she makes careful note of important days or lengths of traveling time; and finally, she redeems herself with her deft determination of exactly how much she is worth for ransom. However, when she tries to count the Indians, she admits, it proves to be "beyond my skil" (*SG*, 79).

Just as Rowlandson the prisoner of war literally wanders along the frontier, beyond the borders of English colonial settlement, so her narrative figuratively takes place along the frontier of developing discourses in which people become countable numbers. When she writes of her experience, Rowlandson relies on quantification of various kinds to lend a sense of order to the chaos around her. As Christopher Castiglia has argued, "Rowlandson's text refuses to produce coherence," but she does try to restore a sense of "social order" using methods of counting, only to repeatedly fail.[2] Colonialism required this kind of population counting, this need to map both bodies and territory with measurable systems. Rowlandson attempts, on the ground, to apply this strategy of counting bodies to ensure her own survival: numeracy helps create a mental border between enemy and friend; it helps her find her children when they are taken from her; and when she negotiates her ransom, it ultimately sets her free. Her narrative is a sustained dramatization of an individual attempting to see the world through the colonial lens of population numbers—numbers that offer the promise of drawing clear borders between peoples, even as they mask the permeability of those boundaries.[3] In testing these ideas about countable bodies, Rowlandson's narrative provides a window into the inconsistencies within a perfectly enumerated colonial worldview. Even as Rowlandson tries to render her environment familiar by numbering the people she encounters, she reveals the inability of numerical categories to serve as a means of separating kin from enemies. Numbers cannot corral bodies in a stable count: they can only induce the act of counting, and this tension between the desire to enumerate and the mutability of bodies arises especially around the appearance of the reproductive bodies of women and children. By contrast, official histories of the colonists' encounters with the Indians, such as Increase Mather's history of King Philip's War and Cotton Mather's narrative of Hannah Dustan's captivity, insist on the ability of both friend and foe to remain quantified and separate in the midst of conflict. Even when women and children are on the front lines of battle, the Mathers can always keep count of them.

So far I have considered writings by witnesses to some of the earliest colonial experiences, who apply existing theories of population to make sense of their encounters. In the book's second half, starting here with writing about King Philip's War, I show how counting population becomes ingrained as a way to structure relationships within the colonies. As the previous two chapters demonstrated, reproduction again becomes a fraught site as a result of this heightened focus on counting in the narratives produced in the wake of this late seventeenth-century war. Like her female Puritan elders (Anne Bradstreet especially), Rowlandson focuses on the vulnerability faced by children in the process of becoming the right kind of numbers in population counts. However, Bradstreet's major focus is on the perils of Atlantic migration, and the way this migration alters the significance of family relationships. For Rowlandson, like Ligon, emerging ideas of race influence her approach to counting. Writing about her experience of a brutal and pivotal war, Rowlandson turns to population counts as a way to draw distinct racial lines among intermingling people. In this way, her writing about her own and her captors' children begins to resemble David Hume's method of linking personhood and population counts in the next century: as Frances Ferguson describes regarding Hume, "You must be a person to be allowed to reproduce, and liberty is the power not only to count but to have one's reproductive capacity counted in the ratios of population increase."[4] Like Hume, Bradstreet searched classical antecedents for answers to her concerns about population in a settler colony, but Rowlandson links these concerns to urgent questions, borne out of her direct confrontation with indigenous people, about what kind of people matter and what liberty truly means.

By tracing the sustained focus in Rowlandson's narrative on the bodies of children—both her own and those of the English and Indians around her—we can see the persistent problems reproduction poses to separating people into quantifiable groups in the midst of conflict. First, children might switch categories and alter the count, especially white captive children encountering the highly successful adoptive practices of indigenous people in New England.[5] But also, pregnant and nursing women—intertwined with infants who are dependent upon them for survival—each could count both as one person and as two. Given the superiority of Indians' acculturation practices relative to those of the English, Rowlandson may have been cognizant of her children's vulnerability to adoption by Indians—a possibility that would increase her enemies' population count. And to complicate matters further, Rowlandson's act of counting herself as an isolated number separate from her children conflicts with her insistence on feeling a persistent bodily connection with them. Population counts imply that individuals are each distinguishable from one another (like numbers), but this view of subjectivity fits uncomfortably with the way Rowlandson repeatedly describes her children as interdependent with her and other adults around them. Her attempt to enter into the colonial discourse of population developing around King Philip's War shows the fraught, yet central, role played by women and children in this newly calculating worldview. Mathematically inflected views of social life emerged as ways of coming to terms with the constantly shifting lines between imperial subjects and those outside imperial control, and Rowlandson's narrative illuminates the role reproduction plays in both producing numbers of bodies and calling definitive counts of those numbers into question, especially in the midst of war.

Rowlandson attempts her counts in the midst of a profound transition in thinking about human numbers, one in which the tendency toward counting people outpaced the development of vocabulary that described this activity. As I have argued here, nearly all of the words we now use to describe the political arithmetic that royal advisers were advocating from London during King Philip's War came into familiar use long after policies tracking populations were put into place: words like "population," "statistics," and "demography." Even the term "reproduction," which equates women's bodies, sex, childbirth, and childrearing with calculable rates, did not begin to replace "regeneration" to refer to human fertility until after John Wesley railed against the word as heretical in a 1782 response to Comte de Buffon's *Natural History*. The *OED* definition for "reproduction" quotes John Wesley's magazine review of Buffon: "He substitutes for the plain word *Generation*, a quaint word of his own, *Reproduction*, in order to level man not only with the beasts that perish, but with nettles or onions."[6] Yet comparative rates of reproduction are precisely the battleground in the settler colonial war Rowlandson witnessed: a war in which homes are spheres of warfare and the captive bodies of women and children, like hers and her daughters and son, are used as weapons. There was a gap between the experience of social life increasingly inflected with numerical language and the words available to describe that experience, and Rowlandson's text is essential for, as David Glimp describes in his study of Renaissance texts about population, "imagining the relation between literary practice and these early efforts to record and count people."[7]

In the 1680s, the same decade that Rowlandson wrote of her attempts to enumerate her captors, court adviser William Petty set to work calculating how to increase the number of whites born to English settlers in America. He insisted, regarding the American plantations, "[t]hat no youth of between 18 & 58 yeares old, nor woman of between 16 & 41 yeares old, bee unmaryed"[8] without being taxed, and in order to ensure that "every family have in it a Teeming woman of between 16 & 42 yeares old"[9] the colonial governors should "[a]dmit the Native women into freedome."[10] In an effort to produce the demographic statistics England wanted,

Anglo-American colonies had to invent systems to register births and deaths: as historian James Cassedy has noted, "[t]he original vital statistics legislation of Massachusetts Bay was revised or renewed seven times between 1639 and 1692" (32). The thirst for knowledge of Native American numbers was just as strong, if not more so. Petty asked for a meticulous demography of Native Americans living in Pennsylvania in 1685: "Suppose there bee 1000 of them, within a certain scope of ground. Q. How many of them are under 5 yeares old? How many between 5 & 10, 10 & 15, 15 & 25, 25 & 35, 35 & 45, 45 & 55, 55 & 65, 65 & 75, & how many above 75?" (115).

Imperial control demanded an accurate account of human habitation and human reproduction, and this newly numerical social discourse revolves centrally around the bodies of women and children—bodies that have the potential to alter the count. The frequent preoccupation with the bodies of pregnant, laboring, or lactating women in captivity narratives reflects a colonial fascination with reproductive bodies that arises in part from their simultaneously central and vexing relationship to efforts to track population. Metropolitan mathematicians, and a small but growing circle of colonial leaders like the Mathers with advanced training in arithmetic, moved calculation from the realm of bookkeeping into that of social relations, making women's bodies silent centers of imperial inquiry.

Colonial writings about spheres of conflict, such as King Philip's War, helped population science spread from the realm of policy into the perceptions of ordinary people. These colonial texts participate in an epistemological shift, beginning in the seventeenth century, toward the idea that all living people—not just fighting men—*could* be counted, and that societies could be represented numerically as populations. Rowlandson fights for survival and searches for her children among her Indian captors in the midst of this shift, encountering the unfamiliar idea that humans are quantifiable entities in the context of colonial war. Mathematics was a skill only rarely formally taught until the nineteenth century, let alone one that would have been used on a daily basis to organize social life.[11] While *The New England Primer* shows how the alphabet can be used to form syllables, words, and finally texts for the child reader, it does not apply numbers to an instrumental purpose beyond counting time (such as minutes in an hour, or days in a year) and locating Bible passages. When considering the way students in New England generally learned arithmetic, numeracy was subordinate to literacy, and numbers were not commonly deemed relevant to human needs, outside the acts of reading or noting the passage of time.[12] Calculations become vital to Rowlandson's negotiation of these relationships only when violent colonial conflict transgresses the boundaries of home and family.

As a woman, Rowlandson would have achieved a basic level of numeracy not through a primer on arithmetic, but in the process of learning household tasks such as knitting, and as a by-product of learning to read the Bible, as a way to locate verses.[13] Rowlandson relies upon both skills throughout her captivity as a way to mediate her relationship with the Indians, whether knitting in return for food or locating reassuring precedent for her experience in scripture.[14] The numeracy that organizes both of these tasks also enables Rowlandson to attempt to lend the static uniformity of numerical systems to otherwise chaotic social interactions. Pulled violently out of a household that numbers held together—both spiritually through the presence of a carefully enumerated Bible and physically through the numerically governed work of making food and clothing—Rowlandson turns to numbers out of the same desire for control of an unknown environment that drives Petty.

But it is the improvisational, unsophisticated quality of Rowlandson's attempt to count—the kind of counting done in the service of managing homes and families—that enables her narrative, unlike Petty's censuses or the Mathers' accounts of the war, to ask the questions left lingering when bodies become subject to calculation. Rowlandson's narrative is filled with images of attacks on pregnant or nursing women and of threatened English or Indian children, attacks mounted both by the war and by the use of mathematics to track the fluid intermixture of bodies involved in reproduction. Rowlandson herself yearns for the ability to distinguish one individual from another with clarity at the same time as she insists, in her horror and her grief, on the limits of this approach. Her narrative describes in detail how figures of women and children become sites of conflict when colonialism endows numbers with the power to represent not only days, stitches, or verses, but also threatening or threatened bodies.[15]

Between Counting and Chaos

When Rowlandson recounts the siege on her home and family that results in her three months' residence within Indian society, she repeatedly tries to account for this new reality using familiar systems of measurement. Critics have generally focused on Rowlandson's ability to read when they have considered how her prior education sustains her throughout her captivity, but Rowlandson's numeracy enables her not only to locate passages in her Bible, but also to create zones within her control out of sites of chaos.[16] Her narrative juxtaposes fixed quantities with immeasurability: in her opening line, Rowlandson follows the numerical certainty of the date of her capture with the uncertainty about her captors' overwhelming force: "On the tenth of February 1675, Came the *Indians* with great numbers upon *Lancaster*" (SG, 68). Rowlandson does not allow this frightening rupture between chronology and innumerable population to figure as the transition from freedom to captivity, for she immediately begins to try to build a scale that could bring the Indian bodies into a numerical system. At a riverbank, Rowlandson finally gets a view of her captors gathered together, but their lack of stasis renders a census impossible: "I thought to count the number of them, but they were so many, and being somewhat in motion, it was beyond my skil" (SG, 79). Immediately afterward, Rowlandson turns to her knitting and to counting her food: she writes that at least she was grateful to be travelling with a light load of only "my knitting work and two quarts of parched meal" (*SG*, 79).

In contrast to her exasperation at being unable to quantify the large number of Indians, Rowlandson frequently counts the white bodies around her. After she describes the siege in which she was captured, she takes a grave census:

> Of thirty seven persons who were in this House, none escaped either present death, or a bitter captivity, save only one, who might say as he, *Job* 1. 15. *And I only am escaped alone to tell the News.* There were twelve killed, some shot, some stab'd with their Spears, some knock'd down with their Hatchets... yet the Lord by his Almighty power preserved a number of us from death, for there were twenty-four of us taken alive and carried captive. (*SG*, 70)

Again Rowlandson sets up her captivity as a departure from numbered bodies into unnumbered ones, and from surroundings that can be quantified toward ones that thwart quantification.

Following the pattern of this initial violent sequence, the narrative repeatedly uses numbers to mark an initial order that is then lost in disorientation before Rowlandson attempts a new reordering. For example, the third remove begins as usual, with the ordinal in the title and by noting the duration of the Indians' journey with their captives and the time of their arrival in the Indian town. They had not eaten "from Wednesday night to Saturday night" before arriving in "an Indian town, called Wenimesset ... this day in the afternoon, about an hour by sun" (*SG*, 73–74). But then, disorientation: Rowlandson's daughter Sarah dies in her arms in the middle of the night, and Rowlandson contemplates suicide as a result. After Rowlandson describes Sarah's suffering, and her own agony of being unable to relieve it, Rowlandson makes a numerical accounting of the girl's life, the present time, and the duration of her captivity up to that point: "About two houres in the night, my sweet Babe, like a lamb departed this life, on *Feb. 18, 1675*, It being about six *yeares*, and *five months* old. It was *nine dayes* from the first wounding, in this miserable condition" (*SG*, 75). She carefully counts the time from her youngest daughter's birth, and from the day of the siege on Lancaster, as if the logical sequence of numbers were a tether to a familiar place.[17] More tumultuous events follow: an Indian finds a Bible for Rowlandson, a source of spiritual consolation throughout the rest of her captivity, and Rowlandson briefly meets with her two surviving children. At the end of this momentous remove, Rowlandson makes sense of what happened in this place by enumerating the remaining English bodies: "Now the Indians began to talk of removing from this place, some one way, and some another. There were now besides my self nine *English* Captives in this place (all of them Children, except one Woman)" (*SG*, 77). The number "nine" fixes "*English*" identity on this particularly impressionable group of young captives, and Rowlandson's demography here concludes the remove with both a fixed number, and an admission that these particular kinds of English numbers are vulnerable ones: eight children and "one Woman."

Rowlandson's careful inclusion of body counts at times offers a history of the war that runs counter to the earlier one of her presumed advocate, Increase Mather. Rowlandson describes the Indians as keenly interested in enumerating their victory, and her report of their intelligence on how many English died in the notorious devastation of Medfield, another siege in the war, revises upward Mather's record of the toll:[18] "Oh! the outrageous roaring and hooping that there was. They began their din about a mile before they came to us. By their noise and hooping they signified how many they had destroyed (which was at that time twenty-three)" (*SG*, 76).[19] Rowlandson punctuates the "outrageous" commotion and unintelligible "din" or "noise" with the relation of a precise mortality count, "twenty-three." Mather's entry for the same February attack, published in 1676, also includes a body count in a parenthetical aside, but concludes that the

Indians "burnt half the Town, [and] killed several Men, Women, and Children (about eighteen in all)" (*SG*, 23). Mather then turns to focus on shameful English responsibility for their own casualties: after the Indians killed an officer, "his Wife was casually slain by an *English-man*, whose Gun discharged before he was aware, and the Bullet therein passed through the Boards overhead, and mortally wounded Lieutenant *Adam's* wife. It is a sign God is angry, when he turns our Weapons against our selves" (*SG*, 23). In Mather's account, the numbers of English dead mediate a conversation between God and his English people. In Rowlandson's telling, however, the intensity of the Indians' self-congratulatory celebration portrays mortality counts as a fierce contest between warring human groups.

When Rowlandson calculates the razing of Medfield, her allegiances within this competition over numbers become muddled. She reports the English losses to be worse than others presented them to be, repeating the Indians' counts without question. Moreover, Rowlandson describes herself as hearing the "hooping" while "at home" in the Indian camp, and this less than two weeks after her own capture: "Those that were with us at home were gathered together as soon as they heard the hooping, and every time that the other went over their number, these at home gave a shout, that the very earth rung again" (*SG*, 76). Further confusing the idea of where "home" is, she describes the people who "[give] a shout" when others "went over their number" as "those that were with us." The narrative calls into question ideas like "home," "us," and whether numbers of dead bodies are "theirs" or "ours."[20] Exacerbating this confusion, Rowlandson benefits directly from the twenty-three (or perhaps eighteen) deaths at Medfield. In the sacking of the town, one of the Indians carries off a Bible, and this is the Bible that immediately proves to be "such a comfort" and a sign of "the wonderful mercy of God to me" (*SG*, 77) when it reaches her hands.

Coming to her out of the chaos of war, the Bible is itself a perfectly enumerated text. Rowlandson first opens the "28th chapter of Deuteronomy," but finally finds a promise of mercy in "Chap. 30, the first seven verses" (*SG*, 77), and then locates "especially . . . Psalm 27" for strength. The condolence she ascribes to being able to read her Bible emanates outward, to her attempts to make sense of her experience numerically—among the jumble of bodies, space, and time in which she is immersed, exact numbers work, for her, like a reference to a knowable and ordered reality. Like reading, knitting—the site of her arithmetic lessons—also refreshes her and sustains her identity, by helping her to procure food and English clothing. At one point she "knit a pair of Stockins" in return for "a quart of Pease" (*SG*, 83); she also received "some roasted ground nuts, which did again revive my feeble stomach" from an Indian in return for unraveling "a pair of stockings that were too big" and then "[knitting] them fit for him" (*SG*, 90). Toward the end of her captivity, her knitting earns her items of distinctively English goods: "an Indian . . . asked me to knit him three pair of Stockins, for which I had a Hat, and a silk Handkerchief" (*SG*, 97). Numeracy enables Rowlandson both to interact with her Bible and, through knitting, to interact with the Indians around her. Both kinds of exchange ultimately work to protect her English identity, by turning numbers into anchors that tie her to a familiar system in the midst of traumatic events.

Conversely, innumerability leads to terror. Rowlandson describes being immersed within uncountable numbers of Indians by insisting emphatically on the numerical gulf between "one" and "a thousand"—"It seemed as if there had been a thousand hatchets going at once: if one looked before one, there was nothing but *Indians*, and behind one, nothing but *Indians*, and so on either hand, I my self in the midst, and no Christian soul near me, *and yet how hath the Lord preserved me in safety!*" (*SG*, 80). Rowlandson guesses at a number for the bustling aggregate of people around her metonymically, focusing on "hatchets." But when she tries to describe the people themselves, she can only repeat "nothing but *Indians* . . . nothing but *Indians*," filling the space both "before" and "behind one." The only number she can be sure of at this moment is the number one, which she repeats, contrasting "I my self" with the chaos around her. Rowlandson credits God for enabling her to withstand this terrifying moment when, just as during the initial siege on Lancaster, she describes a violent threat using chaotic and innumerable "great numbers."

Rowlandson similarly praises God for intervening to save her when she is surrounded by large numbers of Indians just before being ransomed. A thief steals some but not all of her provisions, and though her Indian companions apologize for the loss she and her escort suffered, Rowlandson describes being outnumbered as the cause of the threat: "*And we may see the wonderfull power of God . . . that when there was such a great number of the Indians together, and so greedy of a little good food; and no English there, but Mr. Hoar and my self: that there they did not knock us on the head, and take what we had*" (SG, 103). Now that she is part of the pair "*Mr. Hoar and myself*" rather than an isolated "one," she shifts the attention away from her body "in the midst" to her "good food" as being vulnerable to Indian threat. Even though she remains outnumbered when she travels with Mr. Hoar, creating a ratio of only two versus "a great number," the companionship of being no longer an isolated "one" mitigates her perception of the threat she faces. Since Rowlandson presents her inability to grasp a definitive number of her enemies as a point of vulnerability, and her ability to count herself and Mr. Hoar creates a zone of enumerated safety, she creates the impression that successful quantification might itself be an essential weapon for self-protection. Indeed, Rowlandson proves that it is: her adeptness at quantification ultimately redeems her. She names the sum of her own ransom to be twenty pounds, and preemptively defends that bold action in her narrative against possible detractors who may have thought she valued herself too highly:

Now knowing that all we had was destroyed by the *Indians*, I was in a great strait: I thought if I should speak of but a little, it would be slighted, and hinder the matter; if of a great sum,

I knew not where it would be procured: yet at a venture, I said *Twenty pounds*, yet desired them to take less; but they would not hear of that, but sent that message to *Boston*, that for *Twenty pounds* I should be redeemed. (SG, 98)

Though in "a great strait" and caught between the possibilities of naming too much or too little, Rowlandson appears powerful in this scene, as she stands in front of the Indian "*General Court*" (SG, 98). She describes the process of freeing herself with her enumerating skills as one filled with deliberating care and extreme mental energy. She speaks in a language that is directly transmittable to colonial magistrates: there is no negotiation or dialogue after her pronouncement, her quantification is the final word, and the messenger departs for Boston. Her voice before the council gives her the opportunity to take control of her destiny, but her ability to assign a number to her own body—a number that corresponds exactly to the competing values of her captors and her husband who must put up the ransom—turns that opportunity into a liberating action.

Even with her quantifying power, she feels at last relieved only when an abundance of Christian bodies replaces those of the Indians. After returning to the empty desolation of her former home of Lancaster, she recalls being elated upon reaching busy Concord: "Now was I full of joy . . . joy to see such a lovely sight, so many *Christians* together, and some of them my Neighbors" (SG, 108). Familiar, personal connections blend together with numerous anonymous faces, and when her social network appears within an anonymous population, she recognizes herself as returned to a group to which she belongs. Being English is a way for her to let go of the need to assert her individual identity by trying to count the bodies that are not her own. It is during moments when counting with the naked eye is not possible that Rowlandson cannot separate herself from the mass around her, and she welcomes this diffusion when she recognizes faces within the mass. Uttering the precise number "twenty" in the politicized sphere of negotiation with Indians leads to her return to immersion in "so many *Christians*," but the moments when Rowlandson searches for or cannot find exact numbers are consistently attended by her strongest feelings of either joy or terror. These unquantifiable emotions lurk beyond her carefully drawn zones of calculability, where one pair of stockings equals a meal, or listing the precise length of her daughter's life can contain her grief, if only for a moment.

Competing for Weaned Children

Reproductive ties throw Rowlandson's demographic attempts to understand herself in relation to masses of bodies into confusion. Between the shattering instability of being incapable of enumerating a mass of people, and the self-liberating power of naming an exact amount, Rowlandson keeps returning to one specific quantity: three, the number of her captive children. Rowlandson does not name them until after she has introduced them by their sex and birth order, and the child for whom she grieves throughout her narrative, Sarah, is named only once, and then indirectly, through the voice of her older brother (meeting while still in captivity, Joseph asks his mother "whether his sister *Sarah* was dead," SG, 76). By this point Rowlandson has already identified Sarah as "my sweet Babe . . . It being about six *yeares*, and *five months* old." The children are numbers first—directly related to her in an ordered system—and named individuals second. In one of her moments of reordering through counting, Rowlandson takes stock of her situation after Sarah's death: "I had one Child dead, another in the Wilderness, I knew not where, the third they would not let me come near to" (SG, 75).

Dejected, Rowlandson buries Sarah but reassures herself that this daughter is now in God's "Wilderness"—not in the hands of a foreign, human power. Immediately after Sarah's burial, she searches for ten-year-old Mary: "*There I left that Child in the Wilderness, and must commit it, and my self also in this Wilderness-condition, to him who is above all.* God having taken away this dear Child, I went to see my daughter *Mary*" (*SG*, 75). Unable to remain with Mary, Rowlandson paces and wanders, unsure whether her reproductive labor has added to the population of her enemy: "I could not sit still in this condition, but kept walking from *one* place to another. And as I was going along, my heart was even overwhelm'd with the thoughts of my condition, and that I should have Children, *and a Nation which I knew not ruled over them*" (*SG*, 75–76). Rowlandson becomes distraught that she might be at once connected to and estranged from Mary and Joseph: that she "should have Children" who are "ruled over" by an entity whose order she cannot interpret, and whose bodies she cannot quantify.

Rowlandson's uncertainty about who is laying claim to her living children remains a source of destabilizing anxiety throughout her narrative. Rowlandson had reason to be concerned that her children might grow to identify with a foreign "*Nation*": when eighteenth-century English colonials tried to redeem their captives, as historian James Axtell records, white children were "so completely savage that they were brought to the camp tied hand and foot" because of their desire to rejoin their Indian families.[21] Sarah lies in God's hands, but Mary and Joseph—still young children in the process of being educated—are vulnerable to this conversion. Through her concern for them, Rowlandson confronts the inherent mutability of colonial populations, who can switch from one column of numbers to another.

Rowlandson describes the Indian incursion into Lancaster as a force ripping children from their mothers: when she recalls her sister's and nephew's murders, she remembers "seeing those wofull sights, the Infidels haling Mothers one way, and Children another" (*SG*, 69); and again when she relates how she was taken, she writes that "the *Indians* laid hold of us, pulling me one way, and the Children another" (*SG*, 70). Rowlandson repeatedly emphasizes that the capacity for regeneration is what is at stake in the war. The first people killed in her narrative make up a nuclear family, which has just reproduced: "the Father, and the Mother and a sucking Child, they knockt on the head" (*SG*, 68). When Rowlandson describes the voices of the besieged crowd, they are voices of mothers and children pleading for help: "Now might we hear Mothers & Children crying out for themselves, and one another, *Lord, What shall we do?*" (*SG*, 69). The population at stake here is reproductive, and Rowlandson frames the conflict from the beginning as an ongoing competition between Indian and English numbers that are always in the process of changing.

The reproductive competition is heightened when Rowlandson interprets the large groups of Indian women and children she sees as even more powerful than the English army: "Holding the English army at bay, *like Jehu, they marched on furiously*, with their old, and with their young: some carried their old decrepit mothers, some carried one, and some another" (*SG*, 79). Blinded to the possibility that these people are war refugees by her fixation on the threat of their fertility, Rowlandson wonders how, even when women are in the majority, the travelling Indians are not vulnerable to attack. Pairing knitting and counting bodies again, Rowlandson describes being forced to knit "a pair of white cotton stockings" (*SG*, 79) for her mistress on a Sabbath, just before she expresses her frustration at the English inability to overtake massive numbers of Indian squaws. "They were many hundreds," she writes, "old and young, some sick, and some lame, many had *Papooses* at their backs, the greatest number at this time with us, were *Squaws*, and they travelled with all they had, bag and baggage, and yet they got over this River" (*SG*, 79). The sight of new generations surviving is "strange" and awful to Rowlandson, and doubtless, the presence of sick or lame young people reminded her of when she carried her own fatally wounded daughter. But watching them "[get] over this River" may have caused Rowlandson and her readers to consider the frightening possibility that unlike Sarah, these children would recover, mature, and further increase the Indians' population.

Rowlandson's narrative maintains focus on the ways reproductive bodies come under intense scrutiny when colonial competition calls for dividing people into countable groups. The narrative depicts a shocking tableau of a woman and her child under attack when she retells the story of the torture of a pregnant woman—a figure who is paradoxically both two and one. She writes in detail of a report she heard from escaped children about how her neighbor, Goodwife Joslin, was killed:

> Being so near her time, she would be often asking the Indians to let her go home; they not being willing to that, and yet vexed with her importunity, gathered a great company together about her, and stript her naked, and set her in the midst of them; and when they had sung and danced about her (in their hellish manner) as long as they pleased, they knockt her on head, and the child in her arms with her; when they had done that, they made a fire and put them both into it, and told the other children that were with them, that if they attempted to go home, they would serve them in like manner: The Children said, she did not shed one tear, but prayed all the while. (SG, 77–78)

In Rowlandson's story, Goodwife Joslin "prayed all the while," but the white children around her noticeably do not. Like Goodwife Joslin, whose Christian faith appears invincible, the adult Indians are completely one-sided characters, as "hellish" as she is Christian. The other white "children that were with them," including those who relate the story to Rowlandson, exist between these culturally identifiable parents: a praying English mother and a group of Indians who seek only to separate the children from "home." These Indians do not want merely to destroy infants and their mothers, but subsequently seek rapaciously to gather the weaned children to themselves. In this diabolical vision, the Indians force children to adopt a new "home" and increase the Indians' numbers as soon as they are no longer physically dependent on their mothers. Rowlandson imagines reproduction as a temporal development of individuation—pregnancy, suckling infant, and weaned child—and Indians can commandeer English population numbers during that vulnerable time between weaning and maturity.[22] For Rowlandson, the colonial frontier is a space of competing numbers, in which women's labor can be exploited by their enemies and turned against them.

Rowlandson feels the loss of her ability to parent her children physically: she is "dizzy," "feeble," with her "body raw" (SG, 78) as she worries about where she can find her three, including Sarah, whose gravesite she has no way of being able to find again. She describes her body faltering at their dispersal: "Heart-aking thoughts here I had about my poor Children, who were scattered up and down among the wild beasts of the forrest" (SG, 78). By registering her feelings of separation from her children on her own "body raw," Rowlandson insists upon a kind of inviolable connection with them, even after they have become transportable numbers within a competition over population. When she considers how her children are now intermingled with "wild beasts," Rowlandson faces their extractability from the families and societies that produced them.

In one scene, buffered by passages in which she establishes contact with her son Joseph, Rowlandson considers the bodies of children who become completely alienated from society. Out in the cold, Rowlandson describes a tableau of two sick children, one English and named, the other an anonymous Indian orphan. The pair mingle together naked on the ground after they have been left to die:

> I went to see an *English* Youth in this place, one *John Gilberd* of *Springfield*. I found him lying without dores, upon the ground; I asked him how he did? He told me he was very sick of a flux, with eating so much blood: They had turned him out of the *Wigwam*, and with him an *Indian Papoos*, almost dead, (whose Parents had been killed) in a bitter cold day, with-out fire or clothes: the young man himself had nothing on, but his shirt and wast-coat. This sight was enough to melt a heart of flint.

> There they lay quivering in the Cold, the youth round like a dog, the *Papoos* stretcht out, with his eyes and nose and mouth full of dirt, and yet alive, and groaning. (*SG*, 89–90)

A scene that depicts the sacrifice of two for the benefit of the group becomes for Rowlandson one that could "melt a heart of flint," but Rowlandson's pity is invoked not just by the Gilberd boy's body ravaged by dysentery, but the doubling of his near-death state by the presence of the "*Papoos.*" Her words "[t]here they lay" tentatively extend the compassion she feels for the exposed English boy to "the Papoos stretcht out." Her concern slips from the English boy to the Indian as the passage continues: at first the Indian child is "almost dead," but by the end it is he who is "yet alive, and groaning," while John Gilberd is "round like a dog." Between animals and human, between dead and alive, the two shivering naked boys tempt Rowlandson into sympathy for both of them. But their mingling, their interchangeability, may have been what truly frightened her about the Gilberd boy's fate. Immediately afterward the narrative disrupts the tableau and Rowlandson jumps into action, dragging the Gilberd boy toward a fire and being threatened with a hatchet for doing so. She does not again mention the Indian child she left "yet alive."

When separated into groups with their parents, the difference between Rowlandson's concern for English and Indian children could not be starker. On the same day she visits her son and works on combing the lice out of his hair, she describes the death of her Indian mistress's child:

> That night they bade me go out of the *Wigwam* again: my Mistrisses Papoos was sick, and it died that night, and there was one benefit in it, that there was more room. I went to a *Wigwam*, and they bade me come in, and gave me a skin to ly upon, and a mess of Venison and Groundnuts, which was a choice Dish among them. On the morrow they buried the *Papoos*, and afterward, both morning and evening, there came

a company to mourn and howle with her: though I confess, I could not much condole with them. (SG, 91)

Beyond not being able to "much condole with" the Indians' grief, Rowlandson directly benefits from the child's death and triumphantly spends the night the child dies eating "a choice Dish" and lying on a mat. In the midst of a war over territorial expansion, Rowlandson frames the battle she is fighting as a population contest: when an Indian child dies, there is now "more room," and more food, for herself.

Rowlandson's insistence on the inviolability of her original connection with her children through birth is simultaneously a rejection of their potential adoptability. When she first sees her son in captivity, together they read from the Book of Job about the unreliability of worldly distinctions: "*Naked came I out of my Mothers Womb and naked shall I return*" (SG, 82). With all of the imagery of pregnant and lactating mothers in Rowlandson's narrative, reading this verse with her oldest child enables her to assert the primacy of this connection in the face of immersion within another family and community. When her ten-year-old daughter Mary is redeemed, Rowlandson finds her attached to an Indian woman who has led her back to English society, and cared for her and taught her to survive during the long journey: "She followed the *Squaw* till night, and then both of them lay down, having nothing over them but the heavens, and under them but the earth. Thus she travelled three dayes together, not knowing whither she was going: having nothing to eat or drink but water, and green *Hirtle-berries*" (SG, 110). The squaw does not ask for money in exchange for Mary, and Rowlandson gives no other reason for Mary's return except God's (or possibly, the squaw's) goodwill. Mary reappears thanks to the temporary caregiving of a woman Rowlandson does not want to claim as a member of her community. Like the verse reminding Joseph that he came "naked" out of his mother's womb, Mary arrives after spending the night under the protection only of the squaw's body, with "nothing over them" or "under them." Despite this unmediated physical connection, Rowlandson reclaims her daughter by asserting that connection through birth trumps any quantifiable value. Speaking of Mary, she recalls, "The *Indians* often said, that I should never have her under *twenty pounds*: But now the Lord hath brought her in upon free-cost, and given her to me the second time" (*SG*, 110). Genealogical connection dispels the worldly power of numerical value here, and Rowlandson imagines a "second" birth for her daughter that reaffirms the connection established in the first. This reaffirmation comes as a response to a moment that lays bare the reality of Mary's adoptability: the Indians are capable caregivers and educators, and Mary's dependence on adults might render her a willing member of whichever society cares for her, or whichever potential mother "[lays] down with her."

Enumerated Histories

When Rowlandson steps out of Lancaster and into her migrating group of captors, she confronts a world where population numbers are unknown. Like a blank space on a map, the social life beyond English colonial settlement appears as an empty column on an imperial ledger. Her own and her children's dispersal among these masses exposes the difficulty of permanently separating people in order to count them—an essential tool of colonial power. Given the impetus for gathering information about population numbers, it is hard to imagine how Increase Mather, who authorized Rowlandson's narrative, tolerated Rowlandson's repeated failure to note how many Indians were alive, or at least dead, around her. A central tactic of his account of King Philip's War, the 1676 *A Brief History of the WARR with the Indians*, is to insist that every English death is matched by a greater number of Indian deaths— and to reinforce this insistence with a careful accounting. When he does not have an English witness to give an estimate of the number of Indian bodies, he produces an Indian rumor to assure his reader that the loss was great:

They took five of six of the English and carried them away alive, but that night killed them in such a manner as none but *Salvages* would have done ... What numbers of the Indians lost in this fight, we know not, onely a Captive since escaped out of their hands, affirms that the Indians said one to another, that they had an hundred fighting men kill'd this day.[23]

Mather asserts the authority of his record by introducing its gaps, and then filling these in with the claims of informants. In a manner that recalls both John Smith's and Thomas Harriot's early interactions with Algonquians, Mather variously presents the Indians as both unreliable in terms of their ability to count themselves, and as attempting to hide their accurate knowledge of mortality, which he nevertheless is able to discover. At times he reports there was a "swarm of Indians" (*HW*, 31), or Indians "in such numbers, as that [a Captain] and his company were in extream danger" (*HW*, 12), but then following these instances "but few [English] men were slain" (*HW*, 12), or the English lost "not one man" while "the Enemy fled, having lost five and twenty" (*HW*, 31). The appearance of a swarm, or the fear of one, always gives way to an ability to count the bodies and compare the numbers to those lost by the English.

Mather claims he risks his integrity as a historian in compiling these mortality tables: "There is not much heed to be given to Indian Testimony, yet when circumstances and Artificial arguments confirm what they say, it becometh an impartial *Historian* to take notice thereof," and so he reports that "diverse Indians ... say that there were three hundred killed at that time," therefore it must not be doubted that "the loss of the enemy was greater then those Captives taken by our Forces abroad did acknowledge" (*HW*, 31). After another battle description, Mather admits that ascertaining enemy losses could be difficult because of Indians' deliberate attempts to conceal them: "How many *Indians* were killed is unknown, it being their manner to draw away their dead men, as fast as they are killed, if possibly they can do it" (*HW*, 12). He claims that "they will venture their own lives" to keep this knowledge from the English, but Mather concludes by asserting that he has obtained it from the Indians themselves: "I am informed that some of the *Indians* have reported, that they lost ninety six men that day, and that they had above forty wounded, many of which dyed afterwards" (*HW*, 12). Be it ninety-six, three hundred, or "an hundred fighting men"—Mather, unlike Rowlandson, can always produce a fixed number of Indians. He marshals the Indians' own power to account for their bodies and puts it into the service of the English record.

Mather obliquely refers to Anglo-Americans' constant fear of overwhelming numbers of Indians when he describes traumatized soldiers panicking in the face of the threat of being outnumbered. After a battle where perhaps "an hundred and thirty" Indians "perished . . . while but one *English-man* killed, and two wounded" (*HW*, 30), an English boy recently recovered from captivity reports that "a thousand *Indians*" are en route to the camp. At this "a pannick terror fell upon" the soldiers, "and they hasted homewards in a confused rout," leaving the shoreline undefended and enabling Indians to arrive from an island and pursue the English "four or five miles," though the English, according to Mather, were "near twice as many as the Enemy" (*HW*, 30). Mather pleads for accurate counts, and insists that these will prove the English outnumber the Indians whenever they meet in conflict. In retelling this incident, Mather also asserts his authority over any redeemed captive's accounts of numbers in the war, rendering disputes over population as self-defeating, even murderous. False reports and the terror of immersion among Indians constitute the greatest threat to English safety, and with this formulation, Mather imagines New Englanders' power to count and maintain an accurate record as the keys to their protection.

Mather ensured that his son, Cotton, received an extraordinarily high level of mathematics instruction, and the younger Mather applied this to the study of smallpox epidemics, earning him entry into the Royal Society. Cotton Mather the population scientist, like Rowlandson, sensed the power of images of reproductive bodies when writing about colonial conflict. When the younger Mather wrote his sermon describing Hannah Dustan's captivity in 1697, he made sure to counter directly the threat of Indian innumerability that Rowlandson introduced. Cotton Mather packs his short narrative with precise numbers of children and adults and exact dates and distances, making sure to surround the exceptionally vulnerable Dustan—taken captive right from her childbed—with quantification. At the moment when Indians memorably smash the body of an English baby, Mather lets his reader know that enemies outnumbered the English by exactly two to one: "About Nineteen or Twenty *Indians* now led these away, with about half a Score other *English Captives*; but e'er they had gone many Steps, they dash'd out the Brains of the *Infant* against a Tree."[24] And Dustan is never immersed among a sea of Indians; instead, Mather's demography of her captors is as meticulous as Dustan's body is conspicuously reproductive: "The *Indian Family* consisted of Twelve Persons; Two Stout Men, Three Women, and Seven Children" (HD, 59). Dustan does not free herself as Rowlandson does with a skillful use of arithmetic, but kills and then sells the scalps of six Indian children and four adults for over twice the amount of Rowlandson's ransom. Dustan does not name the price of her own body, but rather exploits the market value of the body parts of her captors. Mather precedes Dustan's violent self-liberation with the precisely numbered date, "*April* 30" and a more generally enumerated location, "about an Hundred and Fifty Miles from the *Indian* Town": "But cutting off the *Scalps* of the *Ten Wretches*, they came off, and received *Fifty Pounds* from the General Assembly of the province, as a Recompence of their Action" (HD, 60). Cotton Mather offers an antidote to the Indian threat to English women's fertility in the form of mathematical exactitude in demographics and the targeting of Indian children.

As in Rowlandson's narrative, the interest in counting bodies in Cotton Mather's tale of Dustan accompanies interest in the cultural identity of children. The utterly known ratios and market-determined values throughout the sermon on Dustan surround a vision of similarly assembly-line-like reproduction of the young. The father in charge of protecting children in Dustan's story turns them into an organized, marching "army": "Such was the *Agony* of his Parental Affections, that he found it impossible for him to distinguish any one of them from the rest. . . . A Party of *Indians* came up with him; . . . yet he manfully kept at the Reer of his *Little Army* of Unarmed Children, while they Marched off with the Pace of a Child of Five Years Old" (HD, 58). Like Rowlandson, Dustan's husband, in Mather's rousing sermon, suffers "agony" over his threatened children. However, this parent is successful in protecting his band of children from death, capture, or adoption, in part by freezing them in time as all "Five Years Old." These children are numerically invariable, and even as a "*Little Army*" they are simultaneously "unarmed" and in need of protection. These potential-filled bodies are constituted entirely in opposition to the enemy, and therefore incapable of being absorbed within it.

Incalculable Subjectivity

By contrast, Rowlandson's narrative treats captive children's membership in a "*Little Army*" of English as frighteningly precarious. When the Mathers affix numbers to bodies in order to separate Puritans from Indians, they methodically efface the way people can easily move between these categories. In this process, children as potential numbers and women as producers of these numbers garner a heightened focus. Through figures like Hannah Dustan or the marching children, Cotton Mather adamantly denies the possibility that some kinds of subjects might be interdependent or mutable. Rowlandson's narrative, however, departs from these official accounts to question that view of subjectivity, and to point out the complexity of reproductive relationships at the center of the obsession with population. Her counts begin and end with caretaking domestic work—she looks up from counting her stitches to see numerical chaos, and then she looks toward the bodies of her children to see the inadequacy of counting as a means of structuring social relationships. For her, there is a frustrating dissonance between the tantalizingly static world of numbers, and the constant mutability of the social world as she experiences it.

Rowlandson describes her children as interdependent subjects, both shaped by and shaping the adults around them. Her own physical body continues to respond to her children even when she is separated from them, showing how she is acting in a way that is at least as collective as it is individualistic. But all this conflicts with the kind of subjectivity implied in a population count. While the idea of fixed racial categories offers security for Rowlandson, the count also separates each individual from one another as isolated numbers. Population numbers do not express how people can mix and be interdependent with others, even others within the same group.

At one moment, Rowlandson sees her son Joseph in captivity and recalls how, in Lancaster, he used to be surrounded by a network of friends and caretakers that could take his mother's place. Now, that same susceptibility to influence by his community renders him vulnerable to Indian influence or mistreatment. After she visits Joseph and finds him ill and in pain, Rowlandson writes, "I went up and down mourning and lamenting: and my spirit was ready to sink, with the thoughts of my poor Children: my Son was ill, and I could not but think of his mournfull looks, and no Christian Friend was near him, to do any office of love for him, either for Soul or Body" (*SG*, 84). When Rowlandson laments that "no Christian Friend" was there to stand in her place to care for Joseph, she echoes Bradstreet in gesturing toward the possibility of a community that can perform mothering work: the poet expresses gratitude that when her son travelled, "friends raised him" in "country strange." However, when Joseph is captive in this racially marked "country strange," Rowlandson, unlike Bradstreet who focuses on affective ties, emphasizes the physical effects of this separation on not only her son's body, but also her own body. Her son's pain sends her into a restless and anxious state, and upon leaving him she describes herself as "unsatisfied," recalling a word she most often uses to describe her hunger: "He had a boyl on his side, which much troubled him: We bemoaned one another a while, as the Lord helped us, and then I returned again. When I was returned, I found myself as unsatisfied as I was before" (SG, 84). She opens her Bible, and then gets up to look for "something to satisfie my hunger" (SG, 84), closely linking her physical need for sustenance with a similarly embodied desire to be near her children.[25]

Rowlandson often registers her longing for her children on her physical body in this way. When she is finally released, she experiences an almost debilitating angst over how to redeem her children: "My heart was ready to sink into the Earth (my Children being gone I could not tell whither) and my knees trembled under me" (SG, 109). At the moment when she is finally able to wander freely, she is rendered immobile—her "knees trembled"—by not knowing where her living children are. The most intense of these moments in the narrative occurs earlier, when Rowlandson holds the lifeless body of her daughter Sarah. Here Rowlandson surprises herself by being comfortable for the first time in the presence of a corpse: "I cannot but take notice, how at another time I could not bear to be in the room where any dead person was, but now the case is changed; I must and could ly down by my dead Babe, side by side all the night after" (SG, 75). Other corpses disturb her, but she is fiercely attached to her daughter's body—so attached, in fact, that she admits that it was during this time spent embracing her dead daughter that she wanted to die herself: "I have thought since of the wonderfull goodness of God to me, in preserving me in the use of my reason and senses, in that distressed time, that I did not use wicked and violent means to end my own miserable life" (SG, 75). Rowlandson's thoughts of suicide point to the intensity of the grief she suffered, but at the same time reveal her deep identification with the body of her daughter. Just as her trembling legs prevented her from moving freely until her children were also released from captivity, her intimacy with her dead child threatens to kill her as well. At these moments, she senses a physical connection with her children resembling the physical intimacy of pregnancy or birth—a connection that is at odds with the individualized subjectivity mandated by a population count.

Rowlandson's suicidal grief over Sarah could be seen, as Mitchell Breitweiser argues, as a desire to escape mourning. According to Breitweiser, the Puritan "social hermeneutic" was hostile to intense grief that posed "an obstacle to the carefully directed transference of affection from the person to the mandated representation of person."[26] This "representation" could be both an eternal soul and a number to be added or subtracted from the aggregate; these two kinds of figures are similar in that they subordinate the individual's fate to the community, and dismiss bodies as merely "rotting flesh."[27] But there is a dissimilarity, too, when human numbers are put in the service of demographic competition, even if this competition is framed by biblical typology. When quantified so carefully, flesh becomes strikingly visible and intervenes instrumentally in the human world. It must be at once perceived and disavowed as a measure of the community's worth against the Indians. This discourse of the appearance and disappearance of the body as a visible, bounded entity was still emerging when Rowlandson wrote of her trauma. Colonial competition developed ways of seeing bodies as separate, thus obscuring their interdependence. Reproduction is a process at the center of these contradictions, one in which bodies mutate and evolve across time from permeable to impermeable, from dependent and malleable to independent and potentially foreign. Rowlandson testifies repeatedly to instances of this process occurring in a war zone. This catastrophe creates the need for a mortality table, and for representing a person as an isolated integer.[28] Rowlandson thus does not want to die solely in order to escape the directive to forget her daughter's body; rather, she seeks to inflict on her own body the same kind of "wicked and violent" acts that took her daughter's life in order to perform their connectedness. Pain can be a way for them to inhabit the same "body raw," and imagine a record that circumvents mathematical forms of certainty.

CHAPTER 4

The Death and Life of Colonial Mortality Bills

In the first half of the eighteenth century, readers of colonial Anglo-American newspapers began to encounter regularly circulating population statistics about their communities. With this advent of newspaper tallies of local deaths, social enumeration became an increasingly standardized part of ordinary discourse. The subtle addition of regular mortality statistics to the purview of newspapers, especially when these statistics did not appear as part of a larger story about an epidemic, contributed greatly to the wider acceptance of enumeration as a way of understanding communities. Europeans had long seen themselves counted in print after wars, floods, or plagues, but the experience of being counted outside of some catastrophic context implies a changing relationship to the authority doing the counting, whether it was the parish clerk or a magistrate. Regular collection of population data bolstered acceptance of the idea that collectives are inherently enumerable. This view of societies as quantities carries with it implications about how people view each other, and promotes the idea of states as composed of bodies rather than territories, and of individuals rather than social connections. When represented in an enumerated table, the boundaries of social groups appear static and clear.

This chapter asks how eighteenth-century colonial readers felt upon seeing their communities regularly enumerated in print, and how the growing proliferation of public social enumeration affected the way these readers related to their communities. It picks up where the previous chapter left off, in Boston at the turn of the eighteenth century, where Benjamin Franklin was born and was exposed to a print culture heavily influenced by the Mathers and their interest in the science of population. Much like Mary Rowlandson counted as a way to anchor herself as she wandered among indigenous settlements during her captivity, printed mortality counts became a way for colonial cities simultaneously to differentiate themselves from and relate to both each other and Europe. At a time when colonial newspapers mostly reprinted news from abroad,[1] the print circulation of regularly updated numbers of local burials enabled a generation of readers to see their communities enumerated as they never had before. The numbers present the readers' bodies as a form of currency that produces representations of social aggregates, which may then be compared and contrasted with numbers produced elsewhere. The increasing quantification of bodies in print was part of a broad shift in the early modern Atlantic collective unconscious toward viewing the world in terms of populations—a shift largely undetectable at the level of individual writers, readers, or printers. This kind of investigation demands a broader view, asking how and when vital statistics appeared and what forms they took; what frames their appearance on the page, and thus contextualizes their entry into other conversations; when they were intermittent and when they were continuous; and who took the time to comment on them and why.

As both a sophisticated early scientist and a printer intent on disseminating useful knowledge, Benjamin Franklin contributed profoundly to the expansion of population discourse. He circulated much of his work on political arithmetic privately to scholars in England and Europe, but as a printer he also joined an already active public engagement with vital statistics in newspapers around the Atlantic. This chapter positions his work, which bridges elite and popular ways of speaking about people as populations, within a network of colonial printers and readers increasingly interested in quantifying their communities. In 1799, Thomas Malthus drew upon Franklin's calculations about the rate of growth of colonial populations as an example of "unchecked" population, imagining North America as a testing ground for unfettered European regeneration. Given this colonial lineage, the question remains of whether Anglo-American readers of colonial mortality statistics before Malthus saw their own communities as limit cases. What particular pressures accompanied death counts when they appeared in colonial spaces?

Moving between the specific example of Franklin's influential writings and a larger examination across multiple colonial cities, I show how coloniality changes the political and social stakes of burial statistics. The appearance of these seemingly mundane tallies in the colonies, after they had been circulating for a few decades in London, did not merely extend this metropolitan print culture of population data, but rather, created a fundamentally different means of using quantification as a way of telling stories about communities. Colonial mortality notices fostered a form of necropolitics—a means of negotiating social interaction by focusing on deaths. The printing of burial numbers codified and popularized the idea that human beings are materials that can be counted with numbers, and thus raised questions about the meaning of that materiality. Because counting deaths was much more feasible than tracking living bodies, mortality tables were an early way for printers and readers to grasp at this uncounted multitude beyond the page. Reading mortality bills with an interest in calculating population is imaginative work that views people only negatively; it entails looking for life using the evidence of death.

Death appeared in print as a far more public event than births, because burial grounds reported counts more readily than did midwives in an era before birth certificates. A sense of mortal competition looms over charts and graphs that separate death numbers by religion or race. Mortality counts engendered intercity competition and comparisons between colony and metropole, begging the question of which places, and which races, were healthier and more capable of population growth. This data constitutes an attempt to represent a public in print, as well as the kind of reading experiences and conversations that begin as a result.[2] We know from *The Spectator* that the weekly bills of mortality, first circulated as broadsides after the plagues of the later seventeenth century, could be conspicuous reading material in London. In an essay for the January 31, 1712 issue, Joseph Addison describes how the *Spectator* persona likes to read the weekly "Bill of Mortality" while everyone else around him in the London coffeehouse reads the news. "I often draw the Eyes of the whole Room upon me," he writes, "when ... they hear me ask the Coffee-man for his last Week's Bill of Mortality." Seeming to enjoy the curiosity he elicits with this odd choice of reading, Addison's fictional Mr. Spectator describes how his interest in the weekly reports of the number of people who died in London from various illnesses leads other readers to mistake him variously "for a Parish Sexton, sometimes for an Undertaker, and sometimes for a Doctor of Physick." But he is none of these: "I am guided by the Spirit of a Philosopher, as I take occasion from hence to reflect upon the regular Encrease and Diminution of Mankind ... I am very well pleased with these Weekly Admonitions, that bring into my mind such Thoughts as ought to be the daily Entertainment of every reasonable Creature."[3] Mr. Spectator suggests there is evidence of the divine in the neat proportions between males and females, baptisms and burials; he then muses on how the bills present life as merely a way station on a longer journey. The essay ends with a tale set in the East about a dervish who mistakes a king's grand palace for a common caravansary, or inn. When the king is astonished by such a mistake, and the king shares that his ancestors there lived before him and his young prince will abide there in the future, the dervish responds with a meditation on the transience of life: "a House that changes its inhabitants so often, and receives such a perpetual Succession of Guests, is not a Palace but a *Caravansary*." For Addison's Mr. Spectator, the mortality bills communicate quotidian data as well as social and moral lessons that hold the potential to spur the narrative imagination.

But the Bills of Mortality also conjure a unique and imaginatively rich scene of reading in public. Mr. Spectator does not just read the bills; he describes how others *see* him reading them, and how the other coffeehouse patrons try to fix his professional identity as a result. Death statistics are a way of representing a community, and this *Spectator* essay dramatizes a scene of a public made self-conscious of its exposure in print. Population data in the form of death statistics turns everyone into a number—women or men, friendless or prominent, child or adult—replacing social distinctions with bodily ones like age, sex, and mortal illness. This inclusiveness is precisely what entices Mr. Spectator to read the London bills: "The General, the Statesman, or the Philosopher, are perhaps Characters which we may never act in, but the dying Man is one whom, sooner or later, we shall certainly resemble."[4] Unlike other types of reading, the reader encounters himself in the public record when he scans printed burial data—or more precisely, he encounters a space on the page that stands ready to interpolate him upon his death in the future. By dying or being baptized, individuals enter into a human economy that can be measured, compared, and tracked across time. Puzzling over whether Mr. Spectator is a sexton or a doctor is a way for those around him to reassert these social ways of organizing people in the face of the bills' leveling uniformity.

By exploring the printing history of burial numbers in Anglo-American colonies, I change the setting of this scene of reading to Charleston, or Boston, or New York, or Philadelphia. At the same time that population numbers connected colonial readers to readers in London, these numbers also cultivated local communal identities. Cities could compare their relative health with that of others when reprinting reports of mortality resulting from a far-off plague, and the way the numbers appeared visually on the page reflected the distinctiveness of the kinds of people who inhabited a place. Moreover, newspapers' frequent placement of burial numbers next to advertisements and lists of prices of local goods fosters a sense of readerly participation in a broader economy, as if the record of corpses could be represented with the same currency as the traffic in goods. The line after the weekly burial numbers was often reserved for short communications between printers and readers, cultivating the sense that the paper was directly addressing, directly representing, and directly inviting the reader into a larger conversation. These forms of communal identity flow from the representation in print of human bodies as quantifiable numbers.

Though statistics were a means of connecting disparate communities, at the same time they were also a way to keep certain kinds of bodies separate from the community. People from different religions or races regularly mingled in places like Philadelphia or Boston, but the burial notices comprised categories, specific to each city, that segregated bodies into distinct categories. Addison's Mr. Spectator transplanted to America may still have pondered the metaphysical implications of burial numbers, but would likely have also confronted relations of similarity and difference that were unique to each particular colonial site. For colonists reading English-language newspapers, mortality data presented a means of telling a story about themselves and, through print, of alternately avowing and disavowing their relationships with others. By understanding the way this form of human accounting sifts certain people out of society and subsequently mirrors a city back to its newspaper readers, we can grasp the colonial tensions underlying the collection and interpretation of population data.

From colonial bills of mortality up through Malthus, visions of positive human numbers in discourses of population—in terms of either birth rates or enumerated communities—remain haunted by death.[5] For Franklin, the living can be represented by performing calculations of numbers of the dead. For Malthus, potential wars, plagues, or famines loom in the future if states do not monitor population growth. But before Malthus's frightening predictions of the consequences of overpopulation, and before Franklin provided Malthus with calculations about how quickly the number of Americans could double, colonial Anglo-Americans read and printed burial statistics that publicized assumptions about which deaths counted, and why. Drawing these historical connections tells a story about population science that bears witness to prior violence and social divisions, rather than solely warning of those to come.

Cultivating a Numerical Identity

The weekly London Bills of Mortality began appearing in the seventeenth century, and John Graunt published his analysis of this data in 1662 as *Natural and Political Observations Made Upon the London Bills of Mortality* (see fig. 4.1). Testifying to the London bills' influence, American colonial newspapers in Boston, Philadelphia, New York, and South Carolina all printed tallies of local deaths soon after they began circulation. In London they had been published not in newspapers themselves, but as broadsides printed by the Company of Parish Clerks. By contrast, colonial printers became compilers as well as printers of burial data, and included it alongside other kinds of local information—prices of commonly sold goods, lists of ships arriving and departing, and advertisements or other messages to readers. Anglo-American colonial newspapers were (especially at first) largely mouthpieces for the governing authorities, but burial numbers became a kind of participatory conversation with readers as a result of their inclusion among the mundane economic data expected to be available about a city. This was the place in the paper when the reader himself would (someday) appear, and also where the reader could potentially spot an ordinary neighbor represented instead of, as Mr. Spectator put it, "the General, or the Statesman, or the Philosopher" who

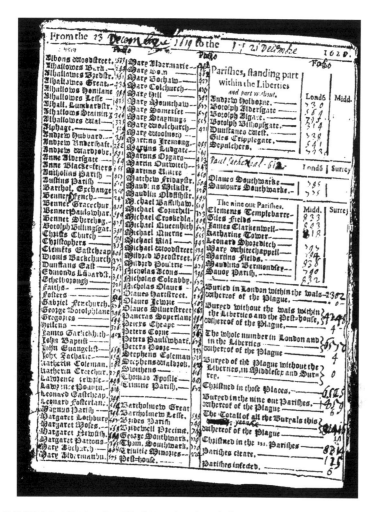

FIGURE 4.1 1621 London Bill of Mortality (broadside). Early English Books Online, STC / 1731:07.

occupied the paper's main articles. Just as it had in London, colonial printing of burial records often began as a response to local plagues, but then continued as the plague subsided. With this transition to printing regularly updated numerical representations of people in a territory, a generation of readers around the English Atlantic became accustomed to seeing themselves serially enumerated in print for the first time. At the turn of the eighteenth century, local death statistics became the kind of ubiquitous, non-narrative print information that inconspicuously shaped reading practices. By circulating these burial numbers, printers brought population-based visions of community into wider public consideration than ever before.

Given the vast differences in the social landscapes across places like South Carolina and Massachusetts, reading experiences of mortality data surely varied greatly, as did the visual appearance of the statistics did on the page. Only a few months after the newspaper began circulating in 1704, *The Boston News Letter* printed a Bill of Mortality collecting annual numbers of colonial deaths (see fig. 4.2). With this table, the printer-editor John Campbell began the first regular series of publicly circulating mortality tables in the Anglo-American colonies. "Because it may carry some useful Information in it," Campbell printed in the *News Letter*'s eleventh number, from June 26 to July 3, 1704, "we have thought it not amiss, to give the Publick, the **Bill of Mortality** for the Three Years last past [boldface in original]." The chart is divided by month and year, with annual totals added together at the bottom, under the heading "*Persons, besides Negro's and Indians, which were buried in the Town of Boston.*" The table acknowledges significant numbers of "Negro's and Indians" but segregates them from the total Anglo-American counts. Immediately after the table ends, however, Campbell qualifies it: in the plague year of 1702, "the Number of *Negroes* and *Indians*, which has a Singular Share in the Mortality, made the Number of the Buried, arise to about, 500." Thus, from the beginning of Anglo-colonial public interest in vital statistics, numbers of Africans and indigenous people play a crucial yet negative role—rather than being ignored, they serve as the boundaries limiting the count (even visually, mentioned both above and below the table). Paradoxically, they also intervene inside the mortality table to give context to the frightening

Bold Becaufe it may carry fome ufeful Information in it, we have thought it not amifs, to give the Publick, the **Bill** of **Mortality** for the Three Years laft paft.

The Number of Perfons, befides Negro's and Indians, which were buryed in the Town of Bofton.

Annq.	1701.	1702.	1703.
March	11	9	21
April	6	13	14
May	11	8	16
June	13	7	12
July	15	20	10,
Auguft	15	32	13'
September	17	47	29
October	12	55	15
November	15	74	8
December	7	87	18
January	17	69	6
February	7	20	7
	146	441	159

Note 1. In that Mortal year, 1702. the Number of Negroes and Indians, which had a Singular Share in the Mortality, made the Number of the Buried, rife to about 500.

Note 2. Many Inhabitants of Bofton, have their Employments at Sea; and many of thefe Dying abroad (in proportion, much more than at home) they are not reckoned in our Catalogue.

Note 3. It has been obferved by fome, that in Times of Health, (fuch as we now Enjoy,) Mortality ordinarily carries off, fomewhat about a Fiftieth Part of the People Every year. Quare How far will that Obfervation hold for this Town?

Note 4. It might be of ufe, if fome other of the principal Towns in the Country, would preferve their **Bill** of **Mortality**, and Communicate it.

FIGURE 4.2 From The Boston News Letter, no. 11, June 26-July 3, 1704 (Courtesy, American Antiquarian Society).

numbers from 1702—however badly Bostonians suffered, Negroes and Indians suffered "singularly."

This early table presents population data as an incitement to conversation between printers and readers. Campbell refers to existing calculations of how many deaths occur annually in a normal city ("It has been observed by some, that in times of health ... Mortality ordinarily carries off somewhat about a *Fiftieth Part* of the People Every year"), and asks how the example of Boston reflects on these theories: "How far will that Observation hold for this Town?" Then, Campbell directly asks readers to participate in the collection of these statistics: "It might be of use, if some other of the principal Towns in the Country, would preserve their **Bill of Mortality**, and Communicate it" [boldface in original]. Campbell does not present the bills of mortality as inert reading material, but instead introduces them as a spark to debate among Boston readers about the accuracy of the count, and about ways to make these numbers more accurately reflect their own experiences. The bill of mortality is a way to involve readers in the representation of themselves as a collective: they passively view a visualization of their communities as numbered columns, as well as actively participate in the conversation about mortality and population through their own calculations.

After 1704, the *News-Letter* went on to print the annual bill of mortality for Boston "usually in March, every year."[6] In the ensuing years, questions of how to gather and—more pressingly—how to interpret meaning from public health data grew as a topic of discussion in New England. In 1712 (the same year that Addison's Mr. Spectator wrote that reading mortality bills caused his fellow coffee shop patrons to mistake him for a "Parish Sexton"), Cotton Mather published a sermon on the bills of mortality after a Connecticut epidemic in which he preached that, "The *Lively Thoughts* of *Death* will have a singular Tendency to make us *Lively Saints.*"[7] As these kinds of numbers continued circulating, especially as a result of epidemics, discussion of the meaning of vital statistics continued to grow until it reached a fevered pitch during the smallpox inoculation controversy of 1721 and 1722.

Intriguingly, the public debate that took place in Boston's newspapers over whether to require inoculation shows how *little* mortality numbers as a form of reliable public health information had by this point actually influenced the majority of people facing the specter of disease. Mather advocated widespread public inoculation, but James Franklin—Benjamin's older brother—turned his newspaper *The New England Courant* into a forum for criticism of the inoculation plan. As Patricia Cline Cohen points out, both sides based their arguments on appeals to quantitative thinking, even though they were working against one another.[8] Mather and Zabdiel Boylston promoted figures in the *Boston Gazette* and the *News-Letter* that showed that inoculated people were less likely to die than those who contracted smallpox naturally, but doctors like William Douglass, writing in the *Courant*, questioned these figures and argued that no controlled studies had been done to prove the efficacy of inoculation before unleashing it on every healthy body. Thus, as Cohen points out, "the two groups who could be called quantifiers worked against each other."[9] And throughout this exchange, no systematic counts were in place; instead, numerical tracking of the epidemic "was rather a sporadic effort stimulated by perceptions of being at the beginning, end, or critical turning point in the progress of the disease."[10] Quantification worked more as a rhetorical tool for articulating widespread disagreement than a policymaking plan of action. Carla Mulford views empiricism as a central issue in the smallpox crisis, but primarily as a means of working out new ways of speaking and creating spaces for dissent. The competition between a "technology of print and its implications for press freedom" and a "technology of the body in the form of determining a medical cure for smallpox" marked "a crossroads in the formation of liberal subjectivity."[11] There is another crossroads here, further complicating matters: one that consists of multiple avenues for applying quantitative data to human life. The smallpox crisis showed the ways in which the openness of quantitative data to interpretation, and the lack of standardized methods for collecting it, fostered new opportunities for speaking and writing about community.

While the quantitatively inclined factions argued over whether to inoculate and neglected to institute any comprehensive tracking of the progress of the disease in the city, another group of Bostonians did not turn to quantification at all to decide whether inoculation was lawful. God sent epidemics, insisted these commentators, and therefore only God could protect the people's health. Speaking for religious objectors to inoculation, Samuel Grainger—who himself "ran a school for writing, arithmetic, and advanced mathematics"[12]—wrote that "arguments of Example, Number, and Success, are very insufficient, though supported with the Testimony of the News Paper. . . . For should Success become a sufficient plea for the Lawfulness of any action, Every wicked action successfully acted, would become Lawful at that rate."[13] The kind of arguments of "Number" presented within the pages of "News Paper" are hardly sufficient, in Grainger's view, for dispensing useful truths about a community. Despite decades of annual mortality counts in Boston and weekly London bills of mortality circulating for decades before that, large numbers of New Englanders still did not view population data as having any actionable purpose, even in a time of political and mortal crisis. A smaller circle of physicians and printers like Mather, Boylston, Douglass, and the Franklins expressed awareness of the potential usefulness of public health statistics, but they immersed quantitatively based appeals within larger debates about colonial authority and freedom of speech. Although bills of mortality had been circulating in Boston since the turn of the century, their primary function remained plague documentation. Among Anglo-American readers in the 1720s, quantification still served a rhetorical purpose subservient to other kinds of appeals. Even the quantifiers neglected to check the numbers presented by the other side as evidence, or even to systematically collect their own supporting data.[14]

A central column of the first mortality bill in the *Boston News-Letter* in 1704 shows a spike in local deaths in 1702: there were 441 deaths that "Mortal year," up from 146 the year before. Benjamin Franklin was born in 1706—between two terrible smallpox epidemics. This first bill recorded the last visitation of smallpox on the town before the inoculation controversy in 1721. Those left alive in Boston in 1703 likely protected the town from smallpox during the intervening years with what epidemiologists now refer to as "herd immunity," but by the 1720s a new generation, with newly vulnerable immune systems, had come of age.[15] Franklin was apprenticed to his printer brother when James was sent to jail for four weeks in 1722 for his role in the innoculation controversy, and the intense debate spurred by the smallpox crisis became a formative event in Benjamin Franklin's life.[16]

Newspapers and Burial Numbers

The younger Franklin began expressing his lifelong interest in mortality bills and public health not long after his arrival in Philadelphia. When Benjamin Franklin became printer of *The Pennsylvania Gazette* in 1729, the rival Philadelphia-based *American Weekly Mercury* had already been publishing monthly numbers of christenings and burials from Christ Church for eight years (see fig. 4.3). The paper announced that the first totals inserted into the paper in January 1721—precisely when Boston was in the throes of smallpox—were intended "For the Satisfaction of many" in Philadelphia.[17] Franklin began printing weekly burial numbers less than two months after he took over the *Gazette*. He included the first mortality totals without remark in November of 1729, in no. 51 (see fig. 4.4). Though not explicitly occasioned by an epidemic, the totals do appear in the same column as the last line of a report from Boston relating that "The Small Pox spreads here." Like the bills circulating in the *Mercury* and in Boston around this time (see fig. 4.5), Franklin includes the local totals on the second

Births and Burials in the City of Philadelphia, for the Month of January.

	Chu. of England.	Presbyterians.
Males Christned,	2	2
Females Christned,	1	0
Males Buried,	2	1
Females Buried,	0	0

People called Quakers.

Males Born, Females, In all
Males Buried, 4. Females, 3. . In all 7.

Buried in the Strangers Burying-Ground, 2.
Negroes, None.

FIGURE 4.3 From *The American Weekly Mercury* January 30th to February 6th, 1722 (Courtesy, American Antiquarian Society).

The Small Pox spreads here.
Custom House, New York, Nov 17
Entred inwards. V. Bodin from Curacoa, Jona. Tucker and J Phenix from Jamaica, G. White from South Carolina. Entred outwards G. Frazer for Perth-Amboy, B. Greenhill for New London, T. Vater for Antigua, J. Smith for Curacoa. Cleared out. D. Aubin to London from Jamaica, Ifa Overy to Lisbon, B. Arnold and B. Greenhill to New London, G. Frazer to Perth-Amboy

Custom-House, Philadelphia.
Entred inwards None
Entred Outwards
Brigt. Anne and Elizabeth, John Searle, for the West Indies.
Cleared Out
Brigt. Mary, John Sim, to St. Christophers.
— Amity, Mark Wheldon, to Ditto.
Sloop Elizabeth and Mary, Richard Evans, to Boston.
— St. Andrew, John Bragg, to Bermuda.
— Dove, John Howell, to Barbados
Snow, Joseph and Benjamin, Wm. Fellows, to Liverpool.
— Satisfaction, Cornelius Davis, to Milford.
Buried in the several Burying-Grounds of this
City in the Week past.

Church ——— 5	⎱ ⎰ Baptists ——— — —
Quakers ——— 1	⎰ ⎱ Strangers, ⎰ Whites ——— 2.
Presbyterians — 1	⎱ Blacks ———
In all 7	Increased in the Burials this Week 6

No further Accounts yet, relating to the Peace with Spain

Advertisements.

FIGURE 4.4 From *The Pennsylvania Gazette* no. 51, November 17th—November 20th, 1729 (Courtesy, Readex/Newsbank).

FIGURE 4.5 From *The Boston Gazette* no. 380, March 6th—March 13th, 1727 (Courtesy, Readex/Newsbank).

page of the newspaper, near the advertisements and the schedule of ship arrivals and departures. However, the Boston *Gazette*, like the *News-Letter* there, printed the city's mortality numbers only annually. Also in the Boston papers, the mortality bills call attention to themselves as stories in their own right, visually conspicuous in their tall, racially separated columns and multiple lines for each month, and included in the penultimate column of the paper, rather than the last.

Philadelphia readers, especially after Franklin's arrival, saw their communities enumerated on a much more regular basis. The *Mercury* published monthly lists of both births and deaths, and once Franklin took over the *Pennsylvania Gazette*, the city's mortality numbers circulated weekly. In other words, Franklin ensured that burial numbers were a regular feature of every single issue of the paper. But the particular form that burial numbers take when they appear as quotidian printed information shapes assumptions about what kind of materials bodies are, especially at this early stage of their entry into public conversation. Both the *Gazette* and the *Mercury* in Philadelphia included vital statistics directly above the advertisements and below the customs-house information. This placement in the paper associates vital statistics—or the comings and goings of bodies between life and death in the city—with both the regular commerce of ships' arrivals and departures, and the business within the city itself, as announced in the advertisements. Franklin's *Gazette* also began to include the prices of commonly purchased goods in the city—"wheat, flour, middling bread, mixt ditto, brown ditto, rum, mellaffes"—above the burial numbers. Thus, readers encounter lists of commodities assigned specific numbers just before they see a list of enumerated human groups, such as Quakers, Presbyterians, and white or black Strangers. The burial numbers create a sense of bodies as a kind of exchangeable currency, with Philadelphia's numbers able to be compared with those in Boston or London, for example.

The placement of the burial numbers above the advertisements further underscores how they work to include individual bodies in a commercial exchange. Advertisements are direct appeals to the individual newspaper reader, creating moments of economic connection and inclusion between public matters and individual lives. Before the advertisements appeal to his discretion, the mortality numbers mark each individual body as relevant to public concern, thus making the reader conscious of his own inclusion in this exchange. Indeed, the lines between the mortality bills, in Franklin's *Gazette*, became moments reserved for direct communication between the printer and the reader—at times, even a specific individual reader. The first list of burial numbers ends with the printer relating that there are "*No further accounts yet, relating to the Peace with Spain.*" In future issues, this becomes a moment when the newspaper reminds subscribers to send in their payments, or when readers are warned that a slow news season will likely result in a shorter newspaper.[18]

As in the apology for the lack of updates about "the Peace with Spain" or the call for missing money, the newspaper uses this space to point out a lack—to provide the reader with a sense of what is missing. This absence could be a lack of news because of the winter season or a lack of payments from subscribers, but Franklin's paper also at times hints at items that were either not ready or not fit to print. The issue for April 23–30, 1730 notifies the reader that "*A Letter signed* Philoclerus, *in Answer to that in our last concerning the* Drum, &c. *came too late to be inserted in this Paper, but will be in our next,*" and in issue number 138, from July 1732, the paper uses this line to "thank the Gentleman who sent us the ingenious Criticism on the Word *That*"—a letter that was not printed. More provocatively, number 63 from January 20–27 of that year uses the lines after the burial numbers "*to inform the Writer of* A certain Letter, giving a certain Account of a late certain Difference between a certain ----------- and his Wife, with certain Animadversions upon their Conduct, &c. *That, for certain charitable Reasons, the said Letter is at present thought not fit to be published.*" These genial missives about what is outside, absent, or missing from the newspaper signal an absence as a way to, paradoxically, acknowledge the readers' presence.

When the mortality bills appear just above these short messages, they have the effect of drawing the reader into a larger world of commerce and conversation. The reader does not appear in the enumerated list of local deaths, separated in the *Pennsylvania*

Gazette by burying grounds, but as Mr. Spectator points out, it is the place where the paper reminds him that someday, he will be. Like the husband's uncharitable letter or Philoclerus's answer sent too late, the burial numbers mark the reader as present as a form of currency within a broader market by his or her absence from the count. Scanning through the paper, learning about acts and actions abroad, colonial Philadelphia merchants reading *The Pennsylvania Gazette* could keep track of the economy and find, through the weekly burial counts, the moment in the paper where they and their neighbors would someday be recorded. This negative inclusion of readers in the local news underscores the importance of the individual as a category—a person who can be counted as clearly as a whole number. Bodies appear worthy of representation in the world of print because they are numerable, because they fit within one of the predetermined categories in the pre-formatted table. But since no count is possible without set limits, burial counts also identify individuals as members of certain social categories within the city, by offering separate totals for different religious and racial groups.

Burial numbers at first glance appear to be a mundane addition to the newspaper, situated as they are beside ads, local prices, and customs-house news, but the printing history shows that these notices could be a source of competition between rival newspapers and rival colonial cities, as well. One of Franklin's missives below the burial numbers points to this environment of self-conscious competiveness, chiding *The American Weekly Mercury* for stealing his paper's stories: "*When Mr.* Bradford *publishes after us, and has Occasion to take an Article or two out of the* Gazette, *which he is always welcome to do, he is desired not to date his Paper a Day before ours, (as last week in the Case of the Letter containing* Kelsey's *Speech, &c.) lest distant Readers should imagine we take from him, which we always carefully avoid.*"[19] At times the appetite for intercity comparison appears innocuous, as when Franklin's *Gazette* reprints Boston's annual mortality notice from the previous year in February of 1730, or the annual totals of christenings and burials in London, reprinted in April 1731. Over the course of three issues in August 1731, Franklin reprints an article about how to extrapolate total population data from burial numbers by Edmund Halley, showing how the appetite for burial numbers from other cities was driven by curiosity about norms of population growth and loss. Halley analyzes London's bills to estimate the total living population of London and the number of "fighting men," which he deems to be 204,250. To do so, Halley concludes that, outside of times of crisis, "it appears, that about a 29th Part of the Inhabitants die every Year."[20] At the end of the last installment stating these conclusions, Franklin reprints Boston's collective data since it began circulation with that first bill of mortality in 1704. Based on this data, the paper states, "*By comparing the Number of Inhabitants in* Boston *with the above Account, it appears, that not above a 40th Part of the People of that place die yearly, at a medium.*" By reprinting the London and Boston numbers side by side, the *Gazette* boasts of colonial health and longevity relative to London, presenting colonial population data as a vital limit case for any studies of population being done in Europe.

Burial data begs the question of comparison between cities, because compilers searched for truths about human growth and death rates. But the need for comparison to establish norms also fuels competition about where these growth rates might be higher, or mortality rates might be lower. As James Cassedy describes, the printing of burial numbers during epidemics could provoke intercity competition, in which a city so far untouched by the latest spreading disease would reprint other city's ghastly data as a form of lightly veiled schadenfreude: "It was common practice for colonial printer-editors to minimize, distort, or suppress these kinds of local data in hopes of promoting the economic well-being of their communities. Conversely, they were happy enough to print the death figures of other cities."[21] At the end of the same month in which Franklin reprints Halley's calculation, he also reprints news of a smallpox epidemic in New York: "The Small-pox now spreads in this City pretty much. *Buried in the City of* New-York *last Week*, viz. Church of England 4. Dutch Church 8. French 0. Presbyterians 0. Lutheran church 0. Quakers 0. Baptists 0. Jews 0. In all 12."[22] The paper prints Philadelphia's weekly total in its usual place, which in this issue was ten.

Over the next few months, the *Pennsylvania Gazette* follows intensely the story of New York's epidemic, reprinting that city's grave lists of numbers weekly, and even apologizing to readers if the New York *Post* did not come in time to reprint its count that week.[23] Two weeks later, Franklin's paper reprints New York's mortality totals below those of Philadelphia, making for quicker comparison (see fig. 4.6). That week, a total of "60 Whites" and "14 Negroes" died in New York, whereas the uncalculated total from all the various burial grounds in Philadelphia is only 16.

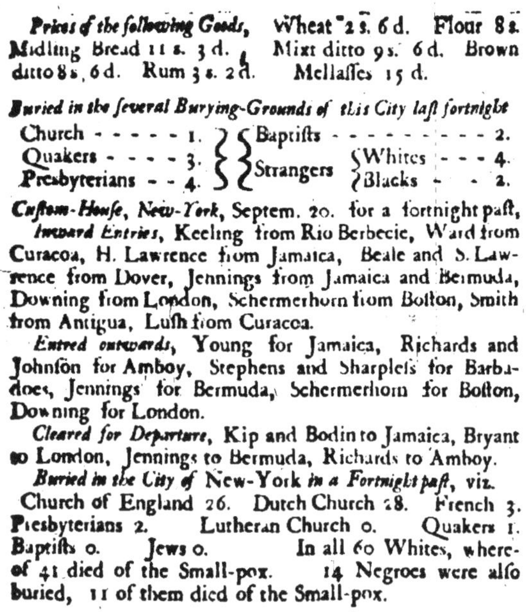

Prices of the following Goods, Wheat 2 s. 6 d. Flour 8 s. Midling Bread 11 s. 3 d. Mixt ditto 9 s. 6 d. Brown ditto 8 s. 6 d. Rum 3 s. 2 d. Mellaſſes 15 d.

Buried in the ſeveral Burying-Grounds of this City laſt fortnight

Church - - - - - - 1.
Quakers - - - - 3.
Presbyterians - - 4.
Baptiſts - - - - - - - - - - 2.
Strangers { Whites - - - 4. / Blacks - - 2.

Cuſtom-Houſe, New-York, Septem. 20. for a fortnight paſt,

Inward Entries, Keeling from Rio Berbecie, Ward from Curacoa, H. Lawrence from Jamaica, Beale and S. Lawrence from Dover, Jennings from Jamaica and Bermuda, Downing from London, Schermerhorn from Boſton, Smith from Antigua, Luſh from Curacoa.

Entred outwards, Young for Jamaica, Richards and Johnſon for Amboy, Stephens and Sharpleſs for Barbadoes, Jennings for Bermuda, Schermerhorn for Boſton, Downing for London.

Cleared for Departure, Kip and Bodin to Jamaica, Bryant to London, Jennings to Bermuda, Richards to Amboy.

Buried in the City of New-York *in a Fortnight paſt,* viz. Church of England 26. Dutch Church 28. French 3. Presbyterians 2. Lutheran Church 0. Quakers 1. Baptiſts 0. Jews 0. In all 60 Whites, whereof 41 died of the Small-pox. 14 Negroes were alſo buried, 11 of them died of the Small-pox.

FIGURE 4.6 From *The Pennsylvania Gazette*, no. 148, September 23, 1731 (Courtesy, Readex/Newsbank).

Well into October, these side-by-side totals amount to 81 in New York, of whom "most died of small-pox," while the readers of Franklin's *Gazette* see that only 6 died that week in their city.[24] The picture the *Gazette* reports from New York in September 1731 is bleak: "The Small Pox, Flux and Fever, prevail very much in this City, and many Children die of the said Distempers as well as grown Persons; and the country people are afraid to come to Town, which makes the markets thin, Provisions dear, and deadens all Trade."[25] The news from New York reports that charities have been set up for the city's poor, who are hardest hit by the epidemic. Throughout November, Franklin repeatedly prints New York's burial data next to Philadelphia's own.

To mark the end of the epidemic, and the end of the *Pennsylvania Gazette*'s inclusion of New York's weekly burial data, Franklin reprints the burial totals left in the wake of smallpox in Philadelphia's neighbor city:

> The Distemper having gone thro' the Town, it appears by adding our Weekly Accounts together, that since the Mortality began, which is about 11 Weeks, there have been buried in the several Burying Grounds as follows; Church of England 229, Dutch Church 212, French Church 15, Lutheran Church 1, Presbyterians 16, Quakers 2, Baptists 1, Jews 2. In all 478 Whites. Blacks 71. Total 549.[26]

The act of adding together the weekly totals marks the containment of the deadly distemper, giving the epidemic a conclusion through arithmetic. After this story is printed, Franklin no longer prints New York's weekly burial numbers. Meanwhile, between August and November Philadelphia's burials have hummed along at a reassuringly low rate, appearing steadily each week, and yet never venturing beyond the realm of ignorable reports.

Franklin's printing of New York's numbers during an epidemic alongside numbers indicating (albeit negatively, through mortality) Philadelphia's relative health may have been driven by competitive schadenfreude, by sensational interest, or by genuine economic or personal concerns. Regardless, the dual printing has the effect of creating a space in the paper for enumerated normalcy alongside one for enumerated catastrophe. In the past, burial numbers would circulate chiefly in the context of a crisis like a fire, war, plague, or flood. Across Franklin's early career, counting people became a part of everyday discourse, and ceased to signal an emergency. Thus people's consciousness of themselves as individual numbers within some kind of defined, and therefore enumerable, social whole arises not out of a state of heightened concern, but rather as a mundane part of literate and numerate culture. The appearance of enumerated lists of bodies lingers after the panic of spreading disease subsides, acclimating readers to the sight of numbers of humans listed next to values of circulating commodities in print.

After the epidemic of late 1731, the *New York Gazette* continued weekly inclusions of the city's burial numbers without interruption for over a year. Before smallpox began to spread in the city in August, weekly burial numbers had not been a regular feature. The week in November after the final mortality totals at the end of the epidemic appeared in both New York and Philadelphia, *The New York Gazette* included the weekly burial numbers—a total of eleven—without comment before the advertisements (see fig. 4.7). The *South Carolina Gazette* has a similar history of printing weekly burial totals. In August of 1732, the South Carolina paper printed this note about a recent

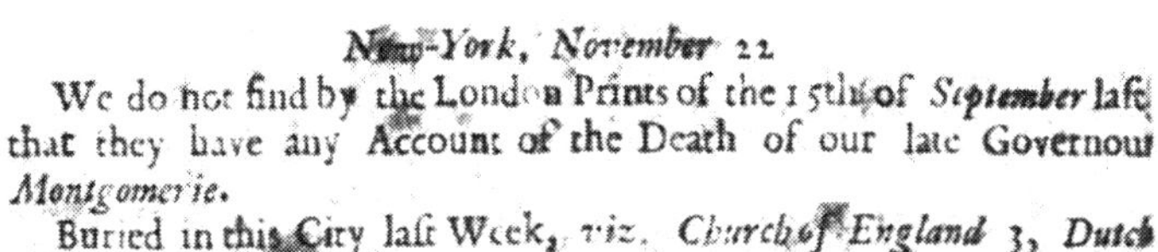

New-York, November 22.
We do not find by the London Prints of the 15th of September last, that they have any Account of the Death of our late Governour Montgomerie.
Buried in this City last Week, viz. Church of England 3, Dutch Church 4, Blacks 4. In all this Week 11.

FIGURE 4.7 From *The New York Gazette*, no. 317, November 22, 1731 (Courtesy, Readex/Newsbank).

epidemic above the prices of local goods: "The Sickness, which has afflicted this Town, is (by the Blessing of God) now almost over."[27] Two weeks later, the paper printed a mortality bill for the city: "Buried in Charlestown from the 1st of July to the 28th of August [. . .] Church of England 55 Men, 25 Women & 12 Children Presbyterians 12 Men, 4 Women, and 4 Children. French Church 8 Men, 3 Women. Quakers 1 Man In all 144 exclusive of Negroes."[28] The Charleston paper ceases printing of mortality tables until the following January, when rumors surface that "*the Small Pox is in 2 Families at* Winyaw."[29] Above the prices of rice as measured by "Baggs" or "barrels" and of other commodities like tar or turpentine, the paper prints that there were "Buried in Charlestown this Week past 7. Baptized 1" (see fig. 4.8). Though neither this week's nor subsequent burial notices record an uptick in deaths, *The South Carolina Gazette* then begins printing the numbers of local deaths every week for the next two months, in this same format and place in the paper. As in London, as in New York, and as in Charleston, the fear of epidemics spurred interest in counting the number of local deaths, but as the crisis passed, this fear gave way to the frequent print circulation of enumerated bodies as quantities just like rice or turpentine. Burial numbers became a way for newspapers both to integrate their readers into a larger Atlantic social marketplace, and to distinguish their cities among others by comparison and competition. Catastrophe brought burial numbers to the attention of readers

We hear, the Small Pox is in 2 Families at Winyaw.
Buried in Chareftown this Week paft 7. Baptized 1,
Exported from this Place fince Nov. 3, 1732, to Jan. 19.
1732-3. Rice 12,820 Barrels, and 628 Baggs. Pitch 2,970.
Tar 1,242. Turpentine 295. Whereof 4,532 Barrels,
and 538 Baggs of Rice for Foreign Markets.

FIGURE 4.8 From *The South Carolina Gazette*, no. 53, January 13th to 20th, 1732/3 (Courtesy, Accessible Archives).

as a piece of worthwhile local news in an era when most colonial newspapers only reprinted stories from abroad, but spectacular death was only the beginning. Burial numbers continued to appear in print across North American cities, despite the absence of catastrophe as a way for newspapers and their readers to monitor their communities.

Visualizing the Dead

Unlike rice, which is sometimes listed as being shipped in bags and other times in barrels, mortality numbers do not change in the manner they are quantified from place to place. Seven deaths in Boston is quantified in the same manner as seven deaths in London or Charleston, and the printed statistics thus create a population marketplace for comment and comparison, and for reprinting other city's statistics across the Atlantic—indeed, like its sister newspaper in Philadelphia, *The South Carolina Gazette* reprints both Boston's and London's bills of mortality in 1732 and 1733, respectively. Vital statistics create an economy of bodies across colonial spaces, while simultaneously revealing fundamental social differences. The manner in which these numbers appear on the page in different newspapers—and what kinds of numbers appear above or below them—provides commentary on the social character of the city, and how each of its enumerated categories of bodies relates to the whole. Mortality tables turn certain predetermined bodies into clearly visible and valuable forms of currency, which can then be networked with other counted bodies. By counting the burials in Philadelphia, newspaper readers could feel that their bodies were more closely connected to the enumerated dead appearing in bills of mortality in London coffeehouses than to the living indigenous bodies that walked beside them on the streets, or lived and died just beyond the borders of the city. Enumerating bodies fostered both a sense of connection to the metropolitan center across the Atlantic, and a sense of alienation from potentially hostile bodies closer to home.

The local prices printed next to the mortality tables offer as much of a commentary about the social life of a community as does the enumeration of the traffic in the city's local burial sites. The *Pennsylvania Gazette* lists the prices its readers want to know: wheat, bread, rum, and "mellasses." However, the Charleston paper has a much longer and more varied list: the price of rice, pitch, tar, turpentine, skins, wine, Indian corn, Barbados rum, lime juice, salt, and "pease" in addition to flour and bread. Just as the types of local goods listed above the weekly burial numbers change between papers in different cities, so does the visual form in which the bodies are enumerated on the page. Despite the unique panoply of social influences made apparent in the Charleston paper's listing of the price of its city's famous African-cultivated "rice," "pease," and "Barbados rum," its presentation of burial numbers contains no different categories for race at all. After the epidemic that initiated the weekly burial counts, the *South Carolina Gazette* did not count a single Negro death: the final total was "144, exclusive of Negroes." Unlike the 1704 Boston *News-Letter's* mortality bill, the paper did not then go on, outside the list, to comment on how, say, Charleston's black population had a "singular share" in the mortality. The *South Carolina Gazette* instead refuses to acknowledge black deaths in print at all. In the following weeks, as regular burial numbers outside of a time of crisis begin, the Charleston paper does not subdivide the number of local deaths by church burial ground and by race, as do other papers in colonial cities. The numbers each week in early 1733 are presented as merely separated by death and birth: "Buried in Charlestown this Week past 1. Baptized 1," as the issue of February 24 states. Each week the burial numbers appear, Charleston newspaper readers see undeniable evidence of their city's remarkable diversity and activity in the list of local goods, but the mortality bills point to social uniformity in the way they enumerate the dead.

As the annual mortality bill from 1727 shows (see fig. 4.5), the *Boston Gazette* enumerated deaths from all races in the city, albeit with a firm separation between columns of "Whites of every Age and Sex" and "Indians and Negroes." Both during and after the New York smallpox epidemic of 1731, that city's *Gazette* enumerated "Blacks" weekly, though at the end of a longer prose list subdividing the rest of the town by church affiliation, such as "Church of England" or "Dutch Church," for example. The New York paper added together black and white deaths to give its readers a total number of the city's death in the previous week, inclusive of races, religions, and strangers. For example, in the May 8, 1732 issue, the *New York Gazette* prints that there were "Buried in this City last Week, viz. French Church 1. Presbyterians 1, And Blacks 3. Buried in all 5" (see fig. 4.9). When Franklin started printing burial numbers, the *American Weekly Mercury* had already been printing both black and white deaths in Philadelphia, albeit placing the numbers of "Negroes" at the bottom of their monthly lists (see fig. 4.3). The *Mercury*, like other papers, did not include numbers of African Americans in their counts of christenings or baptisms.

Like the *Mercury* and the Boston *News-Letter*, but unlike the New York or South Carolina papers, Franklin printed the weekly burial numbers in carefully aligned columns set off from the flow of other prose sentences printed in the paper (see fig. 4.4). "Church," Quakers, and Presbyterians appear in the left column, while Baptists and "Strangers" appear in the right. Noticeably, and unusually in comparison with other weekly mortality notices, numbers of deaths in the African American community appear enumerated as a subset of "Strangers," a group divided by race into numbers of "Whites" and "Blacks." Most of the time, Franklin sums all the counts together into one overall total number of bodies "*Buried in*

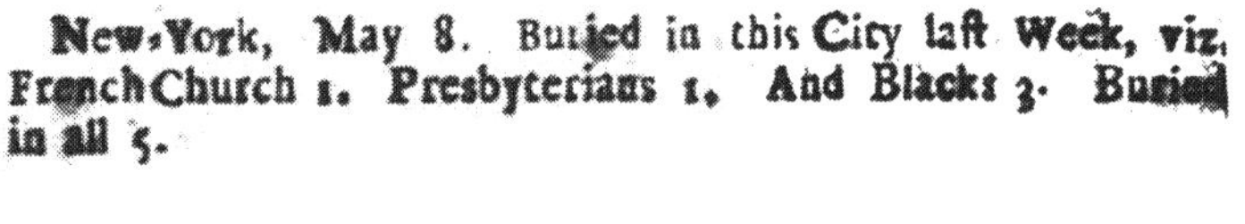

New-York, May 8. Buried in this City laft Week, viz, French Church 1. Presbyterians 1, And Blacks 3. Buried in all 5.

FIGURE 4.9 From *The New York Gazette*, no. 341, May 8th, 1732 (Courtesy, Readex/Newsbank).

the several Burying-Grounds of the City in the Week past." Printing a
comparison across different weeks is Franklin's invention. After the
total number, Franklin regularly includes the amount by which
the current week's total number of burials increased or decreased
in relation to the week prior. Franklin's mortality notices thus
offer Philadelphia readers a portrait of the city's social divisions
and health on a more frequent basis than the city had yet seen, or
that was commonly printed in other colonial newspapers. Tellingly,
whites are only racially marked in the column when they appear so
close to African Americans. The heading marking off the graphic
from other lists or lines of prose creates an inclusive umbrella that
prepares the way for the total number of deaths—in the case of
November 20, 1729, the number was "In all 7"—to negatively
represent all the different groups living in Philadelphia who have
means enough to bury their dead. By including so often a comparison between weeks, Franklin fosters the sense that the newspaper
is monitoring Philadelphia's health (and indeed he was), as though
public health is a concern that creates community through numbers as well as burials. Local deaths are a phenomenon that, at least
in Philadelphia, fosters calculation and tracking and creates a way
of circulating numerical representations that craft categories of
race and social difference. Some papers used death accountings to
align racial groups explicitly, as in Philadelphia, or to explicitly exclude certain groups, as in the 1704 Boston *News-Letter*'s mortality
bill; and even the *South Carolina Gazette*, by refusing to count or
even (most of the time) to refer to black deaths, comments just as
strongly on race and community through its conspicuous silence.

Michel Foucault describes in his *Security Territory Population*
lectures that bills of mortality were crucial precursors to modern
forms of biopolitics. [30] Before the state could track life effectively, statisticians in Europe had to make extrapolations on
death numbers seem routine. However, this seems insufficient
to understanding the particularly colonial complexities of these
eighteenth-century Anglo-American bills. Rather than simply
filing these bills away as a transition toward something else, the

social, political, and racial implications of ushering colonial deaths into print warrant attention in their own right. For this, Achille Mbembe's concept of "necropolitics" provides a useful tool, even though Mbembe is explicitly concerned with late modern colonial occupation in places like apartheid-era South Africa and contemporary Palestine. Mbembe defines necropolitics as "contempororary forms of subjugation of life to the power of death," and is careful to differentiate "[l]ate-modern colonial occupation" from "early-modern occupation," while still emphasizing the roots of necropolitics in slavery, which he terms "one of the first instances of biopolitical experimentation."[31] Crucially for the understanding of colonial mortality bills circulating in an Atlantic world shaped by slavery, Mbembe defines "*[c]olonial occupation*" as the "writing on the ground a new set of social and spatial relations," and part of this "writing" involves "the classification of people according to different categories."[32] When they experiment with how to classify and publish colonial deaths, colonial printers invent a way of printing and circulating "a new set of social and spatial relations" of their own design. Mbembe also asserts that "colonial occupation entails first and foremost a division of space into compartments," and compartmentalization is key to any mortality table, which divides bodies according to that city's particular social divisions, sometimes even in compartments plotted across x- and y-axes.[33]

Moreover, these divisions and spatial relationships are made visible by death; in fact, they instrumentalize death as a way of making the community visible to itself, drawing metropolitan connections while at the same time disavowing or severely restricting cross-racial ones. Mbembe draws on G. F. Hegel and Georges Bataille to describe how necropolitics entails a vision of self (and, ultimately—of community) arising from a confrontation with death. Hegel describes how "the human being truly *becomes a subject* . . . through this confrontation with death . . . [he is] cast into the incessant movement of history,"[34] and Bataille goes further to describe death as "essentially self-consciousness."[35]

Mr. Spectator may have drawn the eyes of the whole room upon him by specifically asking to read the bills of mortality in London, but that sense of self-consciousness could have been enormously compounded by the pressures of being one of the colonial merchant readers of these newspapers, especially eager to be "cast into the incessant movement of history." As Benedict Anderson points out, the idea of the nation as an imagined community was truly an export from the colonies back to the metropole. Anderson cites specifically "early gazettes" like the ones that printed these burial numbers: he writes, "the newspaper of Caracas,"—and presumably of Boston, Philadelphia, New York, or Charleston as well—"quite naturally, and even apolitically, created an imagined community among a specific assemblage of fellow-readers, to whom *these* ships, brides, bishops and prices belonged."[36] These deaths belonged to them too, turning their bodies into numbers that could be compared with numbers in other cities, and that could identify who mattered and who didn't; who was healthy and who was malignant; who counted first and who was only counted in the margins. The lens of necropolitics helps us see how these materials make death matter as a way of publicly representing race and as a means for developing colonial self-consciousness, not simply as stepping stones toward the biopolitics that came later.

Franklin's Calculations

The history of early colonial mortality bills is itself defined by a conspicuous and sudden absence. Within a matter of months, newspapers across the Atlantic coast all inexplicably began to reject these early weekly burial notices. On January 9, 1733, in issue no. 376, the *New York Gazette* printed its final weekly mortality bill without comment. *The American Weekly Mercury*, having printed monthly numbers of burials and Christenings for the previous twelve years, stopped permanently after the chart that appears in no. 680, from January 11, 1733. Franklin printed the last weekly graphic enumerating bodies buried "*in the several Burying-Grounds of the City in the Week past*" in *The Pennsylvania Gazette* the following month, on February 22, 1733. The *South Carolina Gazette*, having only just begun printing weekly burial numbers earlier that year, was the last newspaper to pull them, stopping after the issue from March 3, 1733. Newspapers in Boston continued to print annual bills of mortality uninterrupted throughout the eighteenth century, but the sudden flurry of weekly burial statistics as regular features of the newspaper alongside local prices, customs' records, and advertisements that Franklin had begun in 1729 was over permanently and without explanation. None of these three cities appear to have entered a time of disease or crisis—or, for that matter, exceptional health—in the late winter of 1733 that would account for this seemingly coordinated movement to end this widespread feature, nor was there a clearly responsible set of international events or imperial edicts.

The kind of intercity rivalries about the appearance of relative health that Cassedy describes may have led to the end of weekly bills in the newspapers, although none of the papers from January to March include any unusual commentary on any other city's health of the kind that had appeared over a year earlier between New York and Philadelphia.[37] New York newspapers were occupied at the turn of 1733 with intense political fights taking place in print over the new governor, which resulted in one printer being sentenced to jail for libel, much like James Franklin had been during the smallpox crisis, although this does not explain why both Philadelphia papers and *The South Carolina Gazette* would have stopped printing death rates as well. At the end of 1732, William Bradford, printer of the *New York Gazette*, engaged in what Charles E. Clark calls "the first *intercolonial* newspaper controversy"[38] when he criticized lamentations circulated in a Boston paper about the arrival of regular dancing in that Puritan city. However, intercolonial newspaper rivalries involving Boston papers do not explain why annual bills of mortality continued appearing in Boston uninterrupted, while weekly bills printed in cities to its south permanently ceased. Although the sudden end of the short-lived proliferation of weekly mortality numbers in colonial newspapers remains inexplicable, the coincidence of the timing of their cessation across four Anglo-American newspapers implies that they did not disappear solely as a result of printers' waning interest. These banal lines above the advertisements must have become at least conspicuous enough to merit conscious removal.

When Franklin pulled the annual mortality reports from his newspaper in 1733, his personal lifelong research into vital statistics was just beginning. He continued to read European writings on political arithmetic, and forwarded Philadelphia's bills of mortality, collected at Christ Church, to his friend and fellow at the Royal Society, Peter Collins, for publication in London. Collins in turn sent him publications on mortality statistics from London, most notably the Royal Society's *Philosophical Transactions*.[39] The *Philosophical Transactions* circulated among a few highly educated early Americans like Franklin, and presented them with foundational early demographic essays by English and continental political arithmeticians like William Petty, Edmund Halley, John Arbuthnot, Charles Maitland, and William Kersseboom.[40] After his interest in weekly notices of whether deaths in Philadelphia were increasing or decreasing with each week between 1729 and 1733, Franklin began circulating pieces on mortality again to the general (rather than particularly scholarly) reading public in the 1750s. First, he included a mortality table at the beginning of his 1750 *Poor Richard Improved*, and then in his essay "Observations Concerning the Increase of Mankind," which appeared in *The Gentleman's Magazine* in London in 1755.

Franklin's later publications on population show how he imagined mathematical calculation as a way to turn numbers signifying death into representations of communal vitality. Throughout the decades in which Franklin took an active interest in estimates of Philadelphia's population, births in the colonies remained stubbornly resistant to precise recording. As the small numbers of christening reports in the *American Weekly Mercury* show, women did not regularly register their children with the local church, and thus these announcements produce far lower numbers than what was likely the actual local birth rate. In terms of the world of print then, death appears as a far more public event than birth. A corpse must be buried, but an infant does not have to leave the home to be born. Laurel Thatcher Ulrich describes how before 1750, birth still took place largely within a closed realm of women's knowledge,[41] and Clark admits that despite growing literacy rates, "the English language newspapers of the eighteenth century, wherever they were printed, presented their readers with . . . the world view, by and large, of the upper-class, cultivated, ethnocentric, and fiercely patriotic Protestant English male."[42] Even after the widespread enumeration of bodies, and speculation in Anglo-American newspapers since the turn of the eighteenth century about how to count total population from the numbers at hand, population numbers remained only approachable in the negative sense, through death. Mortality counts become a cipher for the living population numbers they represent. As John Campbell asked in New England's first newspaper mortality bill, "Mortality ordinarily carries off somewhat about a *Fiftieth Part* of the People Every year. How far will that Observation hold for this Town?" The proliferation of mortality numbers make numbers about births and total numbers of inhabitants appear that much more desirable and elusive.

Colonial governors did not maintain reliable birth registries, as Swedish traveler Peter Kalm noticed in his journal of his visit to Philadelphia in September 1748. He describes how his efforts to determine the city's population and birth rates were thwarted:

> I have not been able to find the exact number of inhabitants in Philadelphia. In the year 1746 they were reckoned to be above ten thousand, and since that time their number has incredibly increased. Neither can it be ascertained from the lists of mortality since they are not kept regularly in all the churches. . . .

The number of births cannot be determined since in many churches no order is observed with regard to this affair. The Quakers, who are the most numerous in this town, never baptize their children, though they keep a pretty exact account of all who are born among them.[43]

Kalm does, however, find and include in his journal a *List of Births and Deaths in Philadelphia* for the year 1722, which had been printed in the *American Weekly Mercury*, showing the longevity of the early period of printing regular mortality data that had become less frequent in newspapers by the time Kalm was writing.

When Franklin resumes printing his human accounting, he attempts to get at the positive numbers of living people only hinted at through mortality data. However, these efforts show the tensions between human accounting in the form of narrative prose versus tabulated charts. In the *Poor Richard* almanac for the year 1750, Franklin compares census data from the years 1737 and 1738 for the different counties of New Jersey with those of 1745 and thus calculates the colony's rate of population increase over that time (see fig. 4.10). The table is divided by counties on the left, and the numbers are identified as gathered by a government source: "the Number of People in *New Jersey*, taken by Order of Government." Across the top, the chart is divided into eight rows of numbers, dividing "Whites" from "Slaves," and separating the whites into sex and groups aged under and above sixteen. Slaves are only divided by sex, and as a bridge between these two categories, the word "Slaves" is the only category of people in New Jersey that can be read horizontally across the chart. In the accompanying text below, the almanac qualifies its data to note that one county was split into two between 1737 and 1745, and that "no distinct Account" of Quakers "was taken" by the census in 1737. After these qualifications, Franklin interpolates the population sums into prose and points toward a further mathematical question: "Total of Souls in 1737, 47369; Ditto in 1745, 61403; Increase 14034. *Query:* At this rate of Increase, in what

Counties.	Males above 16.	Females above 16.	Males under 16.	Females under 16.	Slaves. Males.	Slaves. Females.	Total of Whites.	Tot. of Slaves.
Middlesex,	1134	1085	1086	956	272	231	4162	503
Essex,	1118	1720	1619	1494	198	117	6648	375
Bergen,	935	822	876	7??	443	363	3289	806
Somerset,	967	940	799	807	425	307	3773	732
Monmouth,	1508	1339	1289	1295	362	293	5431	655
Burlington,	1487	1222	1190	996	192	151	4895	343
Gloucester,	930	757	784	676	74	48	3145	122
Salem,	1669	1301	1313	1327	97	87	5700	184
Cape-May,	261	209	271	211	21	21	962	42
Hunterdon,	1618	1130	1270	1170	124	95	5288	219
Total,	11631	10725	10639	9700	2208	1773	43388	3981

The Number of People in New-Jersey, taken by Order of Government in 1737-8.

	Males above 16.	Females above 16.	Males under 16.	Females under 16.	Slaves. Males.	Slaves. Females.	Total of Whites.	Tot. of Slaves.
Morris,	1109	957	1190	1087	57	36	4343	93
Hunterdon,	2302	2117	2182	2090	244	216	8691	460
Burlington,	1786	1605	1523	1454	213	197	6373	430
Gloucester,	913	797	785	805	121	81	3304	202
Salem,	1716	1603	1746	1595	90	97	6660	187
Cape-May,	306	272	284	274	30	21	1136	52
Bergen,	721	590	494	585	379	237	2390	616
Essex,	1694	1649	1852	1548	244	201	6543	445
Middlesex,	1728	16??	??	1695	483	396	6735	879
Monmouth,	2071	17??	??	1899	513	386	7728	899
Somerset,	740	67??	??	719	194	149	1896	34?
Totals,	1508?	13704	14253	13752	2588	2018	58797	450?

Numb. of Ditto, taken in 1745, by Order of Gov. MORRIS.

Note, That Morris and Hunterdon Counties, were both in one, under the Name of Hunterdon, in 1737-8. In 1745, the Number of the People called Quakers in New-Jersey, was found to be 6079; no distinct Account was taken of them in 1737-8. Total of Souls in 1737, 47369; Ditto in 1745, 61403; Increase 14034. Query, At this Rate of Increase, in what Number of Years will that Province double its Inhabitants?

Buried in the several Burying Grounds of PHILADELPHIA, belonging to the

In the Years	Church of England.	Swedish Church	Presbyterians.	Baptist Meeting.	Quaker Meeting.	Strangers.	Negroes.
1738	113	24	29	15	46	269	54
1739	109	16	18	7	56	97	47
1740	105	8	22	12	29	80	34
1741	165	30	41	20	120	300	69
1742	126	35	21	9	70	98	50
1743	117		19	21	68	150	50
1744	123	16	29	14	81	100	47
	858	129	179	98	476	1094	351

Note, No Account of Burials in the Swedes Ground, was taken in the Year 1743, and these Germans buried in the new Dutch Burying Ground are numbered among the Strangers, who were chiefly Palatines: The Mortality among them is not owing to any Unhealthiness of this Climate, but to Diseases they contract on Shipboard, the Voyage sometimes happening to be long, and too easy

FIGURE 4.10 From *Poor Richard Improved* (1749), A1 (Courtesy, American Antiquarian Society).

Number of Years will that Province double its Inhabitants?" The first note after the chart, commenting that one county had to be split into two, points to political questions about when population increase might require a redrawing of political boundaries. Just as Campbell had done, and as the placement of the weekly burial totals had implied, population data is a way of including readers into the formation and representation of their communities by participating in the work of mathematical calculation.

Franklin continues to promote mathematical skill as the remedy for the persistent problem of how to represent positive numbers of people when he answers his own query about when the population of New Jersey will double. He introduces, on the bottom half of the page, a chart listing all the deaths in Philadelphia between 1738 and 1744. In this way, growth has to be approached, yet again, by way of interpreting past accounts of death. Because church-run cemeteries provide the numbers, Philadelphia burial data is divided primarily into religious sects—listed as the Church of England, Swedish Church, Presbyterians, Baptist Meeting, and Quaker Meeting—as well as "Strangers" and "Negroes." Strangers are the largest group in this mortality table, though as the almanac notes beside the table, "those Germans buried in the new *Dutch* Burying Ground are numbered among the Strangers," calling into question just how strange these corpses are. This note reveals the shorthand assumptions that structure the seemingly factual charts, if the strangers' origins are mostly known but not specifically recorded. Franklin, however, dismisses numbers of strangers in his calculations of living Philadelphia bodies. Franklin's commentary insists that the high number of strangers' deaths is caused solely by their means of travel, and not by any inhospitability of Philadelphia's ecology: "The Mortality among them is not owing to any Unhealthiness of this Climate, but to Disease they contract on Shipboard, the Voyage sometimes happening to be long, and too great a Number crowded together." The high mortality of sea travel, then, is a problem of disproportion, of assigning too high a number of people to too small a space, thus creating the disproportion evident within the chart of deaths, with the four numerals "1094" crowded into the box assigned to total stranger deaths, whereas the next highest number is "894," for bodies buried by the Church of England.

Employing the generally accepted notion of one death for every thirty-five people per year to a total number of deaths "in seven years ... [as] 2100, which is 300 *per Annum*," the almanac reports that Philadelphia "should have had nearly 10,500 Inhabitants during those seven years, at a Medium." Even in the years since 1744, however, the almanac states that, "the Town is greatly increased." Relying heavily on mortality statistics, Franklin is able to turn death rates into birth rates through quantitative calculation, and to transform numbers that threaten to portray Philadelphia as filled with disease, into numbers that instead paint the city as bursting with life. Investigations into deaths at the time provided a more statistically reliable account of birth rates even than inconsistently performed censuses, but as mortality turns into population, Franklin inserts several unsupported conclusions into his calculations. The death rates of Philadelphia help Franklin count population numbers by applying one of several ratios circulating through the transcontinental writings of political arithmeticians, with Franklin both echoing and amending the mathematical equation that translates mortality into living bodies used by his printer predecessor Campbell: "in a healthy Country (as this is) political Arithmeticians compute, there dies yearly One in Thirty-five." This form of human accounting extrapolates a representation of the living population out of the records left from counting the dead.

There are tensions in Franklin's human accounting, evident in the two forms in which it appears in the 1750 *Poor Richard*. The reader hears from two voices: one the voice of the bounded, firmly categorized chart; the other, the voice of the prose commentary, which makes room for both mathematical calculation and jumbled messes of undifferentiated collections of numbers. When the almanac reports in prose the statistics from Massachusetts,

Franklin includes in full the motley counts he garnered from that state. Without first expurgating the animal numbers from his list, he renders calculations on the human numbers to arrive at a rate of increase of adult men:

> In the Province of *Massachusetts Bay*, in *New-England*, *Anno* 1735, there were 35,427 Polls of white Men of 16 years and upwards, 2600 Negroes, 27,420 Horse-kind of three Years old and upwards, 52,000 Neat Cattle of three to four Years old and upwards, 130,001 sheep of one year old and upwards. In 1742 there was 41,000 Polls of white Men, from 16 years upwards. Increase of Men in seven Years 5573, which is near one Sixth.[44]

When Franklin receives data from Massachusetts and presents it outside of the organizing principles of a chart, numbers of horses, cattle, and sheep are interspersed with different annual counts of "Polls of white Men," with maturity being the only common denominator across species. Franklin pulls out, at the end of this jumbled list of data, the calculation of a "one Sixth" rate of human increase. *Poor Richard* extrapolates the figure from Massachusetts to account for inhabitants of both sexes and all ages by comparing it to the New Jersey data, concluding that "they should have in that Province, in 1742, about 164000 Souls." The almanac as a whole reflects a broader interest in acquiring these types of skills with an advertisement for mathematical instruction: "READING, Writing, Arithmetick, Merchants Accompts, Geometry, Algebra, Surveying, Gauging, Navigation, Astronomy, and all other mathematical Sciences, are taught by, THEOPHILUS GREW, in *Philadelphia*."[45] *Poor Richard* wades through a mess of reports of different types of numbers and brings them into one, "about 164000 Souls," with Franklin's numeracy as the skill that can differentiate so many different quantities from one another and turn them into cohesive and coherent political data.

Ultimately, the conclusion Franklin comes to at the end of these opening pages of this edition of *Poor Richard* is not based on mathematics, but rather on speculation. Franklin cannot pinpoint the exact rate of increase of the colonies, but for the first time he makes the assertion that colonial populations reproduce faster than metropolitan ones. He compares the data he has compiled to what he has read (likely from English mathematician Edmond Halley) of "*Breslaw* . . . a healthy inland City, to which many Strangers do not come," where the "Yearly Increase" is calculated to be sixty-four. But Franklin ends his prose discourse, and his collection of tabular data, with this assertion relating population to the size of a territory:

> Yet I believe People increase faster by Generation in these Colonies, where all can have full Employ, and there is room and Business for Millions yet unborn. For in old settled Countries. . .the Overplus must quit the Country, or they will perish by Poverty, Diseases, and want of Neccessaries. Marriage too, is discouraged, many declining it, till they can see how they shall be able to maintain a Family. (*PR* 1750, unnumbered)

Franklin points to the prospect of "Millions yet unborn" at the end of a prefatory population sketch that includes no record of births as they occur, only deaths. On the next page after the mention of "Family" and "Millions yet unborn," the almanac includes an image of one male body mapped into parts of the zodiac, an image entitled "The Anatomy of Man's Body as govern'd by the Twelve Constellations" (see fig. 4.11).[46] Just when Franklin ponders the expansion of human bodies' reproductive potential into unfathomable millions, he then directs his printer's attention to the dissection of one white and male ideal unit uniting the heavenly forces around it. At this level of extrapolation, Franklin's attempt to comprehend the human potential to reproduce "Millions" seems to collapse into a return to focusing on one archetypal "Man's Body" between the pages of the almanac.

The Anatomy of Man's Body as govern'd by the Twelve Conftellations.

♈ The Head and Face.

Ⅱ Arms
♌ Heart
♎ Reins
♐ Thighs
♒ Legs

♉ Neck
♋ Breaſt
♍ Bowels
♏ Secrets
♑ Knees

♓ The Feet.

To know where the Sign is.
Firſt Find the Day of the Month, and againſt the Day you have the Sign or Place of the Moon in the 5th Column. Then finding the Sign here, it ſhews the Part of the Body it goverus.

The Names and Characters of the Seven Planets.
☉ Sol, ♄ Saturn, ♃ Jupiter, ♂ Mars, ♀ Venus, ☿ Mercury, ☽ Luna, ☊ Dragons Head and ☋ Tail.

The Five Aſpects. ☌ Conjunction, ☍ Oppoſition, ⚹ Sextile, △ Trine, □ Quartile.

Common Notes for the Year 1750.

Golden Number	3	Dominical Letter	G
Epaɛt	3	Cycle of the Sun	23

FIGURE 4.11 *Poor Richard Improved* (1749), "The Anatomy of Man's Body as govern'd by the Twelve Constellations" (Courtesy, American Antiquarian Society).

Colonial "Vacancy," Malthus, and Necropolitics

Likely only two years after he printed the 1750 almanac, Franklin wrote a pamphlet in which he delved into the subject of the "Millions yet unborn." Franklin published *Observations concerning the Increase of Mankind* in 1755 in *The Gentlemen's Magazine* and later included it in his *Experiments and Observations*. It was likely written as a response to the Iron Act of 1751, which asked Britain to recognize the power of emerging demand in the colonial market, but it is probably best known as the document that may have brought Thomas Malthus's attention to Franklin's work on the potential of new world population growth. Malthus cites Franklin directly in the first chapter of his *Essay on Population* (Franklin had died eight years earlier in 1790):

> It is observed by Dr. Franklin, that there is no bound to the prolific nature of plants or animals but what is made by their crowding and interfering with each other's means of subsistence. Were the face of the earth, he says, vacant of other plants, it might be gradually sowed and overspread with one kind only, as, for instance, with fennel; and were it empty of other inhabitants, it might in a few ages be replenished from one nation only, as, for instance, with Englishmen. This is incontrovertibly true. . . . In the northern states of America, where the means of subsistence have been more ample, the manners of the people more pure, and the checks to early marriages fewer, than in any of the modern states of Europe, the population has been found to double itself, for above a century and a half successively, in less than twenty-five years.[47]

After Franklin's musings in the almanac he went on, in *Observations*, to try to calculate the number of years required for an unbounded population to double, which Malthus later claims to be twenty-five. When Malthus tries to imagine human reproduction as a force, isolatable, calculable, and tempered only by social conditions, he turns to Franklin's work from nearly a half-century earlier, attempting to calculate this reproduction using the context of settler colonialism. Malthus bases his vision of an unfettered reproducing body, at least in part, on the example of English bodies in North America, filtered through Franklin's projections. Malthus deletes the multiple columns within Franklin's population tables reserved for strangers and black slaves, and ignores entirely indigenous people, whose numbers were concentrated beyond the borders of cities.

By turning the imperial context of population rates into a universal human standard, Malthus turns non-European groups of people competing for resources into the number zero as a factor in his worldwide population equation. Population growth in America becomes a model for how "one nation only" might come to inhabit a place through multiplication alone. Using Franklin, Malthus replaces the violence of settler colonialism with the fiction of a prior vacancy, of human growth in a monoculture like a sea of fennel. The ideas about rampant colonial population growth that Malthus takes from Franklin are predicated upon a prior lack of variation in a human ecology. In other words, they require the past violent removal of people outside of the "nation." These kinds of thought experiments about population intertwine cataclysm and fantastic fertility, rendering one unthinkable without its opposite. Like mortality bills, Malthus's population science approaches quantitative visions of humanity only through the rhetoric of cataclysm: a cataclysm that may have been in the past, creating a vacancy, or one that looms in the future, as a potential famine or other deadly lack of resources.

Franklin seems to have wanted European thinkers to view his data on English reproduction in America as particularly useful for the study of population, just as Malthus would go on to do. Franklin begins *Observations Concerning the Increase of Mankind* by laying aside all the European political arithmetic he has so avidly studied, claiming that it does not apply to a colonial sphere where so much of the population is dispersed beyond cities:

Tables of the Proportion of Marriages to Births, of Deaths to Births, of Marriages to the Numbers of Inhabitants, etc. form'd on Observations made upon the Bills of Mortality, Christnings, etc. of populous Cities, will not suit Countries; nor will Tables form'd on Observations made on full settled old Countries, as *Europe*, suit new Countries, as *America*.[48]

A major reason Halley's or Graunt's previous observations no longer apply, Franklin argues, is the changed relationship between country and city in the colonial sphere. In the Old World, the relationship of labor supply in the country and labor demand in the city creates a situation where population growth is rare:

In Countries full settled, the Case must be nearly the same; all Lands being occupied and improved to the Heighth; those who cannot get Land, must Labour for others that have it; when Labourers are plenty, their Wages Will be low; by low Wages a Family is supported with Difficulty; this Difficulty deters many from Marriage, who therefore long continue Servants and single.—Only as the Cities take Supplies of People from the Country, and thereby make a little more Room in the Country; Marriage is a little more incourag'd there, and the Births exceed the Deaths. (*IM*, 368)

Franklin in 1750 is fully steeped in a language which can speak easily of people as a form of "supplies." He sets up the dichotomy of country and city as an established pattern of circulating bodies—one that is interrupted by Atlantic colonialism.

In the New World, according to Franklin, the proportion of country to city is vastly different than in England, and land is "plenty" and "cheap." This new ratio doubles the rate of population growth, because access to land makes access to marriage easier:

Hence Marriages in America are more general, and more generally early, than in Europe. And if it is reckoned there, that there is but one Marriage per Annum among 100 Persons, perhaps we may here reckon two; and if in Europe they have but 4 Births to a Marriage (many of their Marriages being late) we may here reckon 8, of which if one half grow up, and our Marriages are made, reckoning one with another 20 Years of Age, our People must at least be doubled every 20 Years. (*IM*, 368–369)

Franklin does not explain why the ratio of city to country in North America leads to a doubling of the marriage rate per annum, but merely joins with the reader in reckoning this as reasonable, subordinating his unsupported assumptions to his mathematical calculations. However, Franklin's ultimate conclusions in this pamphlet proved to be uncannily accurate.[49]

In making the first of these assumptions, Franklin describes a phenomenon in which immigration has a negligible effect on population growth: "[t]he Importation of Foreigners ... will be in the End no Increase of People; unless the New Comers have more Industry and Frugality than the Natives ... but they will gradually eat the Natives out.—Nor is it necessary to bring in Foreigners to fill up any occasional Vacancy in a Country; for such Vacancy (if the Laws are good) will soon be filled by natural Generation" (*IM*, 371). Natives, Foreigners, New Comers— all these categories disappear into the umbrella of the "People," which remains to reflect the number of those who are the most industrious and frugal. Here Franklin points outward in two ways: to indigenous people on the frontier, in relation to whom the English were the "Foreigners"; and to potential immigrants like the Germans in Europe, who made up the column of "strangers" listed in his almanac, and who turn members of the Church of England in Philadelphia into "Natives." Anglo-Americans become simultaneously both Natives and Foreigners by constituting a "People," who, "if the Laws are good," will fill, through "natural Generation," any void left by others who depart.

For Franklin, population growth is a direct result of good leadership. Even when that growth is made possible by the use of "vacant" lands, those lands are always something that a leader had to gain control over or *make* vacant:

> Hence the Prince that acquires new Territory, if he finds it vacant, or removes the Natives to give his own People Room; the Legislator that makes effectual Laws for promoting of Trade, increasing Employment, improving Land by more or better Tillage; providing more Food by Fisheries; securing Property, etc. and the Man that invents new Trades, Arts or Manufactures, or new Improvements in Husbandry, may be properly called Fathers of their Nation, as they are the Cause of the Generation of Multitudes, by the Encouragement they afford to Marriage. (*IM*, 370)

Vacancy of land here always has a history—for Franklin, it is not happened upon accidentally. The opportunity for causing "the Generation of Multitudes" is a sign of good leadership, and the activity of making land available through acquisition or through "[removing] the Natives" is akin to the making of laws or improving cultivation. Elsewhere Franklin again alludes to cataclysmic ruptures as moments that subsequently enable "the Generation of Multitudes." In doing so, Franklin rhetorically ties the previous conditions that created the vacancy to the limits imposed by the production of food and resources: "Privileges granted to the married ... hasten the filling of a Country that has been thinned by War or Pestilence, or that has otherwise vacant Territory; but cannot increase a People beyond the Means provided for their Subsistence" (*IM*, 370). Heaps of corpses left by disasters that have "thinned" a country create the conditions for high rates of reproduction that are adequate to the "Means" supporting that growth.

In the second of Franklin's assertions about political arithmetic, he rounds up his first assessment that the vast territory of North America will enable a doubling of the population every twenty years, and settles on the number twenty-five. As I showed above, Malthus later alludes directly to this passage and its discussion of "fennel" to radically reconceive of the human body, as a power to be unleashed without restraint by social or environmental impediments. But Franklin's observation is almost unchanged from that of mercantilist sixteenth-century philosopher Giovanni Botero, who advocated for colonial expansion because "plants cannot prosper so well nor multiply so fast in a nursery where they are set and planted near together as where they are transplanted into an open ground."[50] Franklin celebrates the reproductive potential of Englishmen on this kind of colonial "open ground":

> There is in short, no Bound to the prolific Nature of Plants or Animals, but what is made by their crowding and interfering with each others Means of Subsistence. Was the Face of the Earth vacant of other Plants, it might be gradually sowed and overspread with one Kind only; as, for Instance, with Fennel; and were it empty of other Inhabitants, it might in a few Ages be replenish'd from one Nation only; as, for Instance, with *Englishmen.* Thus there are suppos'd to be now upwards of One Million *English* Souls in North-America . . . This Million doubling, suppose but once in 25 Years, will in another Century be more than the People of England, and the greatest Number of *Englishmen* will be on this Side the Water. (*IM,* 373)

Franklin employs a simile from plant life, of fennel overspreading a garden, and implies that human, animal, and plant reproduction can be similarly analyzed. Comte de Buffon controversially makes explicit the comparability of these phenomena in his *Natural History,* which he had begun writing in 1749, almost at the same time Franklin began publishing his population analyses.[51] But even as Franklin begins to equate human and plant reproduction, he turns the process into, paradoxically, an inorganic one—inorganic in the sense that both the fennel and the English are isolated entirely from a larger system within which they grow and spread. The English are an isolatable category, divisible from the columns carrying numbers of "strangers or Negroes," and entirely reducible to mathematical calculation.

Franklin may have deliberately used the comparison to fennel, however, to present a caveat to his population predictions—plants grow in ecosystems, interdependent with the prior existence of certain symbiotic animals, plants, or natural disasters like floods or fires. And therefore, his predictions of the growth of English population rely on the assertion that Franklin may well have recognized was questionable, namely that "Was the Face of the Earth vacant of other Plants, it might be gradually sowed and overspread with one Kind only." The essay as a whole maintains this rhetorical strategy of positing an assertion, but then backing away from its implications: it ends memorably with Franklin expressing a wish that someday the earth might be vacant of all non-white faces, but then in his final sentence he undercuts that assertion by recognizing his own perspective within a multitude: "[W]hy increase the Sons of Africa, by Planting them in America, where we have so fair an Opportunity, by excluding all Blacks and Tawneys, of increasing the lovely White and Red? But perhaps I am partial to the Complexion of my Country, for such Kind of Partiality is natural to Mankind" (*IM*, 373). At this moment, human and plant cultivation are perfectly joined in the metaphor of slavery as the activity of "planting" Africans in America, but then Franklin controverts that statement by insisting on the existence of a quality inherent "to Mankind," the existence of "Partiality" to one's own. Franklin thus calls into question his own extended endeavor to represent human reproduction as mathematical calculation when he translates it into prose rhetoric. Whether borrowing botanical metaphors or commenting on complexion and politics, Franklin retains an ironic self-consciousness about the process of classifying people into categories, enabling him (unlike Malthus) to gesture toward the construction of population tables as a particular genre that can express a subjective point of view.

To illustrate his view of the interdependence between different population groups, and how this relationship can cause their

numbers to wax and wane, Franklin points to Caribbean plantation slavery:

> The Negroes brought into the English Sugar Islands, have
> greatly diminish'd the Whites there; the Poor are by this Means
> depriv'd of Employment, while a few Families acquire vast
> Estates; which they spend on Foreign Luxuries, and educating
> their Children in the Habit of those Luxuries; the same Income
> is needed for the Support of one that might have maintain'd
> 100. The Whites who have Slaves, not labouring, are enfeebled,
> and therefore not so generally prolific; the Slaves being work'd
> too hard, and ill fed, their Constitutions are broken, and the
> Deaths among them are more than the Births; so that a con-
> tinual Supply is needed from Africa. The Northern Colonies
> having few Slaves increase in Whites. Slaves also pejorate the
> Families that use them; the white Children become proud, dis-
> gusted with Labour, and being educated in Idleness, are ren-
> dered unfit to get a Living by Industry. (*IM*, 371)

Slaves and whites increase disproportionately to one another on the
island and the continental colonies, in Franklin's view. Although he
gives extensive social reasons for the black Caribbean majority—
lack of opportunities for white servants, the brisk slave trade, and
the excessive "luxuries" white children enjoy—Franklin merely
offers the North American colonies as a counterexample. In these
colonies, Franklin does not offer arguments for why whites retain
a majority in these areas—he merely asserts that, by contrast with
the Caribbean, the North American colonies prove that the white
population grows in inverse proportion to that of slaves.

   Although Franklin writes, sometimes ironically, about the interrelatedness of different groups' population growth, Malthus
later turns Franklin's work on North American reproduction into
a general rule applicable across the human species. Malthus similarly posits a mathematically constant rate of reproduction that
rarely, if ever, translates into reality, in order to turn his discussion

toward an analysis of the social and environmental forces that affect population. Referring to Franklin's *Observations* about the English in North America, he writes, "It may safely be pronounced therefore, that population when unchecked goes on doubling itself every twenty-five years, or increases in a geometrical ratio" (*EP*, 17). Like Franklin, Malthus posits assertions like this only to qualify them later—just after he makes this assertion, he goes on to demonstrate the inevitability that scarce resources become population "checks." But where Franklin deliberately employed a botanical metaphor to embed in his analysis the caveat that any group reproduces in a system alongside other reproducing groups, Malthus ignores discussions of the interdependence of different human groups in order to focus squarely on food supply. In the Malthusian vision, human population comprises one column, and the only relevant mathematical equation to compare it with is the rate of production of natural resources. Malthus does not gesture, as Franklin does, toward the relative planting of different racial groups that may decline or grow in population jointly or conversely.

After repeating Franklin's calculation about the English in North America, extracted from any relationship to other national or racial categories, Malthus turns to an analysis of the island of Great Britain. He compares two rates of growth: the rate of growth possible for food production, and the calculation that the population doubles every twenty-five years. With this analysis, Malthus quickly demonstrates his conclusion that after a century, there would be "means of subsistence only equal to the support of fifty-five millions, which would leave a population of a hundred and twenty-one millions totally unprovided for" (*EP*, 19). On the road to this specter of famine, Malthus appeals repeatedly to the philosophical dispassion of arithmetic. Reproduction, both plant and animal, is a process of neat, clean, and uncontroversial figuration. When positing the most fruitful future possible for cultivation—"[i]n a few centuries it would make every acre of land in the Island like a garden"—Malthus reminds his readers that this paradise is still a calculation (*EP*, 19). And catastrophe looms even in this arithmetical Eden, for he compares "arithmetical ratios" of population growth and growth of resources to render their impending collision:

> Let us now bring the effects of these two ratios together. . . . Taking the population of the world at any number, a thousand millions, for instance, the human species would increase in the ratio of—1, 2, 4, 8, 16, 32, 64, 128, 256, and subsistence as   1, 2, 3, 4, 5, 6, 7, 8, 9. In two centuries and a quarter, the population would be to the means of subsistence as 256 to 9. (*EP*, 19)

Malthus's series of ratio increases—nine for humans, nine for subsistence—line up, row by row, until the final total displays their inequality. Now the competition is not between different groups, but between survival and catastrophe. By comparing ratios, Malthus intertwines population with mortality once again, as his table with only two columns amounts to a ticking clock wherein mathematical reproduction ushers in doom. And like sixteenth-century discussions of the Flood that portray a post-diluvian world as one struggling to recover and reclaim territory through abundant human generation, Malthus's table is a call to action. But this action will be social, and it looks forward to an imbalance to prevent, rather than backward toward a precedent to emulate. Here again, positive numbers in a society are made visible through an investigation into causes of death. Either by guessing at how many people live in a city by counting its dead bodies, by invoking a historical population decline in the past to insist that people need to reclaim their former populousness, or by warning that population rates must be monitored to prevent social catastrophes in the future, mortality persistently serves as the lens through which discussions of aggregate living human numbers can be made visible. Death instigates the work of representing communities in print, and calculating this death determines the conditions of inclusion or exclusion within a quantifiable social whole.

Population extrapolations as articulated by Franklin and Malthus impose a vexed narrative on a community that requires a fictional beginning point of "vacancy" from which to begin telling a story about the future. When, as today, epidemiologists study mortality data, they craft narratives of epidemics by seeking to uncover the first person infected—the "patient zero."[52] In Franklin's *Observations*, the rhetorical starting point is a "population zero," the fiction of empty habitable land available for humans to "fill" it. This "vacancy" recalls the terrifying cataclysms omnipresent throughout early population discourse—except when Malthus quotes Franklin, he leaves out any mention of the causes of vacancy. Malthus draws upon a fiction of colonial America as a population-zero wasteland in order to contrast it with England; and unlike Franklin, he does not gesture toward the colonial warfare undergirding this fiction of vacancy. Franklin owns to the fact that vacancy of land can occur by "[removing] the Natives" through violent and communally traumatic conflicts like the Pequot massacre or King Philip's War in the seventeenth century, or in the many territorial wars fought in Franklin's own time. In a sense, a colonial mortality table wages a representational war through the medium of circulating print. The counts themselves, compiled in part by amateur demographers writing in to the local paper, repeatedly acknowledge and then erase the indigenous and African numbers living in their midst.

Again, Mbembe's concept of necropolitics illuminates the negativity essential to the conceptions of space and community that emerge from colonial mortality bills. Mbembe points out the ways that Foucault's ideas about biopower are insufficient to describe situations in which "the political . . . makes the murder of the enemy its primary and absolute objective," and more generally, insufficient to account for "forms of subjugation of life to the power of death."[53] We can follow Mbembe and look closely at the ways colonial mortality bills deploy "the power of death"— through their placement of bodies next to prices, their rigidly separate columns, and their insistence on representational forms that simultaneously forge transatlantic links and sever possible connections between cultures circulating at home—in order to acknowledge the violence and suffering that is present, yet disavowed, in the population rhetoric of vacancy. Also similarly, the crowding out of the "enemy" is the "primary . . . objective" in a narrative that requires the fiction of a population zero to tell a story of fantastically prolific population growth. Thus the popular bills of mortality circulating throughout the Anglo-American colonies are, in a sense, necropolitical visions of a social multitude, because first, they provide a matter of public affairs that arises from deaths and, second, they innovate ways to count deaths in differential ways. Each of these colonial bills tells a communal story about how to envision the future of a constantly changing and still-violent place. Through vacancy and death, the vitality of a city becomes visible. When the newspapers stopped regularly printing them, the quantification of social life and the measurement of multitudes were, in fact, just beginning.

Epilogue
Mourning the Figure of Three-Fifths

In writing a history of the eighteenth-century slave ship, Marcus Rediker insists on the necessity of recognizing the human story told through economic representations: "It is as if the use of ledgers, almanacs, balance sheets, graphs, and tables—the merchants' comforting methods—has rendered abstract, and thereby dehumanized, a reality that must, for moral and political reasons, be understood concretely."[1] Rediker describes the slave ship as "a strange and potent combination of war machine, mobile prison, and factory," which, alongside manufacturing labor power in the Americas, "also produced 'race.'" Violence created the separation on board the ship between "white men" and "black people," who could then each be represented separately, using the "merchants' comforting methods," and later, in mortality and population tables. As the previous chapter's discussion of mortality bills showed, Achille Mbembe locates the roots of what he calls "necropower" in this history of early modern enslavement. Indeed, one of the ways in which Mbembe defines "necropower" closely recalls the kind of "social death" that Orlando Patterson described specifically in regard to the lived experience of slavery: necropower creates "*death-worlds*, new and unique forms of social existence in which vast populations are subjected to conditions of life conferring upon them the status of *living dead*" in this history of early modern enslavement.[2] In particular, Mbembe focuses on slavery in his effort to understand modern forms of terror, in order to show how "the violent tenor of the slave's life is manifested through the overseer's disposition to behave in a cruel and intemperate manner." Later, when Mbembe defines the plural "manners" as "the links between social grace and social control," he points out that within the system of slavery, violence "becomes an element in manners, like whipping or taking of the slave's life itself: an act of caprice and pure destruction aimed at instilling terror."[3]

Thomas Jefferson devoted a chapter of his only published book, the 1785 *Notes on the State of Virginia*, to describing these violent behaviors characteristic of a slave system: Query XVIII, "On Manners." The book, which draws on Jefferson's extensive knowledge of natural history and population debates to respond to a list of questions about the ex-colonies posed by the French diplomat François Marbois, interweaves commentary on race and the new nation with extensive calculations and taxonomies describing his home state's human and animal inhabitants. In answer to Marbois's question regarding "the *particular* customs and manners that may happen to be received in that state," Jefferson turns immediately to the deleterious effects of slavery: "There must doubtless be an unhappy influence on the manners of our people produced by the existence of slavery among us."[4] After describing, in a way Mbembe echoes, how "the whole commerce between master and slave is a perpetual exercise of the most boisterous passions, the most unremitting despotism on the one part, and degrading submission on the other," Jefferson then warns of the specter of revolution, and finally, of racial "extirpation": "I tremble for my country when I reflect that God is just: that his justice cannot sleep for ever: that considering numbers, nature and natural means only, a revolution of the wheel of fortune, an exchange of situation, is among possible events: that it may become probable by supernatural interference" (*NS*, 169). While Abraham Lincoln and others recalled this memorable passage in the Civil War era, I focus especially on the first signal of a coming race war that Jefferson mentions: "considering numbers." Like colonial writers since Guaman Poma, when Jefferson considers numbers, he also contemplates a fearful implementation of divine justice. For Jefferson, the coming cataclysm that the numbers portend is not a flood or a plague but "a revolution of the wheel of fortune," a topsy-turvy world in which whites fear the terror of black ex-slaves. As Rediker argues, the seeds of this revolution were sown on the slave ship, when the violent rendering of human beings into numbers on a merchant's ledger turned motley collections of sailors and captives into uniformly counted groups of "whites" and "blacks." Jefferson's *Notes* combines an intervention into late eighteenth-century population discourse with an acknowledgment of the violence of a slave system that institutes racial categorization. When his book "[considers] numbers," it reenacts a longstanding trope within colonial writing about population, yet casts the attending cataclysm as a race war.

In this epilogue I juxtapose two texts that circulated in the aftermath of a century and a half of experiments with human accounting in colonial writing: Jefferson's *Notes*, and William Cowper's poetic reflections on the bills of mortality that circulated in American periodicals at the turn of the nineteenth century. Although assuming very different forms and addressing differently imagined audiences, both texts reflect the naturalization of the custom of representing people as populations. These texts appear at the cusp of the entrenchment of the word "population" in everyday English usage, as well as at the moment when population became a fundamental principle of organizing government in the Anglophone world. Yet at the same time that they reflect a changed relationship to the act of counting people, they also evince the persistent link between population discourse and cataclysm, and the colonial legacy intertwining human accounting with racism, slavery, and fears of contagion.

Jefferson's Unaccountable Figures

Jefferson published *Notes* thirteen years before Malthus's landmark *Essay*, well into the era of serious political thinking about population. As this book has argued, various forms of colonial writing about population helped naturalize the increasingly common numerical representation of human groups in response to slavery, war, and settlement. Human accounting, as I have called the early experimentation with forms of applying numbers to bodies, had, by Jefferson's time, given way to an emerging science of population. *Notes* first appeared in Paris fifteen years before Britain established regular state counts in the Census Bill of 1800, and five years before the first US census in 1790 "[considered] numbers" along racial lines in a decidedly peculiar way: each slave was entered in the count as only equaling "three-fifths" of a white person. When Jefferson wrote *Notes*, counting people—as opposed to land, or tax revenue—was about to be a constitutive element of representative democracy in the new nation; and the "merchants' comforting methods," which sublimated violent repression on the slave ship, were about to be instituted as the law of the land. As is repeatedly the case in population discourse, *Notes* shows how this invocation of counting people also brought the attendant specter of divinely retributive "revolution." Writing about population had changed from the early colonial period; the regular practice of counting living numbers of people had taken root and increasingly bore the weight of law. Indeed, one of the complaints Jefferson lodged against George III in his draft of the Declaration of Independence (and maintained in the final version) was that the king had "endeavored to prevent the population of these states," turning a question of population management into an incitement of actual political and military revolution.[5] Impromptu or creative explorations of the application of numbers to bodies had to take place in the perceivable shadow of official statistics and government enforcement. Yet elements of this earlier era lingered into the early national period, and these appear in

Notes in the form of cataclysmic portents of race war and female figures, both of which confound clear numerical distinctions.

Jefferson chose to invoke the complex etymology of the word "population" in *Notes* when he renamed Marbois's query "on the number of its inhabitants" as Query VIII, "Population." Marbois had asked these questions of all of the former colonies then composing the US, yet Jefferson was the only respondent to use the word "population" when giving an account of the state's number of inhabitants.[6] Jefferson's response is unique particularly because it was by far the lengthiest and most detailed, yet the choice to refer to "population" itself points to much that was distinctive about Jefferson's approach. The term had much wider circulation at the end of the eighteenth century than it had throughout the previous century, when it could still be synonymous with "depopulation"; but it still was not nearly as widely used as it would be after Malthus published his *Essay*.[7] In *Notes*, Jefferson's "Population" section follows a lengthy engagement with Comte de Buffon, in which Jefferson refutes the French natural historian's claims about the inferiority of American natural life, and immediately prior to a query Marbois did not ask, on "Climate." Population debates had long been tied to discussions of climate, like those by Montesquieu; by titling a section of his book "Population," Jefferson signals his membership in an international community of natural historians and philosophers engaged in discussing the subject. He also signals his departure from an earlier era, in which the word "population" had conflicted or esoteric meanings.

Besides the shift in terminology, Jefferson also reordered Marbois's questions, transforming what had been a somewhat random list of topics into a narrative that flows from geographic and natural realities at the beginning, toward human activity and social relations at the end (for example, Jefferson moves the query on "Manners"—Marbois's term as well as Jefferson's—later, appearing eighteenth instead of eleventh). Notably, Marbois circulated two separate lists, one with sixteen queries and one with twenty-two; Jefferson apparently had the longer list, but the shorter one asks each colony not only for "the number of its inhabitants," but also "the proportion between the whites & the blacks."[8] Recalling how Richard Ligon invokes aesthetics of proportion as a way to enumerate slaves, Marbois expresses an interest in the racial makeup of states beyond merely their gross quantities of people. The query asks that the numbers tell a relational, social story, rather than solely a quantitative one; and although Jefferson does not signal that Marbois specifically asked about "the proportion between the whites & blacks," he spends much of the chapter he titles "Population" addressing this concern: the response to this query, Jefferson writes, "will . . . develop the proportion between the free inhabitants and slaves." Using his revised ordering of the query, Jefferson here prepares for the consideration of numbers that will appear in his response describing violent "manners."

Beyond the terminology, Jefferson signals the solidification of a new era of population discourse by working solely from counts of living people, rather than from extrapolations of mortality data, as Franklin had done. In order to obtain the total proportion of whites to enslaved blacks in Virginia, however, he has to perform several calculations ameliorating the gaps left by the 1782 census. Reflecting its interest in taxation—those who pay tax and those whose bodies are property to be taxed—the recent census did not count white women or any free person under twenty-one years of age, yet it counted "slaves of all ages and sexes." Black female bodies and the bodies of black children enter into the count, yet white female bodies and white children require Jefferson's calculations to be rendered numerically visible. Jefferson makes an interesting move in equating black and white reproduction in order to close this gap in the count. He begins by turning his attention to the line in the 1782 census that includes the number "23,766" for an amount "not distinguished in the returns, but said to be titheable slaves" (NS, 92): "To find the number of slaves which should have been returned instead of the 23,766 titheables, we must mention that some observations on a former census had given reason to believe that the numbers above and below

16 years of age were equal" (*NS*, 93). Jefferson then doubles the number of titheables, apparently assuming that those reported for tithes were not children, and arrives at a total of "259,230 slaves of all ages and sexes" (*NS*, 93). Then, Jefferson uses the same calculation of proportion on the basis of age—half the population being above age sixteen and half below—to hypothesize the number of white children in Virginia: "To find the number of free inhabitants, we must repeat the observation, that those above and below 16 are nearly equal" (*NS*, 93). Jefferson conjectures using militia data to ascertain a number of free males between sixteen and twenty-one, and assumes that the numbers of men and women are exactly equal. He arrives at a total number of free inhabitants— 284,208—and finally, accounting for counties originally excluded from the census, the total number of people living in Virginia, both slave and free: 567,614. His numbers show that there are only around 25,000 fewer slaves than free people, representing the proportional divide Marbois asked about as only slightly less than equal: "[T]he number of free inhabitants," Jefferson writes, "are to . . . the number of slaves, nearly as 11 to 10" (*NS*, 94).

Despite leaving out Virginia's indigenous people entirely from *Notes*'s query on population, Jefferson does include, in a subsequent query, a table of four different counts of "Aborigines which still exist in a respectable and independent form . . . within, and circumjacent to, the United States, whose names and numbers have come to my notice" (*NS*, 108). Taken from 1759 to 1768, the different counts vary drastically. Although listed as approximated numbers by tribe and "where they reside" (the numbers are all rounded to the nearest fifty or hundred) *Notes* never adds together these counts. This is in keeping with Jefferson's portrayal of them as politically "independent," as well as with his differential treatment of African Americans and indigenous people. With regard to African Americans, Jefferson attributes difference to immutable racial characteristics, yet he attributes indigenous differences entirely to culture and politics (this incongruity results in part from his determination to refute Buffon's claims that all life in America—its people, flora, and fauna—are smaller than in Europe because of the climate).[9] Although *Notes* does not sum its several pages of counts of individual tribes, it enables the reader to do so just as Jefferson did three queries earlier. If added together by the reader, the total sums paint a picture of decline (first signaled by Jefferson's prose describing the list as made up of those nations "which still exist"), or perhaps of incoherence, like that which Rowlandson encountered when she tried to count Indians during wartime. The 1768 numbers add up—if the reader takes the time—to a total of 35,830, and the count taken just eleven years later constitutes only 11,050. Jefferson, however, never adds the counts of individual groups together to arrive at a sum total of indigenous people reported by a particular attempt at a census, despite presenting the data that would enable this.

Jefferson's refusal to add estimates of the North American indigenous population is relatively consistent with his portrayals of these peoples as not constituting a separate race and as not aligned within a unified nation. However, it does appear odd considering that one of the first and most memorable mentions of rates of population growth or decline in *Notes* occurs in relation to questions about indigenous birth rates. In Query VI, a section in which Jefferson extensively engages with Buffon about the environment of the Americas, Jefferson describes how indigenous women "raise fewer children than we do":

> The causes of this are to be found, not in a difference of nature, but of circumstance....[T]hey have learnt the practice of procuring abortion by the use of some vegetable; and that it even extends to prevent conception for a considerable time after...To the obstacles of want and hazard, which nature has opposed to the multiplication of wild animals, for the purpose of restraining their numbers within certain bounds, those of labour and of voluntary abortion are added with the Indian. No wonder then if they multiply less than we do. (*NS*, 65)

Jefferson locates the cause of differential rates of population growth between whites and indigenous people within the life circumstances of women. Before discussing their skills in "the practice of procuring abortion," Jefferson claims that indigenous "women are submitted to unjust drudgery" (*NS*, 64). The labor of indigenous women appears conspicuously here; their bodily autonomy and education in "the practice" of controlling family size also renders them as a socially important group. The reason for the odd disjunction between Jefferson's early attention to indigenous birth rates and then the later absence of a calculation of their population numbers is likely that he is caught in a dilemma: he wants to argue against Buffon to prove that the American climate can sustain population growth (and so he mentions the frequency of abortion), while at the same time prove that the indigenous American population will inevitably disappear. These two contradictory goals work together to serve the purpose of arguing for colonial expansion, but they require disjunctions in Jefferson's approach to population discourse in the process.

Notes devotes extensive attention to women's bodies and reproductive lives in the discussion of indigenous population growth rates, and then, with regard to white women in the query on "Population," he carefully describes the calculations required to render those women's bodies visible within the census count. Yet in these census calucalations, African slave women's bodies do not appear as a distinct group at all within the counts of "titheables" and "slaves of all ages and sexes." Rather than focus intently on them, as Ligon does, Jefferson ignores the lives of black women in his query on population and, for the purposes of his calculations, he assumes that their reproductive "practices" and conditions mirror those of white women.

However, immediately after Jefferson acknowledges the near parity between white and black numbers—numbering "nearly as 11 to 10"—he posits that somehow the slaves' rate of population growth actually exceeds that of whites: "Under the mild treatment our slaves experience, and their wholesome, though coarse, food, this blot in our country increases as fast, or faster, than the whites" (*NS*, 94). Jefferson does not account for why white reproduction would not be "as fast, or faster" given the "mild treatment" and likely less "coarse" food, but instead points toward a lurking, incalculable reproductive force that could eclipse the white majority. When *Notes* describes the black population as a "blot," it is as if slavery is a mistaken explosion of black ink on the paper; a spillage that mars otherwise orderly calculations on a page. Conceived of as a "blot," the slave population in Virginia threatens the representation of the state's social life: it is a blemish, a disfiguration, or an error. When Jefferson began calculating the total population of Virginia—arriving at the 567,614 number—he was amending a census that, because of its focus on adult males and people deemed "titheable," told a story of vast numerical imbalance: 53,289 "free males above 21 years of age" compared to 211,698 slaves. At first glance, this 1782 census presents the power imbalance as it truly was: a minority of powerful whites holding sway over a vast population of subjugated people. Jefferson's calculations, rendering white women and minors visible within the count, helps to revise this numerical story into a very different one—one that suggests near equality (in numbers), and ultimately, a final number free from division between blacks and whites (although it effaces indigenous numbers) and from power imbalance. The arithmetic solution that adds these varied populations together suggests, unlike the census, a coherent statewide unity: "567,614 inhabitants of every age, sex, and condition." This numerical unity achieved, Jefferson can then turn to arguing for the need to thwart and eventually eradicate the slave numbers contained within that sum. Foreshadowing the discussion of racial revolution he will pick up in the query on Manners, he ends this query on population by arguing for continuing the ban on the importation of slaves, which will "in some measure stop the increase of this great political and moral evil, while the minds of our citizens may be ripening for a complete emancipation of human nature" (*NS*, 94).

In Query XIV, on laws, Jefferson returns to the need to subtract the number of blacks from the total calculation of inhabitants, in a frightening passage warning of the threat of genocide
posed by the prospect of emancipation without forced colonization of the freed ex-slaves:

> It will probably be asked, Why not retain and incorporate the
> blacks into the state, and thus save the expence of supplying,
> by importation of white settlers, the vacancies they will leave?
> Deep rooted prejudices entertained by the whites; ten thou-
> sand recollections, by the blacks, of the injuries they have sus-
> tained; new provocations; the real distinctions which nature
> has made; and many other circumstances, will divide us into
> parties, and produce convulsions which will probably never
> end but in the extermination of the one or the other race.
> (*NS*, 145)

Jefferson follows up here on the calculations he made in the query
on population by proposing a social engineering that replenishes
the overall sum of inhabitants "by importation of white settlers"
after forcibly removing the black numbers of the state: "sending
them out," he writes, with the means for colonization (*NS*, 145).
Within the quotidian acts of counting and calculation in Query
VIII, Jefferson plants the seeds of violence and genocide—"the
extermination of one or the other race"—to be taken up later
in the queries on Laws and Manners.[10] Despite the separation of
these discussions of race over the course of *Notes*, Jefferson deliberately chose to place the population calculations first, so that his
subsequent comments could be made "considering numbers." In
so doing, Jefferson retains the twinning of cataclysmic portents of
death and considerations of counts of living numbers of people
that had persisted since the beginnings of human accounting.

Before turning to racial calculations that, over the course of the
book, evolve into discussions of violence and genocide, Jefferson
echoes Anne Bradstreet by devoting the majority of the query

on population to plans for ensuring that the numbers of whites included in the count are the right *kind* of numbers. Whereas Bradstreet's poetry explores the problems involved when numbers are made up of "men but in shape and name," Jefferson warns that relying on European immigration for population growth will "render" Virginia society "a heterogeneous, incoherent, distracted mass" (*NS*, 91). Instead, Jefferson takes pains to calculate the rate of population growth through reproduction, and proves that restricting immigration will result in the same total population number in 1862 that would be achieved with immigration by 1835. In order to ensure that the population numbers are not a "mass," but rather "more homogenous, more peaceable, more durable" (*NS*, 91), Jefferson urges patience and a reliance on "natural propagation" (*NS*, 90) that will enable existing members to "transmit" the "principles" of Virginia society "to their children" (*NS*, 91). It makes sense, then, that the final portion of the query on numbers explains in detail how Jefferson renders white women and children visible in his population calculations. His political goals for Virginia rely heavily on the physical and social reproductive labor performed by women: the work of "natural propagation" that can make immigration restrictions feasible and, in Jefferson's view, cultivate a "more homogeneous" population that continues to grow in terms of numbers. Jefferson's significant interest in education, evident in *Notes* and his founding of the University of Virginia, points to the ways that colonial population discourse has developed since William Bradford used a census to insist on the continuity of his community across time. Jefferson, like Bradstreet, does not take entirely for granted that populations will reproduce homogenously without educational structures to ensure they do so.

Yet Jefferson recalls, if obliquely, a figure from an earlier era of colonial writing about population at another moment when discussing the vagaries of reproduction, this time when his attention turns to albino African slaves. Here, the kind of black female bodies that threaten stability and numerical measurement (which also appeared in early texts considering population including those of Richard Ligon or Henry Neville) reappear tucked away as a nearly marginal "anomaly of nature." This discussion physically appears as an addendum to the larger text, written in the manuscript on a page that Jefferson appended at the end of a long list of the various birds of Virginia and the different ways in which they are classified. This concludes Query VI, "A Notice of the Mines and other Subterraneous Riches; its Trees, Plants, Fruits, &C"—the same query which earlier discussed how the conditions of indigenous women's lives affected population growth rates. The passage describes slaves, mostly women, who do not appear to fit within racial categories because they have the appearance of being white, yet were born of mothers who are enslaved African Americans (and thus inherited their mothers' slave status). In this way, even Jefferson, who is so much closer to the center of political power in his place and time than Bradstreet, Ligon, and Rowlandson were, turns as earlier colonial writers did to descriptions of female reproductive bodies to explore potential difficulties with establishing the categorizations that population counts routinely entail.

Jefferson begins his appended passage abruptly: "To this catalogue of our indigenous animals, I will add a short account of an anomaly of nature, taking place sometimes in the race of negroes brought from Africa, who, though black themselves, have in rare instances, white children, called Albinos" (*NS*, 77). Each of these individuals, Jefferson is careful to state, were "born to parents who had no mixture of white blood" (*NS*, 77). Elsewhere, Jefferson considered the means by which some African Americans—including his own descendants—might come to be recognized as white, but here Jefferson is interested in albinism precisely because it does not involve racial mixture.[11] Quickly it becomes clear that the majority of the "white children" of African descent that Jefferson considers in *Notes* are women: out of seven albino slaves described, five of them are women; one is an infant of indeterminate sex who died "at the age of a few weeks"; and one is a man.

Jefferson includes his prose taxonomy of these seven anecdotally collected specimens by surmising, "Whatever be the cause of the disease in the skin, or in its colouring matter, which produces this change, it seems more incident to the female than male sex" (*NS*, 78). Although sidestepping cross-racial sex and reproduction entirely as means of complicating racial difference, Jefferson still genders as female the racial anomaly that could create problems in counts of "whites" and slaves.

The question of whether and how much the femininity of these albino figures matters has stimulated critical debate, with some focusing on this passage as a moment of "incommensurability" in a book devoted to "all-encompassing" systems of knowledge; others focus squarely on this moment's "misogynistic" echoing of scientific renderings of "reproductive power" as a threat, or on traditions of representing the black female body in particular as containing "an irreducible material remainder" of all the complexity of meaning that racist discourse necessarily disclaims.[12] Charles D. Martin displaces the focus on the femininity of Jefferson's albinos in order to offer this appended anecdote as an example of the frequent notable displays of African Americans of all sexes with albinism in early America that threaten "to expose the fiction of whiteness"; like me, Martin emphasizes the odd placement of this moment in the text, "[s]eemingly not knowing what to do with them."[13] Whether the anecdote is a "residue" of something excised or a "remainder" from a prior calculation, Jefferson's deep investment in population discourse (signaled by his renaming of Query VIII) helps to explain why these "extraordinary" and "incommensurable," and mostly female, figures appear in *Notes*. Uncountable, anomalous female figures are a convention of colonial human accounting from Rowlandson to Ligon because they are liminal figures, who point to the complexities of individuality and social categorization that numerical population tables disavow. Although Jefferson repeatedly describes the albino slaves as "property . . . belonging" to white men (*NS*, 77–78), and therefore would include them in a census's "titheable slaves" category, he also refers to them as the "white children" of African American slaves. As Jefferson's language shows, these figures point to the inherent contradictions of race-based counting that form the foundation of the population discussions that are so essential to *Notes*'s work of representing Virginia.

Rowlandson intimated a similar confusion when cross-racial intimacy made counting more difficult, and Ligon also described his powers of counting and measurement as faltering when he tried to represent black female bodies. Writing about human beings as population numbers imposes arbitrary distinctions between intertwined groups and individuals, and imposes a false sense of stasis and order from which the observer appears to be removed. Colonial writing about population dramatizes both the promise of this emerging form of perception, and the ways in which it falters. Jefferson's inclusion of the wondrous and "incommensurable" albino figures evinces his debt to this discursive legacy of rendering people as numbers and using those numbers to ignore the complexity of their humanity. *Notes* manifests this discursive pattern both by underscoring the importance of countable population categories, and by lingering on bodies that have the potential to unsettle those same categories. Produced by a slave system that enumerated bodies, race is the primary category that organizes Jefferson's population counts, as well as the primary category that the albino African Americans call into question.

Ratios and Censuses

With the three-fifths clause, the US Constitution exhibits similar discursive problems around race and counting—problems that circulated throughout early colonial writing about population. Jefferson wrote *Notes* at the same time this proposal was first being made to enshrine slavery and its peculiar forms of counting people into the new nation's founding documents. James Madison first proposed the notion of counting slaves as three-fifths of a person for the purposes of apportioning representation and taxation in the legislature in the Continental Congress in 1783, while Jefferson was still preparing his manuscript for publication.[14] After the Articles of Confederation failed, the proposal was revived later that decade in the debates during the Constitutional Convention in 1787, and it became the law of the land for nearly eighty years, until the passage of the Fourteenth Amendment after the Civil War in 1868. The idea that population would become a central organizing principle of the new government was by no means assured   Britain would not pass the Census Bill, which advocated the taking of regular censuses, until 1800. It was at the earlier Continental Congress that delegates first proposed apportioning representation and taxation on population, rather than land values, as a way of sidestepping the problem of states misrepresenting their assets to avoid taxes.[15] The three-fifths clause thus not only offered a solution to the problem of how to count slaves, but played an essential role in assuring that population would be the key statistic for representation and taxation for the nation as a whole. Historian Howard Ohline notes that, "[p]aradoxically, it was the issue of how to count the slaves that became the means of assuring that representation would be regulated by a census beyond the control of the national legislature," because Southern legislators feared that Congress might someday vote to count slaves differently.[16] The Constitutionally ordained census therefore came into being because of "slavery and the fears of slaveholders," and these forces, as Ohline argues, "acted to assure a more democratic political system for white men."[17] For the "whole Number of free Persons" to become visible in Article One of the US Constitution, another confounding "three-fifths of all other persons" had to appear as well: a calculation that denies recognition of both the word "slaves" and the exploitative social system slavery enforced. The US Constitution attends acts of human counting that institute order with strangely counted "other persons," and that point to the dissonance between social experience and statistical forms of representation, and in so doing echoes the two centuries of colonial population discourse that preceded it. At the same time, the Constitution both *includes* indentured servants like those whose labor was being replaced by African slaves when Ligon visited Barbados, and explicitly *excludes* "Indians not taxed" from the count—just as *Notes* refuses to sum its various counts of indigenous people. Formerly, applying numbers in a way that defines persons to simulate a sense of order had been a site of experimentation open to many different kinds of writers, but with the Constitution this particular experiment took on the force of law.

Arguing for acceptance of the three-fifths clause, James Madison's "Federalist 54" from 1788 acknowledges the way slaves confound attempts to govern based on population. How could they be included twice in the government's accounts—both as property, in order to determine taxation, and as population, in order to apportion representation? Writing about what "one of our southern brethren" might observe, the Federalist admits that "we must deny the fact, that slaves are considered merely as property, and in no respect whatever as persons. The true state of the case is, that they partake of both these qualities: being considered by our laws, in some respects, as persons, and in other respects as property."[18] As Malick Ghachem points out, because both the idea of representation apportioned by population and the "legal personality of the slave" were legal fictions, "Federalist 54" attempts to justify something that was "a legal fiction that both contains and is contained by another legal fiction."[19] Madison himself, in the persona of the Federalist, admits at the end of the essay that the "reasoning" may be "a little strained at some points," yet he feels fully reconciled with "the scale of representation, which the Convention have established."[20] Nevertheless, in 1788, as population counts were about to take on the force of law in the thirteen ex-British colonies, even the proponents found this way of thinking "a little strained." The two centuries of colonial writing about attempts to organize and understand communities through counting that preceded the Constitution help to explain the overextended effort that the Federalist admits he had to employ to make the three-fifths clause, and the national census it enables, seem plausible.

Cowper's Melancholic Counting

In the decade before 1800, thanks to the first two US censuses, the British Census Bill, and Malthus's essay, the word "population," both as a term and as a tool for organizing government, gained a previously unseen level of reach in a relatively short amount of time throughout the Anglophone world. Exhortations about the "sin of David"—the supposed biblical prohibition against peacetime censuses—lost their political legitimacy. Questions of how and whom to count persisted, but the "fact" of a count and its power increasingly became part of everyday life.[21] British writers like William Wordsworth continued, in the tradition of John Milton's *Paradise Regained*, to produce art that questioned the census's authority to assign meaning to human connections. Aaron Fogel argues that Wordsworth's 1798 poem "We Are Seven" shows how, by dramatizing the tension between a child's count that includes the dead and a questioner's exclusion of those bodies, "[r]omantic poetries resisted the idea that population belongs exclusively to prose-and-statistical narrative," and in so doing they "expose the aesthetics of what we take to be non-aesthetic counting procedures."[22] Yet at the same time that Wordsworth's poem harkens back to a long tradition of poets like Milton, du Bartas, or Bradstreet, who blur the distinction between aesthetics and counting, "We Are Seven" and other "anti-census" works, as Fogel calls them, also signal that an important shift has taken place since the seventeenth century. The census, by Wordsworth's time, is part of the fabric of modern consciousness that writers can estrange and defamiliarize, rather than an already strange form of representation that can be simultaneously alluring and forbidding. "We Are Seven" contains a hierarchal dialogue between a questioning adult "Master" and a young girl whose answers confound both him and the reader, and this initial hierarchy, which the poem complicates, nevertheless shows how powerfully normalized the census has become. The response to the census-influenced way of viewing the world comes in the voice of an insistent child, a

decidedly weaker figure than the Master.[23] For poetry to be re-
actionary, the census has to have become a powerful maker of
meaning; and William Cowper especially, meditating on the bills
of mortality a few years earlier in a series of poems, emphasizes
the mournfulness of this feeling of passivity.

In spaces being forged by slavery and colonialism at the end
of the eighteenth century, the census had to carry a different
valence than it did in Britain, and Jefferson's *Notes* shows how
the destructive resonance of the word "population" lingered in
American writing, when it warns of racial revolution and "extermination." But even the same texts about counting likely carried
different meanings when they appeared in postcolonial spaces, in
the aftermath of brutal calculations like the three-fifths clause.[24]
Cowper was a religious abolitionist poet in England who influenced later poets like Wordsworth and Samuel Taylor Coleridge,
and whose poems were widely popular among readers in the
early American nation. Especially among antislavery advocates,
Cowper's poems endured long after his death (for example,
Harriet Jacobs used lines from his famous long poem *The Task*
in the epigraph to her 1864 autobiographical novel, *Incidents in
the Life of a Slave Girl*).[25] His poem "The Negro's Complaint,"
narrated in the voice of a slave, was reprinted multiple times
in the US. It opens by expressing a keen awareness of the cruelty of assigning a numerical value to a human life: "Men from
England bought and sold me, / Paid my price in paltry gold; /
But, though slave they have enrolled me, / Minds are never to be
sold" (*ll.* 5–8).[26] It was not only in explicitly abolitionist verses,
however, that Cowper expressed interest in the effects of enumeration. Less well-known today than his abolitionist poems are
his series of poems, written around the same time, reflecting on
the emotions conjured by reading the annual tally of local deaths.
Cowper's "stanzas subjoined to the yearly bill of mortality of . . .
Northampton" (1787–1793) were reprinted until at least 1809,
well after the poet's death, in periodicals including the *Connecticut
Magazine*, the *Boston Magazine*, and the *Piscataqua Evangelical*

Magazine. Cowper's mournful verses reflecting on what it is like to encounter a printed bill of mortality seem to conjure a communal experience that white, Christian, Anglophone readers across the Atlantic can share, given that they take a local statistic and extrapolate general metaphysical questions from these numbers. And as in the 1730s, by 1800 bills of mortality appeared regularly in print in both Anglo-America and in Britain. Unlike in the weekly, epidemic-related reports in Philadelphia, New York, or Charleston newspapers, American bills of mortality by this time were now being printed annually in magazines. Seventy years on, they still sparked much public conversation: a 1791 article in the *Bee, or Literary Intelligencer* objects to the way that bills of mortality fail to note the impact of migration in comparing cities and the countryside: "Much false reasoning, and many erroneous conclusions have been founded on these data by political writers, within the present century."[27] Similarly, an 1803 letter above the bill of mortality in the *Medical Repository* lauds recent attention to statistics in the legislature for enabling New York City to "render the bills of mortality … more perfect than they have for some time past appeared." In the process of calling for legislation to increase the bills' accuracy, the same letter praises the salutary effects that regular mortality data have on the reading public: the writer notes that "[t]he public mind, accustomed to weekly reports, becomes less agitated and alarmed at the sound of death."

Yet while the readers become desensitized to reports of death when they appear in statistics—"less agitated and alarmed"—they play a less active role in compiling and responding to the data than they did nearly a century earlier, when Boston's first printed bill of mortality called for readers' submission of local information. This letter writer focuses on "medical men": "To the physician belongs the more important duty to contemplate the subject, to endeavor to counteract the baneful effects of our variable climate."[28] The bills of mortality appear here to be mostly the purview of physicians, and their function in public is to inure everyday readership to the idea of vulnerability to death and disease, so that physicians can communicate to them more effectively about health in a particularly American climate. Further showing the increasingly specialized function of bills of mortality, the Academy of Arts and Sciences in Boston in 1785 printed a broadside sheet of a blank bill of mortality to be sent to physicians across Massachusetts to fill in over the following year, as can be seen in Figure E.1: "For by a regular return of such Bills for the course of a few years, the rate of our population may be determined; . . . and a natural history of the diseases incident to our climate, compiled." This empty medical data sheet provides a "formula" by which the recordings of individual deaths might collectively draw a representation of life in Massachusetts. This resonates with Jefferson's attempts to document the effects of the American climate on human life in response to Buffon, and with international interest in the relationship between climate and population since Montesquieu, yet here the specialized figure of the physician has the power to enter marks on a blank and previously standardized page. The table's rows and columns of squares await the occurrence of deaths, and promise that a meaningful story will eventually emerge from the entries.

The Cowper poems responded to this emerging era of physician-driven public health, and a community of readers inured to the import of data, by infusing the act of reading the bills with resigned melancholy. Beyond even being "less agitated and alarmed," Cowper's persona imagines becoming as lifeless as one about to die and manifest as a number on just such a blank form of medical statistics:

> Could I, from Heav'n inspir'd, as sure presage
> To whom the rising year shall prove the last,
> As I can number in my punctual page
> And item down the victims of the past;
>
> How each would trembling wait the mournful sheet,
> On which the press might stamp him next to die.

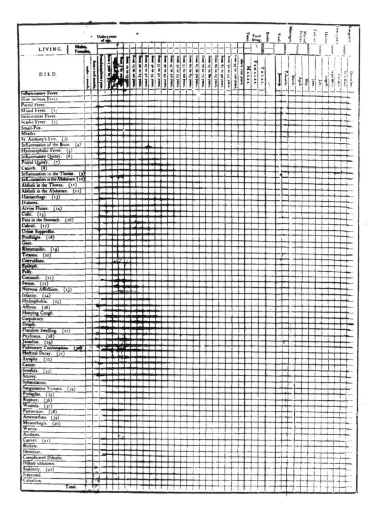

FIGURE E.1 Broadside from Boston, November 10, 1785 (Courtesy, Readex/Newsbank).

Reading the bill of mortality, Cowper imagines being able to know in advance who will become a "number" or "item" in next year's bill, and in so doing the "press" itself seems to gain the power to decide who lives or dies—to "stamp him next to die," rather than merely recording a death. "[T]rembling" before the power of the printed mortality statistics, the melancholic tone of the poem reflects a help-lessness and enervation in the face of printed vital statistics.

Likely British and American readers sensed a similar lethargy in the face of the "press" of statistics when encountering this poem, but when the *Boston Magazine* reprinted it in the January issue, readers may have recalled the yellow fever outbreak in the city the previous summer. Yellow fever epidemics had hit the city nearly every other year between 1795 and 1805 as part of a pandemic—especially deadly in Philadelphia in 1793—that laid bare Atlantic coastal connections and the relationship between the newly post-colonial US and the anti-colonial revolution of former slaves en-gulfing Haiti.[29] Yellow fever, which was endemic in Haiti, played a crucial role in the anti-colonial battles by severely weakening French forces. The deadly mosquito-borne illness hit US port cities along with Creole refugees, inflaming racial tensions and raising questions of race-based immunities—questions that mor-tality data sought to answer. Cowper's "trembling" and desire to "presage" the next year's mortality bill would likely have different resonances for US readers in 1806 that would relate specifically to America's particular ecologies and connections between whites, slaves, and indigenous people.

In 1809, the London-based *Gentleman's Magazine*, widely read in the US, printed an anonymously written poem in the style of Cowper's series of bill of mortality poems in July, the same month in which New York City was hit with another epidemic of yellow fever.[30] The poem's epigraph is the same Horace quotation about the brevity of life that appears in the *Spectator* essay from 1712 about the act of reading the bills, and the first lines describe the anxious anticipation of seeing the annual bill of mortality in print:[31]

> AGAIN we look with fearful eye
> On Death's continued page;
> Again with falling tears descry
> The fall of youth and age. . . .
> Each year the numbers I recount.[32]

The brevity of life, the woeful anaphora "Again," the feeling of incessant return of "each year" having to "recount" the mortality "numbers": for readers in New York facing the onset of another return of yellow fever, all of this may have communicated a particular urgency. Yet the "we" of the poem can only "look" and "descry" with tears and fright at the news; and the "I" cannot even "count," only "recount." Just as before the "stamp" of numbers on a mortality data form seems to itself carry the threat of death, so the bill of mortality here seems to be "Death's . . . page," conflating the power of the record of the feared event with that of the event itself.

In January 1801, in the year after Cowper's death, the *Connecticut Magazine* reprinted another bill of mortality poem after a summer in 1800 when a yellow fever epidemic struck Hartford.[33] In the poem, Cowper asks,

> Did famine, or did plague prevail,
> That so much death appears?
>
> No, these were vigorous as their fires,
> nor plague nor famine came;
> This annual tribute Death requires,
> And never waves his claim.
>
> Like crowded forest trees we stand,
> And some are mark'd to fall.[34]

Again Cowper conflates vital statistics with "Death" itself, as though death is meted out in an "annual tribute," just as the bill of mortality now appears on an annual basis. Cowper here also recalls the mortality bills'—like the word "population" itself—original tie to "famine" or "plague," asking if these depopulating events have induced the tally. The answer is clearly "No," refuting both the prospect that all these deaths resulted from plague or famine, as well as the earlier history that tied population counts to cataclysmic events. Cowper signals with "No" that he and his readers have entered a new era, in which "some are mark'd," again conflating dying with being "mark'd" or recorded in the bill. The passive voice here reflects the resigned, melancholy tone of the poem—a reflection on the act of reading the bills of mortality that expresses a sense of enfeeblement when compared to the *Spectator's* experience of being "very well pleased with these Weekly Admonitions" eight decades earlier. Vital statistics had acquired a sense of permanence and inevitability by becoming a state project on both sides of the Atlantic that mandated the counting of all bodies inside national borders. With this affiliation with state power, it makes sense that Cowper would conflate "Death" itself with the printed tallies, imbuing the bills themselves with an extraordinary force. It also makes sense that each poem conveys resignation and enervation in the face of this power that will eventually encompass everyone—including the reader—within its grasp, as well as a sense of loss, as though Cowper recognizes that an era of playful interactions with the counts of the living and dead, like Mr. Spectator described, has ended.

Yet again there may have been a particular melancholy in reflecting on the mortality bill and this poetic response to it for postcolonial New England readers in 1801, after a summer when yellow fever arose from the Connecticut River. While Toussaint Louverture in Saint-Domingue, after successes with his army of freed slaves, drew up a constitution that abolished both slavery and racial distinctions in the eyes of the law, the US had just completed its second national census, reinforcing the racial exclusions and the disfigurations written into its own Constitution.[35] Certain forms of counting were here to stay. What other possibilities may have been lost with the institution of this fixed accounting? What other powers might have materialized if the count had not garnered such a death-like quality? Whatever we can guess about the particular resonances of texts as they appear in different spaces, Cowper's readers in Connecticut, New York, or Boston had their own distinct reasons to cathect melancholy on printed bills of mortality, and these reasons likely had deep and various roots in the colonial experience.

The "*death-world*," to use Mbembe's term, of early modern colonial occupation and race slavery lingers after the turn of the
nineteenth century in increasingly imperceptible form behind
the population tables that fostered it. For Jefferson, this lingering
presence is the possibility of racial revolution and genocidal violence, a possibility that came to fruition in the new Haiti in 1804,
when Louverture's victorious successor, Jean-Jacques Dessalines,
ordered the killing of thousands of French whites remaining on
the island. During this same time period, US newspapers were
reprinting Cowper's melancholy poems about the bills of mortality, their readers vigilant about the spread of contagion from
the Caribbean. The discourse of counting bodies remained tied,
however obliquely, to the discourse of cataclysm, out of which it
had arisen.

Philosopher Avashai Margolit argues for the essential moral
relevance of mortality statistics in discourses of history and genocide. For him, "[m]orally, numbers should count . . . On the principle that the life of each human counts as one, no less and no
more, the cardinal evil of mass murder should be measured by
cardinal numbers, and by cardinal numbers alone."[36] The abhor-
rence of genocide is the denial of certain kinds of life membership within the category of the human, and the counting of each
body as "one, no less and no more," holds historical actors mor-
ally accountable for each and every murder. But Margolit insists
"we should not toy with ratios,"[37] comparing how many were
killed to how many survived, or who was a child and who was a
soldier. In determining moral weight, we must stop at counting.
Numerical language can redeem the humanity of the dead, but it
can also diminish them. It is a dangerous yet essential discourse, at
once shaping bodies, violating them, and rendering them worthy
of inclusion as (in the words of the Fourteenth Amendment) a
"whole number."

Notes

Introduction

1. Smith adapts this story from Samuel Purchas in 1617, who writes, referring to Uttamatomakkin, "Such is *Tomocomo*, at this present in London, sent hither to observe and bring newes of our King and Country to his Nation . . . This Man therefore, being landed in the West-parts, found cause of admiration at our plenty in these kinds, and (as some have reported) began to tell both Men and Trees, till his Arithmetike failed. For their numbring beyond an hundred is imperfect, and somewhat confused," in *Purchas His Pilgrimage, or Relations of the World and the Religions Observed in All Ages and Places Discovered, from the Creation unto this Present in Four Parts* (London: William Stansby, 1617), 954.

2. Captain John Smith, *A Select Edition of His Writings*, ed. Karen Ordahl Kupperman (Chapel Hill: University of North Carolina Press, 1988), 72.

3. See Helen C. Rountree, *Pocahontas's People: The Powhatan Indians of Virginia Through Four Centuries* (Norman: University of Oklahoma Press, 1990), 62.

4. Paul Ehrlich influenced much contemporary population discourse when he warned that overpopulation would lead to "mass starvation" in *The Population Bomb* (New York: Ballantine 1968), 17. More recently, the website for the 2011 documentary *Mother: Caring for 7 Billion* describes population growth as "the issue that silently fuels our most pressing environmental, humanitarian and social crises," http://motherthefilm. com. The 2008 documentary *Demographic Winter: The Decline of the Human Family*, by contrast, forecasts a crisis as a result of declining

fertility rates among white women, and repeats images of empty playgrounds as warnings of this trend.

5. Michael de Vaan writes that "the meaning 'to devastate' for the deponent probably developed through the usage 'to have an army pass through,'" in *Etymological Dictionary of Latin and the other Italic Languages* (Boston: Drill, 2008), 480. I thank Leslie Lockett for sharing her insights into this etymology.

6. *The Divine Weeks and Works of Guillaume de Saluste, Sieur Du Bartas*, trans. Josuah Sylvester (London: Humfray Lownes, 1621), 269–270. Further references to *Divine Weeks* are to this edition and will be cited parenthetically in the text as *DW*.

7. Elisha Coles, *An English Dictionary: Explaining the Difficult Terms that Are Used in Divinity, Husbandry, Physic, Philosophy, Law, Navigation, Mathematicks, and Other Arts and Sciences* (London: Peter Parker, 1692).

8. See "population, $n.^2$" and "population, $n.^1$, 2.a." in *The Oxford English Dictionary*, 2nd ed. (Oxford: Oxford University Press, 1989).

9. Francis Bacon, *Complete Essays* (Mineola, NY: Dover, [1625] 2008), 91.

10. While examining writings mostly by merchants, accountants, theorists, and policymakers, Poovey asks how numbers came to be seen as "noninterpretive," or even "preinterpretive," "at the same time that they have become the bedrock of systematic knowledge" in *A History of the Modern Fact: Problems of Knowledge in the Sciences of Wealth and Society* (Chicago: University of Chicago Press, 1998), xii.

11. For definitive histories of demography, see Hyman Alderman, *Counting People: The Census in History* (New York: Harcourt, Brace, and World, 1969), and J. Overbeek, *History of Population Theories* (Rotterdam, Netherlands: Rotterdam University Press, 1974). Poovey's *History of the Modern Fact* concentrates on how political science developed in England, while James Cassedy tells the story of social quantification in what became the US in *Demography in Early America: Beginnings of the Statistical Mind* (Cambridge, MA: Harvard University Press, 1969). Patricia Cline Cohen's study of the teaching and learning of arithmetic in colonial and early national America discusses development of population science as well in *A Calculating People: The Spread of Numeracy in Early America* (Chicago: University of Chicago Press, 1982).

12. Alison Games tracks how the "startling growth" of London's population in the seventeenth century led to "an increased rate of migration and travel overseas," in *Migration and the Origins of the English Atlantic World* (Cambridge, MA: Harvard University Press, 1999), 17. Timothy Sweet describes how the colonies provided a means of transforming those who could be regarded as "waste" populations into productive labor power: "[I]n proposing colonization as a means of expelling this

waste from the English economy, [colonial promoters] conceptually transformed it into a productive resource," in *American Georgics: Economy and Environment in American Literature, 1580–1864* (Philadelphia: University of Pennsylvania Press, 2002), 20.

13. Ian Baucom shows how slave ships' insurance records dramatize the "struggle . . . between competing theories of knowledge, a struggle between an empirical and a contractual, an evidentiary and a credible epistemology," in *Specters of the Atlantic: Finance Capital, Slavery, and the Philosophy of History* (Durham: Duke University Press, 2005), 16.

14. Geoffrey C. Bowker, *Memory Practices in the Sciences* (Cambridge, MA: MIT Press, 2005), 184. Lisa Gitelman highlights this assertion in the title of her edited collection, *Raw Data Is an Oxymoron* (Cambridge, MA: MIT Press, 2013).

15. Véronique Petit, *Counting Populations, Understanding Societies: Towards an Interpretive Demography* (Dordrecht, Netherlands: Springer, 2013), 1.

16. Michel de Certeau, *The Practice of Everyday Life*, trans. Steven F. Rendall (Berkeley: University of California Press, 1984), 21.

17. Psychoanalyst D. A. Winnicot called attention to the problems reproduction poses to the notion of an individual subject when he claimed, "'There is no such thing as an infant,' meaning, of course, that whenever one finds an infant one finds maternal care," in "The Theory of the Parent-Infant Relationship," *The International Journal of Psychoanalysis* 41 (1960): 586n4.

18. See M. T. Clanchy's description of how "literate modes could not be imposed by royal decree" between the eleventh and thirteenth centuries in *From Memory to Written Record: England 1066–1307* (London: Edward Arnold, 1979), 12.

19. "The Course of the Exchequer," in *The Dialogus de Scaccario*, ed. and trans. Charles Johnson (Oxford: Clarendon Press, 1983), 63–64.

20. Overbeek writes that "[in the Middle Ages], a systematic treatment of the population problem is nowhere to be found, and the writers of the period—mainly the Fathers of the Church—probably failed to appreciate the influence of numbers on the standard of living and vice versa," in *History of Population Theories*, 26. Hyman Alderman's discussion of the census in the Middle Ages corroborates the link between plagues, wars, and censuses by describing how the next enumeration in England after the Norman Conquest was in 1377, when "the poll-tax rolls needed revision after the Black Death of 1348–1349," in *Counting People*, 39.

21. Jean Bodin, *The Sixe Bookes of a Common-weale*, trans. Richard Knolles (London: G. Bishop, 1606), 32. Further references to *The Six Bookes of Common-weale* are to this edition and will be cited parenthetically in the text as *SB*.

22. Mario Turchetti, "Jean Bodin," in *The Stanford Encyclopedia of Philosophy*, ed. Edward N. Zalta (Winter 2012): http://plato.stanford.edu/archives/win2012/entries/bodin/.

23. Gunnar Heinsohn and Otto Steiger, "Birth Control: The Political-Economic Rationale behind Jean Bodin's Démonomanie," *History of Political Economy* 31, no. 3 (1999): 423–448.

24. Sylvia Federici, *Caliban and the Witch: Women, the Body, and Primitive Accumulation* (Brooklyn, NY: Autonomedia, 2014), 86.

25. Botero is unselfconscious in his admiration of Bodin; in his *Ragion di Stato*, or *The Reason of State*, for example, published the year after *The Greatness of Cities*, "there are more than three hundred quotations" from Bodin's *Six Livres de la République*, as D. P. Waley notes in his introduction to a reprint of the 1606 translation. See Giovanni Botero, *The Reason of State and the Greatness of Cities*, trans. P. J. Waley, D. P. Waley, and Robert Peterson (New Haven: Yale University Press, 1956), x.

26. Ibid., 246.

27. Leslie Tuttle describes how this 1721 epistolary novel by Montesquieu initiated "the depopulation panic," despite the fact that the panic was illusory, in *Conceiving the Old Regime: Pronatalism and the Politics of Reproduction in Early Modern France* (New York: Oxford University Press, 2010), 153.

28. See Carol Blum, *Strength in Numbers: Population, Reproduction, and Power in Eighteenth Century France* (Baltimore: Johns Hopkins University Press, 2002), 18.

29. Montesquieu, *The Spirit of Laws*, ed. and trans. Anne M. Cohler, Basia Carolyn Miller, and Harold Samuel Stone (New York: Cambridge University Press, 1989), 437.

30. Ibid., 433.

31. David Hume, *Essays Moral Political and Literary*, ed. Eugene F. Miller (Indianapolis: Library Classics, 1985), 460.

32. Frances Ferguson, *Solitude and the Sublime: Romanticism and the Aesthetics of Individuation* (New York: Routledge, 1992), 114.

33. See David Quint, *Epic and Empire: Politics and Generic Form from Virgil to Milton* (Princeton, NJ: Princeton University Press, 1993), 338–340.

34. John Milton, "*Paradise Regained*," in *Complete Poems and Major Prose*, ed. Merritt Y. Hughes (Indianapolis: Hackett, 1957), Fourth Book, *ll.* 407–413.

35. "Some remarks on the Bills of Mortality in London, with an account of a late attempt to establish an annual bill for this nation," *Scots Magazine*, April 1, 1771, 170.

36. Aaron Fogel shows how, like Milton did earlier, William Wordsworth as late as 1798 uses poetry to critique the census as a form of representation,

working in the mode that "oppositional counting is an office of rebellion assigned artists," in "Wordsworth's 'We Are Seven' and Crabbe's *The Parish Register: Poetry and Anti-Census," Studies in Romanticism* 48, no. 1 (Spring 2009): 25.

37. The letter is addressed to the Reverend Father Provincial, at Paris, and dated from Port-Royal, January 31, 1612: "Nous avions advance jà bien trois lieuës ... quand voicy que nous descouvrons six canots Armouchiquois venir à nous." *The Jesuit Relations and Allied Documents*, ed. Ruben Gold Thwaites, trans. John Cutler Covert et. al. (Cleveland: Burrows Brothers, 1896), Vol. 2, Acadia: 1612 1614, 34 37.

38. See B. J. Sokol, "Thomas Harriot—Sir Walter Ralegh's tutor—on population," *Annals of Science* 31 (1974): 205–212. See also Timothy Sweet's discussion of Thomas Harriot's calculations in relation to colonization, "Would Thomas More Have Wanted to Go to Mars?," in *Early Modern Ecostudies: From the Florentine Codex to Shakespeare*, eds. Thomas Hallock, Ivo Kamps, and Karen L. Raber (New York: Palgrave, 2008), 272–273.

39. Michael Booth, "Thomas Harriot's Translations," *Yale Journal of Criticism* 16, no. 2 (2003): 357.

40. For a description of Guaman Poma's Yarovilca ancestry, see Rolena Adorno, *Guaman Poma: Writing and Resistance in Colonial Peru* (Austin: University of Texas Press, 1986), 54.

41. See Rountree, 62–63.

42. Samuel Purchas, *Hakluytus posthumus, or Purchas his Pilgrimes*, Vol. 1 (New York: Macmillan, [1642] 1905), 492.

43. Purchas, *Hakluytus posthumus*, Vol. 17, 402.

44. Marcia Asher and Robert Asher state, "The earliest date we can find the museum acquisition of a quipu is 1895" in Germany, in *Code of the Quipu: Mathematics of the Incas* (Ann Arbor: University of Michigan Press, 1981), 157n1(a).

45. Gary Urton with the collaboration of Primitivo Nina Llanos argues against the notion that quipus were mnemonic devices, and posits instead that "the information recorded on the *khipus* constituted something much closer to the units recorded in a system of writing than has heretofore been supposed," even though "all the pieces [are not] yet in place" to analyze these textiles as a form of writing, in *The Social Life of Numbers: A Quechua Ontology of Numbers and Philosophy of Arithmetic* (Austin: University of Texas Press, 1997), 178–179. Frank Salomon describes that "the khipu problem" of interpretation may be "uniquely difficult," in part because "studying the khipu as a single code would be as feckless as trying to study marks-on-paper as one code," in *The Cord*

Keepers: Khipus and Cultural Life in a Peruvian Village (Durham: Duke University Press, 2004), 13.

46. Ralph Bauer has called for US Native American literature scholars to read Guaman Poma's text, arguing that "'Encountering' colonial Latin American Indian counterhistories . . . calls also for a counterhistory of the idea of 'America' in 'Native American literature,' an 'EnCountering' of the conventional narratives of literary history. It means transcending the nationalist boundaries and ideologies that have confined colonial American Indian counternarratives to the archives of oblivion," in "'EnCountering' Colonial Latin American Indian Chronicles: Felipe Guaman Poma de Ayala's History of the 'New' World," *American Indian Quarterly* 25, no. 2 (Spring 2001): 277. Birgit Brander Rasmussen also argues that Guaman Poma's work "deserves greater attention from North American literary scholars . . . as a rare indigenous voice in the cacophony of early colonial documents, as an early contribution to textual studies of the colonial encounter, and as an attempt to recast its terms and possibilities," in *Queequeg's Coffin: Indigenous Literacies and Early American Literature* (Durham: Duke University Press, 2012), 80.

47. See Chadwick Allen's discussion of the term "trans-Indigenous" when reading transnationally, which Allen claims can "invite specific studies into different kinds of conversations, and to acknowledge the mobility and multiple interactions of Indigenous peoples, cultures, histories, and texts," in *Trans-Indigenous: Methodologies for Global Native Literary Studies* (Minneapolis: University of Minnesota Press, 2012), xiv.

48. Guaman Poma's writing on this page may also be arranged to resemble an *unku*, the distinctive sleeveless tunic worn by Inca men; the V-shape at the top indicates this as does the fact that the page describes a count of men. However, the unkus Guaman Poma draws elsewhere are decorated with checkerboard squares, while the horizontal lines of writing on this page recall the dangling, linear shape of quipu strings. I thank Gary Urton for this suggestion. For a detailed investigation into how quipus recorded Incan censuses, see Urton, "Censos registrados en cordeles con 'Amarres.' Padrones poblacionales pre-Hispanicos y coloniales tempranos en los Khipus Inka," *Revista Andina* 42 (2006): 153–196.

49. Felipe Guaman Poma de Ayala, *The First New Chronicle and Good Government: On the History of the World and the Incas up to 1615*, trans. and ed. Roland Hamilton (Austin: University of Texas Press, 2009), 185 (187), 214 (216). Further references to *The First New Chronicle* are to this edition and will be referred to parenthetically in the text as GP. Page numbers refer to where the translated quotations appear in the original manuscript, which is available digitally (See Rolena Adorno, John V. Murra, Jorge L. Urioste, eds., *El primer nueva corónica y buen gobierno*

[http://www.kb.dk/permalink/2006/poma/info/en/frontpage.htm]).
As Roland Hamilton describes, "The original pagination contains an
error after page 155, with the next page numbered 154. The following
pages in this translation have both the original page number . . . and the
corrected page number in parentheses" (*xxv*).

50. Rolena Adorno describes how "Guaman Poma argues for the restitution
of lands and the return of traditional Andean governance" while still
including this "sovereign Andean state" in "a universal Christian empire
presided over by the Spanish king," in *Guaman Poma: Writing and
Resistance*, 5.

51. Sabine MacCormack writes that for Andeans, "*pachacuti* was miracle,
punishment, and judgment all in one. . . . Guaman Poma's divine
punishment, miracles, and judgments occur for reasons that require
no explanation," in "Pachacuti: Miracles, Punishments, and Last
Judgment: Visionary Past and Prophetic Future in Colonial Peru," *The
American Historical Review* 93, no. 4 (Oct. 1988): 993.

52. David Frye translates *unu yacu pachacuti* as "water world-reversal," and
explains that "pachacuti" is an "important Quechua concept" denoting
"when one world age is overturned or gives way to the turn of the next
world age," in Felipe Guaman Poma de Ayala, *The First New Chronicle and
Good Government*, trans. David Frye (Indianapolis: Hackett, 2006), 26n.

53. Guaman Poma's relation of the Incan flood story is corroborated
by sixteenth-century writer Cristóbal de Molina, who includes
a similar report circulating among the Quechua speakers he
interviewed: "During the Flood [most of] the people died because of
the water, except those who could escape to some hills, caves, and trees,
and these were very few. From these [survivors] they began to multiply,"
in Molina, *Account of the Fables and Rites of the Incas*, trans. and ed. Brian
S. Bauer, Vania Smith-Oka, Gabriel E. Cantarutti (Austin: University of
Texas Press, 2011), 5.

54. MacCormack, 961.

55. Mary Louise Pratt offers Guaman Poma as an example of what she
calls an "autoethnographic text," or a text "in which colonized subjects
undertake to represent themselves in ways that engage with the
colonizer's terms," in *Imperial Eyes: Travel Writing and Transculturation*, 2nd
ed. (New York: Routledge, 2008), 9.

56. Michel Foucault describes how statistical thinking in Europe had been
based on mortality data since the fourteenth-century plagues, and as
a result, "the question of the population was not at all grasped in its
positivity and generality. The question of knowing what the population
is and how one could repopulate arose in relation to dramatic
mortality," in *Security, Territory, Population: Lectures at the Collège de France,*

1977–1978, ed. Michael Senellart, trans. Graham Burchell (New York: Picador, 2007), 68.

57. Bruno Latour, *Pandora's Hope: Essays on the Reality of Science Studies* (Cambridge, MA: Harvard University Press, 1999), 15.

58. Giles Deleuze and Felix Guattari point to ways to think outside of both the history of population science and of the way that counting itself separates individuals in their definition of a rhizome: "Unlike roots and their trees, the rhizome connects any point to any other point, and its traits are not necessarily linked to traits of the same nature; it brings into play very different regimes of signs . . . The rhizome is reducible neither to the One nor to the multiple," in *A Thousand Plateaus*, trans. Brian Massumi (New York: Continuum, 1987), 23.

59. Latour, "A Few Steps toward an Anthropology of the Iconoclastic Gesture," *Science in Context* 10, no. 1 (1997): 63.

60. Mignolo, *The Darker Side of the Renaissance: Literacy, Territoriality, and Colonization* (Ann Arbor: University of Michigan Press, 1995), 5. See also Diana Taylor, *The Archive and the Repertoire: Performing Cultural Memory in the Americas* (Durham: Duke University Press, 2003), 37.

61. Jane Bennett defines "assemblages" as "ad hoc groupings of diverse elements, of vibrant materials of all sorts," such as an electric power grid or the worms in a forest's soil, in *Vibrant Matter: A Political Ecology of Things* (Durham: Duke University Press, 2010), 23.

Chapter 1

1. See Ivy Schweitzer, *The Work of Self-Representation: Lyric Poetry in Colonial New England* (Chapel Hill: University of North Carolina Press, 1991), 150–151, and Kathrynn Seidler Engberg, *The Right to Write: The Literary Politics of Anne Bradstreet and Phillis Wheatley* (Lanham, MD: University Press of America, 2010), 17–18.

2. Schweitzer points out that the 1678 posthumous edition of Bradstreet's poems drops the "presumptuous designation" of *The Tenth Muse* and "retains only its descriptive subtitle: *Several Poems, compiled with great Variety of Wit and Learning, full of delight*," resulting in a "revised title [that] shifts the reader's focus away from the author to her works, away from the phenomenon to her accomplishments," in *The Work of Self-Representation*, 130.

3. See Schweitzer, *The Work of Self-Representation*, 169; and Adrienne Rich, "Anne Bradstreet and Her Poetry," in *The Works of Anne Bradstreet*, ed. Jeannine Hensley (Cambridge, MA: Belknap Press, 1967).

4. All citations from Bradstreet's poetry are from *The Works of Anne Bradstreet*, ed. Jeannine Hensley (Cambridge, MA: Belknap Press, 1967.

Line numbers follow the citation. References to prose works included in *The Works of Anne Bradstreet* are to this edition, and will be cited parenthetically in the text as AB.

5. Schweitzer, *The Work of Self-Representation*, 166.

6. See especially Ivy Schweitzer, "Anne Bradstreet Wrestles with the Renaissance," *Early American Literature* 23 (1988): 291–312; and Tamara Harvey, "'Now Sisters . . . Impart Your Usefulnesse, and Force': Ann Bradstreeet's Feminist Functionalism in 'The Tenth Muse,'" *Early American Literature* 35, no. 1 (2000): 5–28.

7. Sir William Petty, *The Petty Papers: Some unpublished writings of Sir William Petty*, vol. II, ed. from the Bowood papers by the Marquis of Landsdowne (Boston: Houghton Mifflin, 1927), 115, 116.

8. Bradstreet was not alone among female colonial poets in blending intimate and global concerns in her writing: the seventeenth-century nun and Hispanophone poet Sor Juana de la Cruz explores similar perspectives in her writing. As was the case with Bradstreet, a printer anointed Sor Juana "The Tenth Muse" on the title page of her book of poetry, in an attempt to represent a female poet as a singular oddity—an attempt rendered absurd when the two colonial poets are considered together because there cannot be more than one "tenth" muse. Tamara Harvey writes that "Bradstreet, [Ann] Hutchinson, and Sor Juana were all treated as *rarae aves*, a term that hardly makes sense in the plural," and points out that criticism seeking out subversion within the writing of early American women like Bradstreet perpetuates "this *rara avis*" vision at the expense of "[identifying] common strategies that link her writings to the works and thought of other women responding to the same or similar social and intellectual traditions." See Harvey, 25.

9. Joyce Chaplin asserts that "William Bradford showed familiarity with Bodin's *De Republica*," in *Subject Matter: Technology, the Body, and Science on the Anglo-American Frontier, 1500–1676* (Cambridge, MA: Harvard University Press, 2003), 127.

10. Kathleen Donegan points out the lengths to which Bradford's history seeks to obfuscate the reality of catastrophic deaths in Plymouth: "How strange, then, that . . . Bradford's history hardly mentions the dead at all," in *Seasons of Misery: Catastrophe and Colonial Settlement* (Philadelphia: University of Pennsylvania Press, 2013), 139.

11. William Bradford, *History of Plymouth Plantation* (Boston: Massachusetts Historical Society, 1856), 450.

12. Bradford redeems even the Winslows, who were originally listed as numbering "5": "2. Mr. Ed: Winslow his wife dyed the first winter; and he maried with the widow of Mr. White, and hath 2. children living by her marigable, besids sundry that are dead. 8. One of his servants dyed, as

also the litle girle, soone after the ships arivall. But his man, Georg Sowle, is still living, and hath 8. children," in Bradford, 451.

13. Charlotte Gordon, *Mistress Bradstreet: The Untold Life of America's First Poet* (New York: Little, Brown, 2005), 278.

14. See, for example, Brian Easlea, *Witch Hunting, Magic and the New Philosophy* (Sussex, UK: Harvester, 1980), 15; and Hugh Trevor-Rober, "The European Witch-Craze of the Sixteenth and Seventeenth Centuries," in *The European Witch-Craze and Other Essays* (New York: Harper, 1969), 122.

15. *The Divine Weeks and Works of Guillaume de Saluste, Sieur Du Bartas*, trans. Josuah Sylvester (London: Humfray Lownes, 1621), 269–270. Further references to *Divine Weeks* are to this edition and will be cited parenthetically in the text as *DW*.

16. Chaplin, 127.

17. Mary Floyd-Wilson calls this Bodin-influenced Renaissance ethnographic favoring of temporal climes "geohumoralism," in *English Ethnicity and Race in Early Modern Drama* (New York: Cambridge University Press, 2003). Du Bartas's adherence to this rejection of "extreme" climates in favor of his own reveals his indebtedness to Jean Bodin, whose writings discuss how states can apply these classificatory principles to understanding their people.

18. Oxford English Dictionary, "list, *v.*[4] 1a.," *The Oxford English Dictionary*, 2nd ed. (Oxford: Oxford University Press, 1989).

19. Max Cavitch, *American Elegy: The Poetry of Mourning from the Puritans to Whitman* (Minneapolis: University of Minnesota Press, 2007), 143.

20. See Michael de Vaan, *Etymological Dictionary of Latin and the Other Italic Languages* (Boston: Brill, 2008), 480.

21. Raleigh, in his *History of the World*, criticizes Darius's troops' lack of training, but focuses mainly on his tactical missteps in not engaging Alexander on the banks of the Euphrates, and on the choice to keep his troops on guard all night while Alexander's army rested: "[N]ot being dismaied at Darius his great armie," Alexander "refresheth his men . . . which Darius did not," and Darius's army had gone "without sleep for fear of surprisal," in Sir Walter Raleigh, *The marrow of historie, or, An epitome of all historical passages from the Creation, to the end of the last Macedonian war* (London: Printed by W. Du-gard, for John Stephenson, 1650), 334.

Chapter 2

1. See Richard S. Dunn, "The Barbados Census of 1680: Profile of the Richest Colony in English America," *WMQ* 26, no. 1 (1969): 8.

David Eltis argues that "in its capacity to generate high-value exports relative to both its physical and demographic size, Barbados was a new phenomenon in the Atlantic world . . . [and] thus one- to two-thirds better off than the society that spawned it," at least in terms of "real per capita income in 1668." See Eltis, "The Total Product of Barbados, 1664–1701," *Journal of Economic History* 55, no. 2 (1995): 335–336.

2. Refining sugar on a hurricane-prone island with few rivers and little food was a risky and complex process that favored larger planters. Dunn, "Barbados Census," 18, footnote 24.

3. Small planters honed their techniques and headed to Carolina; large planters put in their time on Barbados and then retired to England, indentured servants for the most part went either back to England or tried their luck in North America once they had worked off their debt.

4. "In other words," Dunn writes, "he could expect to kill off all his original labor force within seventeen years!" (26). Dunn also bluntly states that "all the evidence points toward demographic catastrophy for the slaves" on Barbados, in *Sugar and Slaves: The Rise of the Planter Class in the English West Indies, 1624–1713* (Chapel Hill: University of North Carolina Press, 1972), 313.

5. See especially Russell R. Menard, *Sweet Negotiations: Sugar, Slavery, and Plantation Agriculture in Early Barbados* (Charlottesville: University of Virginia Press, 2006); and Larry Gragg, *Englishmen Transplanted: The English Colonization of Barbados 1627–1660* (New York: Oxford University Press, 2003). See also Hilary McD. Beckles, *A History of Barbados: From Amerindian Settlement to Caribbean Single Market* (Cambridge, UK: Cambridge University Press, 2000).

6. Dunn, *Sugar and Slaves*, 30.

7. Dunn, "Barbados Census," 3.

8. Along with ships' records, Atkins included all the island's vital statistics records: the "baptismal and burial records for the eleven parishes from March 1678 to September 1679." However, as Dunn describes, the Lords of Trade "suspected—no doubt correctly—that many more than 51 ships had carried sugar from Barbados in eighteen months" ("Barbados Census," 6–7).

9. Richard Ligon, *A True and Exact History of the Island of Barbados* (London: Humphrey Moseley, 1657), 1. Further references to *A True and Exact History* are to this edition and will be cited parenthetically as *HB*.

10. See Karen Ordahl Kupperman, "Introduction," in *A True and Exact History of Barbados* (Indianapolis: Hackett, 2011), 30.

11. Ibid., 20.

12. See Susan Scott Parrish, "Richard Ligon and the Atlantic Science of Commonwealths," *William and Mary Quarterly* 67, no. 2 (April 2010): 220.

13. Barbadian historian P. F. Campbell introduces Ligon's book as "the first published work on social and economic conditions in the island and is an indispensable source for any study of the period," especially because Ligon produced the first map of Barbados, in "Richard Ligon," *Journal of the Barbados Museum and Historical Society* 37, no. 3 (1985): 215.

14. See Kupperman, "Introduction," in *A True and Exact History*, 32; and Tony Campbell, *The Printed Maps of Barbados from the Earliest Times to 1873* (London: Map Collectors' Circle, 1965).

15. Kupperman, "Introduction," *A True and Exact History*, 11.

16. Martin Kemp describes how, for Leonardo da Vinci, "number was ultimately inferior to geometry, since . . . number was limited to separate units, rather plodding kinds of things, and lacked the magic of geometrical proportions, which dealt with surfaces, shapes, and space," in *Leonardo* (New York: Oxford University Press), 84.

17. Myra Jehlen, "History Beside the Fact: What We Learn from *A True and Exact History of Barbados*," in *The Politics of Research*, eds. Ann E. Kaplan and George Levine (New Brunswick, NJ: Rutgers University Press, 1997), 130.

18. "To my much Honoured and Ingenuous Cousin, Mr Richard Ligon, upon his Relation of his Voyage to the Barbadoes," in Ligon, *A True and Exact History*.

19. Viewing the world through the eyes of a bookkeeper was still a new concept in the mid-seventeenth century. As Joyce Appleby argues, the emergence of economic thought in this period required an "imaginative reconstruction" of social relationships: "The advent of the market, and the reorganization of social life through it, made men reconsider the terms of their lives. . . . As men studied the market, they in turn were changed by their studies," in *Economic Thought and Ideology in Seventeenth-Century England* (Princeton, NJ: Princeton University Press, 1978), 22.

20. Kay Dian Kriz notes that, like in Ligon's *History*, the plates in Sloane's "*Voyage to . . . Jamaica* do not picture human beings, which is not surprising, since 'man' became an object of natural history only later in the eighteenth century," in *Slavery, Sugar, and the Culture of Refinement: Picturing the British West Indies, 1700–1840* (New Haven, CT: Yale University Press, 2008), 10.

21. Ligon insists that numerical skill is essential for quantifying these proportions: "In this plantation of 500 acres of land, there was imployed for sugar somewhat more than 200 acres; above 80 acres for pasture, 120 for wood, 20 for Tobacco, 5 for Ginger, as many for Cotton wool, and 70 acres for provisions; *viz.* Corne, Potatoes, Plantines, Cassavie, and Bonavist" (*HB*, 22), and so on.

22. Mary Poovey, *A History of the Modern Fact: Problems of Knowledge in the Sciences of Wealth and Society* (Chicago: University of Chicago Press, 1998), 54, 55.

23. As Poovey writes, the techniques of early bookkeeping, oddly, did not produce a number that referred to any actual verifiable quantity, such as profit or debit: "Because double-entry bookkeeping's sign of virtue— the balance—depended on a sum that had no referent—the number added simply to produce the balance—the rectitude of the system as a whole was a matter of formal precision, not referential accuracy." The point of bookkeeping was not to show the merchant whether he was in the red or the black, but rather to reveal to the reader whether or not this merchant was trustworthy: "The stages by which information was reworked from narrative to number did allow a reader to monitor the accuracy of the entries *in relation to other entries in the books*" (emphasis added), in *History of the Modern Fact*, 55, 56.

24. Elsewhere Ligon addresses the abominably high mortality rate on Barbados, but uses a mathematical ratio to absolve the mercantile trade from accusations that it brings disease to the New World. With regard to a disease on a ship, he observes, "for one woman that dyed, there were tenne men; and the men were the greater deboystes" (*HB*, 21). With the mortality ratio of 1:10, Ligon assures his readers that grave illness attacks "the greater deboystes," rather than being an inevitable hazard of frenzied early colonial trade.

25. The argument with regard to the 1640 numbers is over whether a tax collector can be trusted to offer a complete accounting of the Barbadian population, with Dunn offering the more conservative estimate. Carla Gardina Pestana concludes that by 1660 "there were probably twenty thousand black slaves in Barbados," significantly more than anywhere else in the Anglo-Caribbean and dwarfing Virginia's holding of one thousand, in *The English Atlantic in an Age of Revolution, 1640–1661* (Cambridge, UK: Cambridge University Press, 2007), 194. See also Dunn, *Sugar and Slaves*, 312–313.

26. Pestana writes that the "black population of Barbados surpassed the white shortly after 1660," *English Atlantic*, 194. See also Dunn, *Sugar and Slaves*, 313.

27. Dunn, *Sugar and Slaves*, 203.

28. Parrish reads this anecdote as a theoretical critique about a united people subordinated to the greater good, offered as advice for the English during the interregnum. Parrish argues that the ants—which have a history of being represented to discuss human relationships from Horace to Erasmus—are a model for devotion to the public good that is not embodied (as Hobbes would have it) in a sovereign: "Ligon proposes

through his ant colony experiments . . . [that] [t]he human inhabitants on this sugar island need to learn how to act as unified parts of a sovereignless body politic." Although I agree with Parrish that the ants engage Ligon with a larger theoretical tradition, and that the ants work to critique all the human inhabitants of the island (masters, servants, Indians, and slaves), I focus particularly on their numerousness as a way for Ligon to offer an oblique counterpoint to slaves and servants, whose power is disproportionate to their numbers. See Parrish, 232.

29. Reading Charles Darwin's and Bruno Latour's consideration of worms, philosopher Jane Bennett points out how "worms participate in heterogeneous assemblages in which agency has no single locus, no mastermind, but is distributed across a swarm of various and variegated vibrant materialities," altering ecological landscapes, for example, even against human attempts at intervention. When Bennett or Latour or Darwin think about worms, they begin to ask questions like, in Bennet's terms, "what is the difference between an actant and a political actor?" See Bennett, *Vibrant Matter: A Political Ecology of Things* (Durham: Duke University Press, 2011), 96, 94. Bennett draws upon Charles Darwin's observations about worms in *Formation of Vegetable Mould Through the Actions of Worms on Their Habitats* (1881) and Bruno Latour's *Pandora's Hope: Essays on the Reality of Science Studies* (Cambridge, MA: Harvard University Press, 1999). Given Ligon's concerns with beautiful hierarchical arrangements, he too was likely contemplating the natural orderly formation of a mass of individuals into a powerful unit, or what Deleuze and Guattari might call an "assemblage converter," in Gilles Deleuze and Félix Guattari, *A Thousand Plateaus: Capitalism and Schizophrenia*, trans. Brian Massumi (Minneapolis: University of Minnesota Press, 1987), 324–325.

30. Kriz, 10.

31. Lawrence Marsden Price traces the Inkle and Yarico story in three early Yarico poems and as it moved across England, France, and Germany, in *Inkle and Yarico Album* (Berkeley: University of California Press, 1937).

32. "*The Spectator*, no. 11, March 13, 1711 [Steele on Inkle and Yarico]," *The Commerce of Everyday Life: Selections from* The Tatler *and* The Spectator, ed. Erin Mackie (Boston: Bedford/St. Martins, 1998), 192–195.

33. Joyce Chaplin describes the Anglo-colonial tradition of describing Indian women's painless birth, and the threat this posed because it meant exclusion from the legacy of Eve's curse, in *Subject Matter: Technology, the Body, and Science on the Anglo-American Frontier* (Cambridge, MA: Harvard University Press, 2001), 261–263.

34. Stories of a young woman saving an English adventurer lost in a foreign land were already common by the time John Smith published the

version of his *Generall Historie of Virginie* (1624) that included the story of Pocahontas saving his life from her father, Powhatan. See Rayna Green, "The Pocahontas Perplex: The Image of Indian Women in American Culture," *The Massachusetts Review* 16, no. 4 (1975): 698–714.

35. I am grateful to Kathleen Donegan for first bringing this text to my attention and making the connection between it and discussions of population in her paper, "Fantasy Island: Going Native on Henry Neville's *Isle of Pines*," given at the 2008 Society of Early Americanists Conference in Hamilton, Bermuda.

36. See Michael McKeon, *The Origins of the English Novel: 1600–1740* (Baltimore: Johns Hopkins University Press, 1987), 251–252.

37. Ligon was a sometime political prisoner with unfortunately unreliable Royalist friends, but Neville served as a Member of Parliament and was appointed to Cromwell's council of advisers. An accomplished political theorist, Neville translated Machiavelli and helped James Harrington write his utopian treatise *The Commonwealth of Oceana* (1656).

38. After the English seized control of Jamaica from Spain and demand spiked for knowledge about how to run sugar plantations, Ligon finally found a printer willing to take a chance on his lengthy manual, whose multiple engravings made it expensive to print. Susan Scott Parrish notes that while Ligon dates the prefatory letter to his *History* as 1653, the narrative was not published until 1657, and surmises that this may have been a result of publishers' initial wariness about the volume: "It seems evident that the only explanation for a penniless Ligon finding the means to publish an expensive, engraved folio edition of his *History* was due to its usefulness as a blueprint for setting up sugar plantations and *ingenios* in newly conquered Jamaica" ("Atlantic Science," 220).

39. Amy Boesky points out that political writers of Neville's time invoked Noah explicitly as a figure of paternal power, and Pine can thus be interpreted as a fictionalized new Noah. See Boesky, "Nation, Miscegenation: Membering Utopia in Henry Neville's *Isle of Pines*," *Texas Studies in Literature and Language* 37, no. 2 (1995): 165.

40. Henry Neville, "*Isle of Pines*," in *Versions of Blackness: Key Texts on Slavery from the Seventeenth Century*, ed. Derek Hughes (New York: Cambridge University Press, 2007), 13, 11, 15. Further references to *Isle of Pines* are to this edition and will be referred to parenthetically in the text as *IP*.

41. Like the actual African slaves brought to island colonies, Phillippa is not as healthy as the whites, despite her purported fertility: she is the first of the wives to die, and her death occurs inexplicably—there was not "any thing that ailed her" (*IP*, 15). Phillippa's death seems to instigate Pine's first count of his children, which appears immediately after her death in the text.

42. Elliott Visconsi argues that Neville uses Pine's children's wars to expose the folly of too-severe laws: after the first rebellion on the isle, the death sentence is ordered for everything from blasphemy to missing Bible readings. This exposes the necessity to design, in Visconsi's words, "a balanced constitution and well-framed, equitable rule of law," despite having inherited valuable legal origins. See Visconsi, *Lines of Equity: Literature and the Law in Later Stuart England* (Ithaca, NY: Cornell University Press), 132.

43. Historian Rachel Weil argues that Neville's *Isle of Pines* grew out of a late seventeenth-century emphasis on increasing population, and thus "reflected the spirit of the times, chronicling the peopling of a desert island by a shipwrecked clerk and his four female companions with alarmingly industrial efficiency." See "The Family in the Exclusion Crisis: Locke versus Filmer Revisited," in *A Nation Transformed: England after the Restoration*, ed. Alan Houston and Steve Pincus (New York: Cambridge University Press), 113.

44. James Harrington, The Commonwealth of Oceana *and* A System of Politics, ed. J. G. A. Pocock (New York: Cambridge University Press, [1656] 1992), 94.

45. When the story opens, the island is not ruled by descendants of the original ship's master, but rather by descendants of a servant. Rule over the island passes down from Pine's eldest son, a descendent of the maidservant Mary Sparks, *to his* eldest son, the Prince who greets the Dutch visitors. One of the maidservants was Pine's first wife, and once both maidservants were openly having sex with Pine, "afterwards my Masters Daughter was content also to do as we did" (*IP*, 14). The "Prince or chief Ruler" (*IP*, 9) tells the island's visitors that his father was Pine's "eldest son, and was named *Henry*, begotten of his wife *Mary Sparkes*, whom he appointed governor and chief Governour and ruler over the rest" (*IP*, 17).

46. The "Rule of Three," at times even called the "Golden Rule," was the limit of most students' arithmetical training in England and the colonies until late in the eighteenth century. It provides a way to determine the fourth number in an otherwise known proportion. As Patricia Cline Cohen points out, this rule could be very confusing, especially at a time when logic was not taught, since the first step in the operation—multiplying two numbers—results in a meaningless product. See Cohen, *A Calculating People: The Spread of Numeracy in Early America* (Chicago: University of Chicago Press, 1982), 122.

47. Parrish attributes Ligon's interest in Dürer to his belief, inspired by Bacon and other early modern humanists, that "making (things in a place) and knowing (about a place) are synonymous." This "artisanal

worldview" broke down the previous separation between technical and theoretical knowledge. Thus, instead of judging how each specimen compares to an ideal form, artists and observers like Ligon could make representations based on careful study and appreciate "various forms of tropical beauty" ("Atlantic Science," 222, 223). I take Parrish's description of Dürer's influence on Ligon in a different direction, however, by exploring how Ligon adopts the artist's struggle with applying science to art. More than being known as an advocate for the use of proportion, Dürer's work exemplified the problems and losses inherent in replacing metaphysics with mathematics as source of human knowledge.

48. In this sense, quantification becomes a seductive trap: Ghent writes of the mathematicians, "Whatever they think is a quantity, or is located in quantity as is the case with the point. Therefore such men are melancholy, and become excellent mathematicians but very bad metaphysicians, for they cannot extend their thought beyond location and space which are the foundations of mathematics," quoted in Erwin Panofsky, *Life and Art of Albrecht Dürer* (Princeton, NJ: Princeton University Press, 1955), 168.

49. Dürer is quoted in Panofsky, 171.

50. As Panofsky describes, art theory in Dürer's time was evolving away from a commitment to representing ideal forms. A Northern European who studied in Italy, Dürer committed himself to directing this new theory toward da Vinci-esque natural scientific research that could identify the various proportions of complex phenomena. Not to be confused with a more modern "craving for verisimilitude," beauty in Renaissance aesthetics arose from the harmony between parts in a whole, as well as in predictability and exactness: "Perspective, one might say, is a mathematical method of organizing space so as to meet the requirements of both 'correctness' and 'harmony,' and is thus fundamentally akin to a discipline which sought to achieve precisely the same thing with respect to the human and animal body: the theory of proportions" (*Life and Art of Albrecht Dürer*, 260, 261). Dürer enthusiastically took up this challenge to formulate a theory of proportions by studying different kinds of human faces.

51. Panofsky, 269.

52. Morgan describes, with regard to Ligon, how representations of beautiful and monstrous African woman work together as symbols of "the deceptive beauty and ultimate savagery of blackness." Whereas Morgan argues that Ligon's portrayals of reproductive women are "seductively [disclosing] their monstrosity" (14), I view Ligon as equally troubled by both kinds of representations of African women: the virgins that are paragons of beauty, and the slave mothers who seem almost inhuman.

By placing African women outside the realm of the countable or the proportionate, Ligon inadvertently acknowledges their uniquely powerful role in the slave system and the need to police that role. See Morgan, *Laboring Women: Reproduction and Gender in New World Slavery* (Philadelphia: University of Pennsylvania Press, 2004), 14.

53. Ibid., 16.

54. Panofsky describes *Melencolia I* as "the first representation in which the concept of melancholy was transplanted from the plane of scientific and pseudo-scientific folklore to the level of art," and asserts that the engraving's influence "extended all over the European continent and lasted for more than three centuries," *Life and Art of Albrecht Dürer*, 170.

55. Panofsky, 168.

56. Even the Roman numeral in the "Melencolia I" banner and the title is probably not a reference to counting, according to Panofsky. Instead, it refers to a plane of knowing greater than sequence: since the engraving was never intended to be part of a series, "[t]he number 'I' may thus imply an ideal scale of values, rather than an actual sequence of prints," *Life and Art of Albrecht Dürer*, 168.

Chapter 3

1. Mary Rowlandson, *The Sovereignty and Goodness of God* (New York: Bedford/St. Martins, 1997), 68. Further references to *The Sovereignty and Goodness of God* are to this edition and will be noted parenthetically in the text as *SG*.

2. Christopher Castiglia, *Bound and Determined: Captivity, Culture-Crossing, and White Womanhood from Mary Rowlandson to Patty Hearst* (Chicago: University of Chicago Press, 1996), 49.

3. Nancy Armstrong and Leonard Tennenhouse examine the spike in circulation of Rowlandson's narrative a century after it was written to place it in dialogue with Barbary captivity narratives, and treat these stories as "two sides of the same narrative coin." Armstrong and Tennenhouse view Rowlandson's narrative as taking a theological approach to problems of incorporating subjects into governmental authority, as opposed to the Barbary narratives, which espouse "a commercial ethic" preoccupied with quantities like prices and numbers of commodities. However, in the process of differentiating these narratives as opposite ways of solving "the problem of population," or the problem of imposing a nation on an aggregate mess of numbers, Armstrong and Tennenhouse overlook the way Rowlandson, too, struggles directly with quantification, and confronts a colonial system that turns people into numerical abstractions. See "The Problem of

Population and the Form of the American Novel," *American Literary History* 20, no. 4 (2008): 669, 673.

4. Frances Ferguson, *Solitude and the Sublime: Romanticism and the Aesthetics of Individuation* (New York: Routledge, 1992), 120.

5. James Axtell describes how, contrary to the dismal record of the English in converting Indians to Christianity in colonial New England, "large numbers of French and English settlers had chosen to become Indians— by walking or running away from colonial society to join Indian society, by not trying to escape after being captured, or by electing to remain with their Indian captors when treaties of peace periodically afforded them the opportunity to return home." Though Axtell focuses mainly on unredeemed captives in the eighteenth century, and admits that in earlier periods ransom was the primary goal, the educational practices that succeeded in bonding white children to Indian society were likely already sophisticated among the Algonquian tribes Rowlandson encountered in the 1670s. Rowlandson, Sarah, Mary, and Joseph were exactly the kind of captives that were most in danger of adoption, as "most of the colonists captured for adoption by the Indians . . . were children of both sexes and young women, often the mothers of the captive children." See Axtell, *The Invasion Within: The Contest of Cultures in Colonial North America* (New York: Oxford University Press, 1985), 302, 304.

6. Ludmilla Jordanova has considered in depth this etymological history: "For Wesley, the existence of an abstract term that applied to the entire organic world strips away from human beings something that should elevate them. It is a denial, for Wesley, of human kinship with God to 'level man' in this way." See Jordanova, "Interrogating the Concept of Reproduction in the Eighteenth Century," in *Conceiving the New World Order*, eds. Faye D. Ginsburg and Rayna Rapp (Berkeley: University of California Press, 1995), 372.

7. David Glimp, *Increase and Multiply: Governing Cultural Reproduction in Early Modern England* (Minneapolis: University of Minnesota Press, 2003), xiv.

8. Sir William Petty, *The Petty Papers: Some unpublished writings of Sir William Petty*, vol. II, ed. from the Bowood papers by the Marquis of Landsdowne (Boston and New York: Houghton Mifflin, 1927), 113.

9. Ibid., 114.

10. Ibid., 115.

11. Patricia Cline Cohen describes how it did not occur to seventeenth-century Puritans to count declining church membership, even when it was a frequent subject of concern in sermons and elsewhere: "[A]rithmetic was not among the subjects considered

basic for Puritan children to learn. . . .They could not conceive of any way to measure purity or piety, and numerical thinking did not, in the seventeenth century, develop into a common mode of cognition among them. . . . [T]he religious crisis of declension in the second half of the seventeenth century has been easily and readily comprehended in numerical terms by modern historians, who think of a falling-away from faith in terms of a decline in church membership. For the Puritans, considerations about church membership lay completely outside the realm of things countable." See Cohen, *A Calculating People: The Spread of Numeracy in Early America* (Chicago: University of Chicago Press, 1982), 49.

12. The 1727 primer's list of numbers (up to one hundred) comes after the entire lesson on the alphabet has concluded, under the heading, "The numeral Letters and Figures, which serve for the ready finding of any Chapter, Psalm, and Verse in the Bible." As Patricia Crain argues, basing literacy on the learning of the alphabet had effects beyond pedagogy, and shaped readers' ideologies and cultural assumptions: "[A]lphabetization in the modern period establishes the very possibilities of authorship and readership, permeating the formation of both persons and texts." Turning this analysis to the decidedly subordinate place of numbers in the *Primer* as tools for interpreting the world, I argue that colonialism's demand that bodies be counted was in tension with established modes of thinking about the relationship of individuals to social aggregates. Rowlandson's narrative directly grapples with this deep tension. See Crain, *The Story of A: The Alphabetization of America from* The New England Primer *to* The Scarlet Letter (Stanford, CA: Stanford University Press, 2000), 5.

13. Cohen describes how girls in early New England would have learned arithmetic through adapting recipes and making clothing: "Weaving, knitting, and crochet designs required the use of counting, arithmetic, and geometric progressions and a well-developed sense of spatial relations, all considered today to be part of a mathematical intelligence. But there was no attempt to teach girls written arithmetic, simply because it was assumed that women had no need of it in adult life" (140).

14. Rowlandson knits throughout her captivity as a means of bartering with the Indians for food and favors, and may have associated the counting, basic arithmetic, and measurement involved in this activity with ways to survive cognitively and socially as well.

15. Rowlandson's narrative offers insight into the murky beginnings of ideas about population which, over a century later, would serve as a breeding ground for the "profoundly ambivalent" depiction of reproducing bodies in Thomas Malthus's *Essay on the Principle of Population*, as Catherine Gallagher has argued: "Malthus . . . sees the unleashed power of

population, the reproducing body, as that which will eventually destroy the very prosperity that made it fecund, replacing health and innocence with misery and vice." See Gallagher, *The Body Economic: Life Death, and Sensation in Political economy and the Victorian Novel* (Princeton, NJ: Princeton University Press, 2006), 37.

16. Although Armstrong and Tennenhouse revise this argument in their 2008 article, they largely maintain the reading of Rowlandson's narrative they established in their earlier book as one in which literacy, and the theological interpretation that accompanies it, is the primary tool for her survival. Whereas Armstrong and Tennenhouse first posited that Rowlandson's Bible-reading "testifies to the presence of a peculiarly English consciousness," I argue here that Rowlandson's counting testifies to her peculiarly *imperial* consciousness. See Armstrong and Tennenhouse, *The Imaginary Puritan: Literature, Intellectual Labor, and the Origins of Personal Life* (Berkeley: University of California Press, 1992), 207.

17. Listing the age of the dead, especially the precise age with respect to months and days in the case of children, is a convention of Puritan elegy; but so was the declaration of the dead person's full name. Here Rowlandson oddly participates only halfway in a conventional public performance of Sarah's death.

18. Kathryn Zabelle Derounian concludes that Rowlandson wrote her narrative "within several years of her release in May 1675," and had "almost certainly . . . composed the account before Mather's request for providential experiences, that is, prior to 1681," as a result of which the narrative came to be published. Mather published his *A Brief History of the WARR with the Indians* in 1676. See Derounian, "The Publication, Promotion, and Distribution of Mary Rowlandson's Indian Captivity Narrative in the Seventeenth Century," *Early American Literature* 23 (1988): 240, 242.

19. Jill Lepore describes Indians' vigilance during the war at broadcasting their own counts of English dead, of which this scene described by Rowlandson is an example: "[W]hile hiding the extent of their own losses, Algonquians celebrated English losses by making marks on trees and shouting or 'co-hooping' to count the enemy dead—messages designed to be seen and heard by Indians and colonists alike" in Lepore, *The Name of War: King Philip's War and the Origins of American Identity* (New York: Knopf, 1998), 62.

20. I thank Betty Booth Donohue and Zabelle Stodola for bringing Rowlandson's conflicting use of the word "home" to my attention with their paper "'Home' and 'Homelands' in Mary Rowlandson's Indian Captivity Narrative (1682)," presented at the 2011 Society of Early

Americanists Seventh Biennial Conference, Philadelphia, Pennsylvania, March 3, 2011.

21. Axtell, 307. According to Axtell, by separating captive family members from one another (as Rowlandson is separated from Mary and Joseph), beginning social education early (like teaching captives how to forage for food), and ultimately performing rituals intended to "beat" and "wash out" the whiteness of captives in an "Indian baptism," Indian societies were adept at attaining "cultural conversion." See Axtell, 314, 326.

22. Mitchell Breitweiser also argues that time is the central problem in the Goodwife Joslin episode. Breitweiser, however, sees it as a clash of "imposed itineraries" versus chosen ones, and therefore a clash with providence, not as a cycle from invulnerability to vulnerability, and back again, as I do. See Breitweiser, *American Puritanism and the Defense of Mourning: Religion, Grief, and Ethnology in Mary White Rowlandson's Captivity Narrative* (Madison: University of Wisconsin Press, 1990), 112.

23. Increase Mather, *A Brief History of the WARR with the Indians* (Boston: Printed and sold by John Foster over against the Sign of the Dove, 1676), 27. Further references to *A Brief History of the WARR with the Indians* are to this edition and will be referred to parenthetically in the text as *HW*.

24. Cotton Mather, "A Notable Exploit; *wherein*, Dux Faemina Facti. From *Christi Americana* (1702)," in *Women's Indian Captivity Narratives*, ed. Kathryn Zabelle Derounian-Stodola (New York: Penguin, 1998), 59. Further references to Hannah Dustan's narrative are to this edition and will be referred to parenthetically in the text as HD.

25. For a similar reading of how Rowlandson inadvertently offers clues to how modern ideas about the body developed when her spiritual and bodily desires intermingle in her narrative, especially in relation to satisfying her hunger, see Jordan Alexander Stein, "Mary Rowlandson's Hunger and the Historiography of Sexuality," *American Literature* 81, no. 3 (2009): 469–495.

26. Breitweiser, 51, 55–56.

27. Breitweiser, 70. Breitweiser recognizes the ways numbers are folded into the discourse of community redemption, a process Rowlandson wants to forestall: "[T]he 'us' that is returned to normality is a diminished us, us minus (at least) one, the dead daughter Sarah, an us that is therefore not a return to or of what was, but a new thing. The present is a subtraction from rather than/as well as an addition." He does not acknowledge, however, that conceiving of herself as "one" and others as additions or subtractions would have been radically new and unsettling in Rowlandson's epistemology. See Breitweiser, 20.

28. Reading William Bradford, Kathleen Donegan describes the colonial body as imagined out of the wreck of catastrophe: "[T]he body, as

a privileged site of mediation between 'inner' and 'outer,' became a
crucial location for catastrophic reckoning when interior and exterior
worlds fragmented in response to those colonial ruptures." Catastrophe
is also always inextricably bound to population—as I noted in the
introduction, the word was first a synonym for "depopulation" before
positive numbers became a conceivable phenomenon over the course
of the seventeenth century. See Donegan, "'As Dying, Yet Behold
We Live': Catastrophe and Interiority in Bradford's 'Of Plymouth
Plantation,'" *Early American Literature* 37, no. 1 (2002): 11.

Chapter 4

1. See Charles E. Clark, *The Public Prints: The Newspaper in Anglo-American Culture, 1665–1740* (New York: Oxford University Press, 1994), 114.
2. Scholarship on the eighteenth century has focused intently on questions about print cultures and public spheres. Responding to Jürgen Habermas's theories of the emergence of a public sphere in Europe (*The Structural Transformation of the Public Sphere: An Inquiry into Bourgeois Society*, trans. Thomas Burger with assistance of Frederick Lawrence [Cambridge, MA: MIT Press, 1991]), see especially Michael Warner, *The Letters of the Republic: Publication and the Public Sphere in Eighteenth-Century America* (Cambridge, MA: Harvard University Press, 1992); Elizabeth Maddock Dillon, *Gender of Freedom: Fictions of Liberalism and the Literary Public Sphere* (Stanford, CA: Stanford University Press, 2004); and Trish Loughran, *The Republic in Print: Print Culture in the Age of U.S. Nation Building, 1770–1870* (New York: Columbia University Press, 2007).
3. Joseph Addison, *Spectator* no. 289 (31 January 1712), in *The Spectator*, ed. Donald F. Bond, Vol. 3 (New York: Oxford University Press, 1992), 29.
4. Ibid.
5. Michel Foucault writes about how "the famous mortality tables" in Europe worked to create biological norms in the negative sense before population could be "grasped in its positivity and generality": "[Y]ou know that eighteenth century demography could only begin inasmuch as some countries, and England in particular, had established mortality tables that made a quantification and knowledge of the causes of death possible," in *Security, Territory, Population: Lectures at the Collège de France, 1977–1978*, ed. Michael Senellart and trans. Graham Burchell (New York: Picador, 2007), 67.
6. James H. Cassedy, *Demography in Early America: Beginnings of the Statistical Mind* (Cambridge, MA: Harvard University Press, 1969), 120. Later bills "included figures on Negroes and Indians as well as of Whites," 120.
7. Cotton Mather, *Seasonable Thoughts upon Mortality* (Boston: T. Green, 1712), 3.

8. Patricia Cline Cohen, *A Calculating People: The Spread of Numeracy in Early America* (Chicago: University of Chicago Press, 1982), 95.

9. Ibid.

10. Ibid., 100.

11. Carla Mulford, "Pox and 'Hell-Fire': Boston's Smallpox Controversy, the New Science, and Early Modern Liberalism," in *Periodical Literature in Eighteenth-Century America*, ed. Mark L. Kamrath and Sharon M. Harris (Knoxville: University of Tennessee Press, 2005), 7–8.

12. Cohen, 98.

13. Samuel Grainger, *The Imposition of Inoculation as a Duty Religiously Considered in a leter [sic] to a gentleman in the country inclin'd to admit it* (Boston: Nicholas Boone, 1721), 7.

14. See Cohen, 100.

15. Cristobal Silva discusses the role of a lack of herd immunity in relation to the 1721 smallpox epidemic in Boston, in *Miraculous Plagues: An Epidemiology of New England Narrative* (New York: Oxford University Press, 2011), 113.

16. See a detailed description of the controversy, and James Franklin's role in it with relation to the *New England Courant*, in J. A. Leo LeMay, *The Life of Benjamin Franklin: Vol. I: Journalist, 1706–1730* (Philadelphia: University of Pennsylvania Press, 2005), 84–101.

17. See Susan E. Klepp, *"The Swift Progress of Population": A Documentary and Bibliographic Study of Philadelphia's Growth, 1642–1859* (Philadelphia: American Philosophical Society, 1991), 44.

18. Issue number 108 of *The Pennsylvania Gazette* includes the line, "It is now above 14 Months since we undertook the Publishing this Paper; Those Subscribers who have taken it a Year, are desired to send in their respective Payments," December, 8, 1730. Similarly, the issue from December 3 of that year (number CVII) included these lines warning readers of a slow news season in the same place after the burial numbers: "During the three Winter Months, while the Post performs his Stage but once a Fortnight; This Paper will be Published on Tuesdays. And as the Winter generally occasions a Scarcity of News in these Parts; and it being very little Satisfaction to the Reader to have a whole Sheet, when half of it must be fill'd with Trifles, or Things of small Consequence; we shall for the above time publish it in half Sheets, which we doubt not will be equally entertaining."

19. *The Pennsylvania Gazette*, March 19, 1730, number 70.

20. *The Pennsylvania Gazette*, August 26, 1731, number 145.

21. Cassedy, 125.

22. *The Pennsylvania Gazette*, September 2, 1731, number 146.

23. A note at the end of Franklin's *Gazette* from October 7, 1731 states: "*3 a clock P.M. New-York Post not come in.*"

24. *The Pennsylvania Gazette*, October 21, 1731, number 152.
25. *The Pennsylvania Gazette*, September 30, 1731, number 149.
26. *The Pennsylvania Gazette*, November 18, 1731, number 156.
27. *The South Carolina Gazette*, August 19, 1723, number 31.
28. *The South Carolina Gazette*, September 2, 1732, number 33.
29. *The South Carolina Gazette*, January 20, 1733, number 53.
30. See Foucault, 73.
31. Achille Mbembe, "Necropolitics," trans. Libby Meintjes, *Public Culture* 15, no. 1 (2003): 40, 27, 21.
32. Ibid., 25–26.
33. Ibid., 26.
34. Ibid., 14.
35. Ibid., 15, 38.
36. Benedict Anderson, *Imagined Communities: Reflections on the Origin and Spread of Nationalism* (New York: Verso, 1991), 62.
37. See Cassedy, 124.
38. Clark, 185.
39. Clark, 124–125.
40. Clark, 129.
41. See Laurel Thatcher Ulrich, *Good Wives: Image and Reality in the Lives of Women in Northern New England, 1650–1750* (New York: Vintage, 1991), 126–145.
42. Clark, 11.
43. Peter Kalm, *Peter Kalm's Travels in North America*, Vol. 1, ed. and trans. Adolph B. Benson (New York: Wilson-Erickson Inc., [1770] 1937), 32.
44. Benjamin Franklin, *Poor Richard Improved, 1750* (Philadelphia: Printed and Sold by B. Franklin and D. Hall, 1749), Early American Imprints, series 1, no. 6320.
45. Cohen estimates that there were probably "just under three dozen teachers of the mathematics of navigation and surveying in evening schools in the colonies in the hundred years preceding the Revolution," and advertisements like that of Theophilus Grew for specialized education actually "perpetuated the segregation of the mathematical arts from general education" and thus kept numeracy from diffusing into the general population. See *A Calculating People*, 85.
46. The astrological content of almanacs was steeped in mathematics, but as Cohen points out, almanacs "made no arithmetic demands on the user . . . There was no effort to instruct the readership on any of the mysteries of mathematics or astronomical calculations" (*A Calculating People*, 85). T. J. Tomlin debunks the idea that astrological content like this illustration was at all considered occult at the time, arguing that astrology was "the liturgy of American popular culture" ("Astrology's from Heaven Not Hell: The Religious Significance of Early American Almanacs,"

Early American Studies [Spring 2010]: 289). As in liturgical structure, the Philomath who made the almanac's calculations was the sole interpreter of astrological numbers, not inviting readers to do their own calculations. The pairing of mortality tables and astrology here work together to expose readers to the possibilities for mathematical skill to explain the world around them, as well as simultaneously present it as rarefied and authoritative.

47. Malthus, *Essay on the Principle of Population*, ed. Antony Flew (London: Penguin 1985), 16. Further references to *Essay on the Principle of Population* are to this edition and will be cited parenthetically in the text as *EP*. Historian Conway Zirkle considers at length the corresponding passages in the works of Malthus and Franklin in "Benjamin Franklin, Thomas Malthus, and the United States Census," *Isis* 48, no. 1 (1957): 58–62.

48. Benjamin Franklin, "Observations Concerning the Increase of Mankind," in *Writings*, ed. J. A. Leo Lemay (New York: Library of America, 1987), 367. Further references to "Observations Concerning the Increase of Mankind" are to this edition and will be cited parenthetically in the text as *IM*.

49. Conrad Zirkle compares Franklin's *Observations* with the first hundred years of United States Census data (which was first taken the same year Franklin died, in 1790) to conclude that two of Franklin's predictions were more or less exactly correct: that the population doubled every twenty-five years, and that, as Zirkle paraphrases, "emigration does not reduce the population of a country and that immigration does not increase it," thus proving Franklin's insistence on discounting the influence of "strangers," who appeared in large numbers in Philadelphia mortality tables. See Zirkle, 61.

50. Giovanni Botero, *The Reason of State and the Greatness of Cities*, trans. P. J. and D. P. Waley and trans. Robert Peterson (New Haven, CT: Yale University Press, 1956), 246.

51. See the *Oxford English Dictionary* entry for "reproduction," which cites John Wesley as one of the first to use the word in relation to humans in English, paradoxically at a moment when Wesley is criticizing Buffon's use of the term in French: "He substitutes for the plain word *Generation*, a quaint word of his own, *Reproduction*, in order to level man not only with the beasts that perish, but with nettles or onions."

52. Priscilla Wald describes how early discourse about the AIDS epidemic sensationalized the idea of a "Patient Zero," who, like an earlier story circulating in American culture about "Typhoid Mary," was depicted as an early "superspreader" of the disease. The Patient Zero or Typhoid Mary figure is an essential feature of what Wald calls

"the outbreak narrative": "The description attributed intentionality to the superspreader . . . The metamorphosis of infected people into superspreaders is a convention of the outbreak narrative, in which human carriers rhetorically (or, in some of the fiction, literally) bring the virus itself to life," in *Contagious: Cultures, Carriers, and the Outbreak Narrative* (Durham: Duke University Press, 2008), 4. For a discussion about epidemiology as narrative, see Silva, *Miraculous Plagues*.
53. Mbembe, 12, 40.

Epilogue

1. Marcus Rediker, *The Slave Ship: A Human History* (London: John Murray, 2007), 13.
2. Achille Mbembe, "Necropolitics," trans. Libby Meintjes, *Public Culture* 15, no. 1 (2003): 40. Both Patterson and Mbembe draw on Hegel, and although Mbembe does not cite Patterson, he draws extensively on the history of slavery to understand contemporary colonial and postcolonial spaces. Orlando Patterson writes, "Perhaps the most distinctive attribute of the slave's powerlessness was that it always originated . . . as a substitute for death, usually violent death," and he describes how the the slave is defined "as a socially dead person." See Patterson, *Slavery and Social Death: A Comparative Study* (Cambridge, MA: Harvard University Press, 1992), 5.
3. Mbembe, 21.
4. Thomas Jefferson, *Notes on the State of Virginia*, ed. Frank Shuffelton (New York: Penguin, [1785] 1999), 168. Further references to *Notes on the State of Virginia* are to this edition and will be cited parenthetically in the text as *NS*.
5. Thomas Jefferson, "Original rough draft of the Declaration of Independence," Holograph with minor emendations by John Adams and Benjamin Franklin, June 1776, Library of Congress, https://www.loc.gov/exhibits/declara/ruffdrft.html.
6. All four responses other than Jefferson's repeat Marbois's phrasing asking for the state's "number of inhabitants," instead of using the term "population." Two of these four respond to the version of Marbois's list of questions that asks about the "proportion between the whites & blacks": Thomas Bee of South Carolina responded, "The number of white inhabitants were computed at the beginning of the present dispute at Sixty Thousand and the Negroes at from Eighty to one hundred Thousand or thereabouts"; and John Witherspoon of New Jersey asserted to Marbois that the "number of inhabitants in New-Jersey at present, is certainly not less than two hundred thousand . . . There are

negroes, but they are certainly not above one seventh or one tenth part of the whole." Major-General John Sullivan wrote of New Hampshire, "The number of Inhabitants are about one hundred Thousand"; Roger Sherman of Connecticut wrote that he had "enclosed the names of the counties with the number of Towns and Inhabitants in each County." See Thomas Bee and Lexander Moore, "Thomas Bee's Notes on the State of South Carolina," *Journal of the Early Republic* 7, no. 2 (1987): 118; John Witherspoon, *The Works of the Rev. John Witherspoon* (Philadelphia: William W. Woodward, 1801), 305–306; John Sullivan, *Letters and Papers of Major-General John Sullivan, Continental Army*, Vol. 3, ed. Otis G. Hammond (Concord: New Hampshire Historical Society 1939), 235; and Roger Sherman, "Letter from Roger Sherman to François Marbois (draft)," [18] November 1782, from Miscellaneous Bound Manuscripts, Massachusetts Historical Society, http://www.masshist.org/objects/2010april.php.

7. A search for "population" on Google Ngram supports the claim that use of the word surged after 1800; and the etymological citations in the *Oxford English Dictionary* appear mostly during and after the nineteenth century. See Jean-Baptiste Michel, Yuan Kui Shen, Aviva Presser Aiden, Adrian Veres, Matthew K. Gray, William Brockman, The Google Books Team, Joseph P. Pickett, Dale Hoiberg, Dan Clancy, Peter Norvig, Jon Orwant, Steven Pinker, Martin A. Nowak, and Erez Lieberman Aiden, "Quantitative Analysis of Culture Using Millions of Digitized Books," in *Science* 331, issue 6014 (January 14, 2011): 176–182; and "population, *n.*²" and "population, *n.*¹, 2.a." in *The Oxford English Dictionary*, 2nd ed. (Oxford: Oxford University Press, 1989).

8. "Francois Marbois queries concerning New Jersey (copy), undated [December 1780?]," Massachusetts Historical Society Collections Online, http://www.masshist.org/database/viewer.php?item_id=1847.

9. Rather than being incongruous with his devotion to science, scholars trace Jefferson's inconsistent definitions of "race" directly to his interest in scientific discourses such as taxonomy and natural history. As Bruce Dain points out, Jefferson's discursively powerful invocation of taxonomy with regard to humans was peculiarly influential not because of its legacy within scientific circles, but because "his words were in their contradictions profoundly effective" in giving voice to the contradictions inherent in race slavery, where people are at once intimately recognizable as human and yet quantified as commodities. Timothy Sweet traces these contradictions to problems inherent in natural history, arguing that its paradigm "lacked clarity in regard to the question of 'man': what kind of object was being identified here?" See Dain, *A Hideous Monster of the Mind: Race Theory and the Enlightenment* (Cambridge, MA: Harvard

University Press, 2002), 5; and Sweet, "Jefferson, Science, and the
Enlightenment," in *The Cambridge Companion to Thomas Jefferson*, ed.
Frank Shuffelton (New York: Cambridge University Press, 2009), 110.

10. Jefferson displays his racism when he claims that "blacks" cannot
be "[incorporated] into the state" because of their "colour": "The
circumstance of superior beauty, is thought worthy attention in the
propagation of our horses, dogs, and other animals; why not that of
man?" (*NS*, 145–146).

11. Douglas R. Egerton describes how Jefferson applied extensive
mathematical calculation to determining how many generations of
reproduction with whites it would take for a black person's descendants
to become entirely white, and thus free. Jefferson applied these theories
to his "mixed-race kinsmen," and Egerton points out that three of
Jefferon's children with Sally Hemings, who was a slave, "passed into
the white community, thereby demonstrating the absurdity of their
father's scientific categories." See Egerton, "Race and Slavery in the Era
of Jefferson," in *The Cambridge Companion to Thomas Jefferson*, ed. Frank
Shuffelton (New York: Cambridge University Press, 2009), 80.

12. See Mitchell Breitwieser, "Jefferson's Prospect," *Prospects* 10 (1985): 333;
Christopher Looby, "The Constitution of Nature: Taxonomy as Politics
in Jefferson, Peale, and Bartram," *Early American Literature* 22, no. 3
(1987): 267; Dana Nelson, *National Manhood: Capitalist Citizenship and the
Imagined Fraternity of White Men* (Durham: Duke University Press, 1998),
56; and Eva Cherniavsky, *That Pale Mother Rising: Sentimental Discourses
and the Imitation of Motherhood in 19th-Century America* (Bloomington:
Indiana University Press, 1995), 17.

13. Charles D. Martin, *The White African American Body: A Cultural and
Literary Exploration* (New Brunswick, NJ: Rutgers University Press,
2002), 15, 22.

14. See David Brion Davis and Steven Mintz, eds., *The Boisterous Sea of
Liberty: A Documentary History of America from Discovery Through the
Civil War* (New York: Oxford University Press, 1998), 242; and Frank
Shuffelton, "Introduction," in *Notes on the State of Virginia, xiv*.

15. Davis and Mintz, 242.

16. Howard A. Ohline, "Republicanism and Slavery: Origins of the Three-
Fifths Clause in the United States Constitution," *WMQ* 28, no. 4
(1971): 568.

17. Ibid., 584.

18. Alexander Hamilton or James Madison, "Federalist No. 54: The
Apportionment of Members Among the States," From the New York
Packet (Tuesday, February 12, 1788), Library of Congress, http://thomas.
loc.gov/home/fedpapers/fed_54.html.

19. Malick W. Ghachem, "The Slave's Two Bodies: The Life of an American Legal Fiction," *WMQ* 60, no. 4 (2003): 817–818.

20. Hamilton or Madison, "Federalist No. 54," http://thomas.loc.gov/home/fedpapers/fed_54.html.

21. Mary Poovey describes how the reception of Malthus's *Essay* created a crucial turning point toward the widespread acceptance of what we now think of as social science "facts." Viewing this development in light of the history of counting social life, Poovey writes, "will help us to see why [Malthus's *Essay's*] many incarnations constitute a crux in the history of the modern fact and to understand how the form of representation that late twentieth-century readers associate with disinterestedness or impartiality acquired those connotations partly through Malthus's revision of the modern science of wealth." Poovey, *History of the Modern Fact: Problems of Knowledge in the Sciences of Wealth and Society* (Chicago: University of Chicago Press, 1998), 280.

22. Aaron Fogel, "Wordsworth's 'We Are Seven' and Crabbe's *The Parish Register*: Poetry and Anti-Census," *Studies in Romanticism* 48, no. 1 (2009): 65, 24.

23. Ibid., 26.

24. Although I am discussing a poem printed in a newspaper and Elizabeth Maddock Dillon discusses publics gathered for a performance, the way I view the different effects and possible readings of the same text in the colonies as compared to England resembles what happens when, as Dillon describes, the same theatrical performance moves from London to a colonial stage: "The same black body," Dillon writes, "that appeared on stage . . . in London and galvanized a weeping public there had a far different stage life when (re)transported to the new World . . . that meaning had to do with questions concerning the performance of a public collectivity." Similarly, the same reflections on enumerated bodies would provoke notions of "public collectivity" that would be strikingly different in Boston than in Northampton, especially given the particular context of colonial discourse about population. See Dillon, *New World Drama: The Performative Commons in the Atlantic World, 1649–1849* (Durham: Duke University Press, 2014), 131.

25. Harriet Jacobs takes the title of chapter XXI, "Loophole of Retreat," in which she describes the small garret in which she hid to escape slavery for seven years, from Cowper's *The Task*. See Jacobs, *Incidents in the Life of a Slave Girl* (New York: Penguin, 2000), 128. For a description of Cowper's abolitionist poems in the US, see Mukhtar Ali Isani, "Far from 'Gambia's Golden Shore': The Black in Late Eighteenth-Century American Imaginative Literature," *The William and Mary Quarterly* 36, no. 3 (1979): 368.

26. William Cowper, *Cowper: Verse and Letters*, ed. Brian Spiller (Cambridge, MA: Harvard University Press, 1968), 95.

27. "Observations on Bills of Mortality," *Bee, or Literary Intelligencer*, May 11, 1791, 24.

28. Manasseh Cutler, Francis Dana, Edward Wigglesworth, Benjamin Guild, and Joshua Fisher, Committee, "Broadside" (Boston: S. Hall, November 10, 1785).

29. J. M. Toner, "Reports Upon Yellow Fever: The Distribution and Natural History of Yellow Fever as it has Occurred at Different Times in the United States," *Public Health Papers and Reports* 1 (1873): 374. For a discussion of yellow fever in this period as a pandemic, see also Cristobal Silva, "How to Name a Plague: The History of Yellow Fever in the Age of Epidemic," Paper given at the Americas Before 1900 Working Group, The Ohio State University, Oct. 11, 2013.

30. Toner, 376.

31. The epigraph to both is "*Vitae summa brevis spem nos vetat inchoare longam.* HOR. [Our brief sum of life forbids us to embark upon a protracted hope]." See Joseph Addison, *Spectator* no. 289 (31 January 1712), in *The Spectator*, ed. Donald F. Bond, Vol. 3 (New York: Oxford University Press, 1992), 29.

32. Sylvanus Urban, "On the Annual Bill of Mortality," *Gentlman's Magazine*, July 1, 1809, 592.

33. Toner, 367.

34. "The following Verses, printed at the bottom of the yearly Bill of Mortality of the town of Northampton, Dec. 11, 1787, we are assured were written by Mr. Cowper," *Connecticut Magazine*, January 1, 1801, 45.

35. See C. L. R. James, *The Black Jacobins: Toussaint L'Overture and the San Domingo Rebellion* (New York: Vintage, 1963), 263.

36. Avishai Margolit, *On Compromise and Rotten Compromises* (Princeton, NJ: Princeton University Press, 2010), 180, 181.

37. Ibid., 181.

Index

Printed in Poland
by Amazon Fulfillment
Poland Sp. z o.o., Wrocław

26233572R00170